Praise for Steve Mariotti's *The Young Entrepreneur's Guide to Starting and Running a Business*

"For the real goods, go straight to Mariotti's book."

—*Inc.* magazine

"*The Young Entrepreneur's Guide* provides the two things that young people need the most to succeed: inspiration and the tools to achieve their dreams."

—*Albert Abney,*
National Minority Manufacturer of the Year

"*The Young Entrepreneur's Guide* provides a first-class education for anyone interested in starting a business. It brings to life the excitement of going out on your own in a vivid and practical way."

—*William Bygrave,*
director of the Center for Entrepreneurial Studies at Babson College

"Steve Mariotti has heart—and it shows by the way he understands and communicates business principles to young people in this exciting new startup guide."

—*Bonnie Drew,*
author, *Fast Cash for Kids*

"Without question, Steve Mariotti and NFTE are pioneers and major leaders in the field of youth entrepreneurship education. Reading Steve's insightful and practical book will show you why!"

—*Verne C. Harnish,*
founder of the Young Entrepreneur's Organization

"The best book for young entrepreneurs—the whole process of starting and running a business—from deciding on what kind of business you want to run to creating a successful business plan."

—*George C. Hescock,*
executive vice president,
Direct Selling Association

"*The Young Entrepreneur's Guide* is the bible of self-help. It not only tells the story of many young people who have made the journey to success and self-respect, it shows step-by-step how you can do the same."

—*Jack Kemp,*
former secretary of housing and urban development and
founder of Empower America

"The entrepreneurial spirit is part of what made America great. *The Young Entrepreneur's Guide* is an excellent source for the next generation of young people who want to continue that tradition."

—*Bennie L. Thayer,*
president and CEO,
The National Association for the Self-Employed

"No one in America is more experienced working with aspiring entrepreneurs than Steve Mariotti. *The Young Entrepreneur's Guide* is loaded with practical advice and know-how that will benefit young people in pursuit of the entrepreneurial dream."

—Jeffry A. Timmons,
Franklin W. Olin Distinguished Professor of Entrepreneurship,
Babson College

The Young Entrepreneur's Guide

to Starting and Running a

Business

The Young Entrepreneur's Guide

Guide

TO STARTING AND RUNNING A

Business

Steve Mariotti

with **Debra DeSalvo** and **Tony Towle**

TIMES BUSINESS

RANDOM HOUSE

An earlier edition of this work was published in 1996 by Times Books, a division of Random House, Inc.

ISBN 0-8129-3306-0

Random House Website address: www.randomhouse.com

Manufactured in the United States of America

98765432

SPECIAL SALES
Times Books are available at special discounts for bulk purchases for sales promotions or premiums. Special editions, including personalized covers, excerpts of existing books, and corporate imprints, can be created in large quantities for special needs. For more information, write to Special Markets, Times Books, 201 East 50th Street, New York, New York 10022, or call 800-800-3246.

---

*To Liz, Charles, and David Koch, John Whitehead,
and Diana Davis Spencer of the Shelby Collum Davis Foundation*

CONTENTS

PREFACE

A LETTER TO THE YOUNG ENTREPRENEUR FROM STEVE MARIOTTI

When I was a teacher in some of New York City's toughest high schools, I discovered that even my most difficult students could become successful entrepreneurs. What's more, learning about entrepreneurship gave these young people, who were born into poverty and violence, the feeling that they could take charge of their future. It motivated them to improve their math, reading, and writing skills, and to stay in school. Entrepreneurship education is still in its infancy, but my goal is for it to eventually become an invaluable addition to school curriculums nationwide. If my students could learn to start and operate small businesses, so can you—whether you live in a city, a rural area, or the suburbs.

The Young Entrepreneur's Guide to Starting and Running a Business is for *any* young person who wants to start a business. No matter where you live or what your background may be, if you follow the tried-and-true methods in this book, you will be able to create your own business. I say this with confidence because so many of my students have become business owners.

Will every reader of this book start a business? Probably not, although that would be nice. My ultimate goal is to give you the skills you'll need to become financially independent. Even if you don't become a lifelong entrepreneur, by learning how to start your own business you will develop an understanding of the business world that will make it much easier for you to get jobs and to create a fulfilling work life for yourself. After all, no matter who your employer is, managing your money wisely is not unlike being in business for yourself.

When I saw how much learning about entrepreneurship increased my students' self-esteem, confidence, math and reading skills, and prospects for the future, I wanted every young person to learn about it. So, in 1987, I founded the National Foundation for Teaching Entrepreneurship, Inc. (NFTE, pronounced "Nifty"). Today, we teach entrepreneurship to thousands of students in the United States, Europe, and South America. In 1998, NFTE students won eighteen out of twenty-five national awards for top entrepreneurs under age twenty, and fourteen of twenty-two youth entrepreneurship awards in New York City.

This book will teach you the same skills NFTE students have used to start great businesses and win all those awards. By the time you've turned the last page, you will have negotiated with a wholesale dealer, opened a bank account, registered your business, made flyers and business cards, checked out lots of cool Web sites for entrepreneurs, and sold your product at a flea market. You'll have read about how entrepreneurs like Russell Simmons of Def Jam, Bill Gates of Microsoft, and Anita Roddick of The Body Shop, Inc. got their businesses off the ground. This book will even show you, step-by-step, how to write a detailed business plan that you can use to raise money for your business.

Bear in mind as you read this book that *you have unique knowledge* that can be turned into a money-producing business. What is this unique knowledge? It is how well you know your schoolmates, your friends, and your neighbors. What problem might they have that your business could solve? What product can't they find that you could sell to them? Start thinking like an entrepreneur!

Entreneurship is really about freedom—the freedom to work how and when you want. The freedom to create your life from scratch and make it truly enjoyable and rewarding. As an entrepreneur you can work when you know you are the most productive (designing Web pages at 3 A.M., for example!). You create your own schedule (one that also meets your clients' needs, of course) and your own opportunities. You create a work environment that reflects *your* values, not someone else's. And, in a world where corporations no longer provide the life-long security they used to, you can create your own job security by creating your own job.

Don't think you can't compete with huge companies, either. As an entrepreneur you will have a lightning-fast ability to react to changes in your business environment that big corporations only wish they could command. Once tiny startups like Amazon.com, Ebay and many other exciting new entrepreneurial Internet companies have consistently beat big corporations in the newest marketplace—the Internet—for exactly that reason.

Entrepreneurship is an act of creation. It is an art, not a science. It's the art of creating products and services that your friends and neighbors will want to buy. Like any art, it needs to be practiced and enjoyed. Above all, entrepreneurship should be fun. It's really not just about making money—plenty of people with lots of money are miserable! So, please, don't just read this book—use it to create some fun and excitement in your life! And don't forget that your business could have a powerful impact on your community and perhaps on the world.

Please feel free to write to me—I'd love to hear from you!

STEVE MARIOTTI
National Foundation for Teaching Entrepreneurship, Inc.
120 Wall Street, 29th Floor
New York, New York 10005
SteveM@nfte.com

P.S. to Parents, Mentors, and Teachers

If you have purchased *The Young Entrepreneur's Guide to Starting and Running a Business* for a young person, you have made an excellent choice. The New York Public Library named the first edition of this book one of the top ten books in its field for young people in America.

This revised edition offers new chapters on technology, philanthropy (including mentoring), and opportunity recognition, as well as new Internet-oriented business ideas for young entrepreneurs. To keep topics clear and manageable, business terminology and usage have been slightly modified on occasion, but only after extensive consultation and field testing. The terms I use are in keeping with my belief that instruction in how to start and operate a small business will make a young person more independent, more employable, and a better citizen.

Here are some of the things your young entrepreneur will learn to do:

Negotiate.

Keep accounting records.

Prepare an income statement.

Calculate the return on an investment.

Read *The Wall Street Journal*.

Write memos and business letters.

Make sales calls.

Write a business plan.

Use the phone as a business tool.

Prepare a marketing plan.

Raise venture capital.

I firmly believe there should be a national effort to teach every young person the fundamentals of starting his or her own business. One of my great concerns, however, is that our complex tax code and bewildering array of permits and licenses are dispiriting barriers to entrepreneurship. High tax rates make it very difficult for poor people to accumulate enough capital to start their own businesses. Would-be entrepreneurs are also discouraged by red tape. A streamlining of the business-licensing process and a radical overhaul of the tax code would encourage entrepreneurs to enter the marketplace. So would the establishment of special enterprise zones in impoverished areas. I encourage you to get involved with these issues.

If I can ever be of help to you in any way, or if you are interested in purchasing additional educational products, please write to me.

The Young Entrepreneur's Guide

TO STARTING AND RUNNING A

Business

PROLOGUE

WHY I CREATED THE NATIONAL FOUNDATION FOR TEACHING ENTREPRENEURSHIP (NFTE)

From 1982 to 1988, I worked as a business, math, and special education teacher in New York City public schools, in such notorious neighborhoods as Bedford-Stuyvesant in Brooklyn and "Fort Apache" in the South Bronx. My experiences led me—at first subtly and then increasingly more directly—to introduce lessons in entrepreneurship into the standard academic curriculum.

I saw firsthand that, as a group, inner-city youth had no idea, or a completely distorted notion, of how our economic system worked. This was the root cause of their powerlessness to function within that system. Desperate to reach my students, I began teaching them simple business concepts, such as return on investment. As I saw previously disinterested and disillusioned children light up, I realized that their stressful environment was a factor in making them natural entrepreneurs. I became more and more excited by the positive results I was having in my classes. I also realized that what I was doing could be applied in many other communities.

In 1987, I founded the National Foundation for Teaching Entrepreneurship (NFTE, pronounced "Nifty"), a nonprofit organization whose mission was, and is, to bring basic business and entrepreneurial skills to disadvantaged young people. I am convinced that entrepreneurship can help these young people to achieve financial independence and that, by doing so, they can improve their lives and the economic lives of their neighborhoods.

STARTING MY OWN BUSINESS

I came to this vision by an indirect route. I graduated from the University of Michigan's School of Business in 1977 with an MBA. In graduate school, as a result of a scholarly paper published in the prestigious economics journal *Public Choice,* I won a scholarship to study economics at The Institute for Humane Studies. I was one of twenty economists selected. Our reward was four months of pure economic theory, discussion, and research under the guidance of F. A. Hayek, the Nobel Prize winner for Economics in 1974.

At the end of the summer, armed with a basic knowledge of Economics, I went to work as a financial analyst for Ford Motor Company's legendary finance staff, where my youthful enthusiasm and knack for international finance earned me the nickname "Stevie Wonder." I led a team that managed to lower Ford's interest payments by several million dollars a year. I had a lot of responsibility, considering my age, and I got an inside look at how one of America's largest corporations operates. But I also learned that infighting and intramural politics are often part of the corporate world.

I moved to New York City and tried the other end of the business spectrum. I started my own small sole proprietorship, an import–export firm. That was a revelation. At Ford, I was near the bottom of the corporate hierarchy. In New York, I was making less money, but I was my own boss. It didn't matter that I didn't have high capitalization or thousands of employees. Being an independent businessperson had an immediate beneficial effect on my self-esteem and outlook.

Plus, I felt really good about the fact that I was helping the craftspeople whose work I was importing from Africa and other distant places. I was helping them make money and improve their lives, too. I loved being self-employed and started thinking about expanding into other ventures.

But then I learned another of life's lessons; this one was about living in a large city. One evening in 1981, while jogging on the Lower East Side, I was approached by a group of kids who demanded ten dollars. I was wearing a jogging suit and was carrying very little money. They roughed me up and humiliated me. Afterward, the entrepreneur in me wondered why these kids would mug someone for a few dollars when they could make more money running a small business together.

Becoming an urban statistic was a traumatic experience. My constant and painful flashbacks of the experience soon became more painful than the experience itself. The memories took on a life of their own, and I knew I had a serious problem. My strategy was to confront my fears directly. I decided to become a public school teacher in neighborhoods like the one that the young people who had mugged me called home.[1] I wanted to be assigned to the "worst" areas, to test myself. The school administration was happy to oblige: I was assigned to Boys & Girls High School, in the Bedford-Stuyvesant area of Brooklyn. Although I had asked for it, I was a little nervous. Boys & Girls had recently been the subject of such headlines as: "Teacher's Hair Set on Fire at Troubled Boys & Girls High"; "Teacher Beaten and Dragged Down Stairs at Boys & Girls"; and "Principal Brings Calm to Chaotic City School."

Although the school had only opened in 1976 and had cost $30 million to construct, Boys & Girls had quickly established itself as the worst school in the New York City public school system, and perhaps in the country. Primarily as a result of the negative publicity, seventy-two teachers simply refused to report for duty at Boys & Girls—they preferred to be unemployed. The dropout rate at the school quickly reached 50 percent. In 1978, the New York State Board of Regents took the unprecedented step of putting the entire school on probation.

BECOMING A TEACHER

For me, though, my strategy appeared to be working. Within an hour of arriving at the school, I began to view the kids with less animosity and fear. I also knew that I would like teaching; I was sure I had found a vocation.

Reality set in quickly, however. There were fifty-nine students in my first remedial math class—a number far too high, in the best of circumstances, to teach effectively. There were only forty-two seats and thirty-nine books. If 76 percent of the class showed up, I'd be in trouble.

"Are you the new teacher?" a gigantic youth asked. At first I thought he was a security guard. He turned out to be nineteen-year-old Robert, whose math was at the seventh-grade level—and this was a class of seniors.

"Yes I am. My name is Mr. Mariotti."

"OK, Mr. Manicotti."

"Hey Robert, where did you get the midget?" yelled out the next student coming through the door.

"Sit down, please," I said, trying to keep my voice as low-pitched as possible.

"Who says?"

"I do. I'm the teacher."

"You're a shorty—what's it like being a midget?"

"Please sit down, now."

"Hey, he thinks he's a bad homeboy."

"Chill out, teach, ain't nobody hurting you."

"Please sit down."

"Bust the move, teach."

"Nice suit, homeboy. Too bad you didn't get it in the right size."

There were now forty-six students in the room, which meant that four had to stand and seven didn't have books. They were actually quiet as I gave my standard speech and wrote my class rules on the board. I closed with a plea for them to learn basic math because without it they'd be embarrassed in later life and would find it difficult not only to find a job but to function effectively in their personal lives. I then passed out the books (as far as they would go) and gave a basic diagnostic test. I found out that 20 percent of the class didn't even have pencils or paper, and I had to go in search of supplies. I gave the test to each of my five classes, with disheartening results as to the scores. For the most part, the students were relatively well behaved.

This appearance of good behavior in my remedial classes turned out to be an illusion as the days went on. When I started my lesson on fractions (only a third of the class could add $\frac{1}{3}$ and $\frac{1}{6}$), I soon realized everyone was talking—to everyone else. Two girls in the back of the room were showing each other new dance steps. The boys in the back rows were talking louder than I was. "Please be quiet," I said calmly. No effect. "Please be quiet!" I yelled. Still no effect. Then I just sat down, hoping I would shame them into silence. Instead, they accelerated their conversation. After a few minutes, I continued the lesson for the five or six students who were paying attention as I tried to be heard over the noise.

LOSING CONTROL OF MY CLASS

The situation got worse. I began to lose control on almost a daily basis. One student actually set fire to the back of another's coat—the student with the coat was as astonished as I was. I ordered the arsonist out of the class in a rage, and he was expelled the same day. On another occasion, I was locked out of my eighth-period class. The students would not open the door, for what seemed like an eternity. Finally, one of the girls took pity on me and opened it, just as I was going to admit total defeat and find a security guard.

In each of my three remedial classes, there was a group of six or seven kids whose behavior was so disruptive that I had to stop the class every five minutes or so to get them to quiet down. In my third-period class, I threw all the boys out. Ironically, these young men provided me with the valuable insight that set me on the road to teaching entrepreneurship. I took them out to dinner and asked them why they had acted so badly in class. They said my class was boring, that I had nothing to teach them.

Didn't anything I'd said in class interest them? I asked. One fellow spoke up: I had caught his attention when I had discussed my import–export business. He rattled off various figures I'd mentioned in class, calculated my profit margin, and concluded that my business was doing well. I was dazzled to find such business smarts in a student the public schools had labeled borderline retarded. This was my first inkling that something was wrong not only with my teaching, but also with the standard remedial curriculum.

In my eighth-period class, I was too afraid of the boys to throw them out. The most disruptive boys were Mills, Braddock, and Morrow. They seemed to really hate me, and I didn't like them much, either. They would disrupt the class by making animal noises, cursing me viciously, and treating their fellow classmates with great hostility. I would calmly threaten them with failure. I tried not to lose a joking manner, which, it turned out, they saw as a sign of weakness. One day I knew I was off to a particularly bad start when I sat in my seat and felt something stick to the back of my jacket. I got up, looked at my chair, and saw a large wad of gum. The class roared. Then, seeing the hurt and disgust on my face, they fell silent. A student named Therese came up to me and said: "You all right, Mr. Mariotti, you have gum on your back; let me help you." She pulled off as much of it as possible. I tried to make it humorous: "Judging from the amount of gum, I'd say it came from someone with a big mouth." No one laughed.

I tried to start a new subject, decimals, but asking them to learn something new at this point just made them anxious. A radio suddenly blared from the back of the room.

Me: "Please turn off the radio."

Ramon: "It's not the radio, it's the P.A."

The noise level soared, and Mills and Braddock got out of their seats and began dancing at the front of the room. The rest of the class began to clap in unison. I ran to the back of the room and threatened Ramon: "Turn it off or I'm going to fail you." By this time, Ramon was dancing too and totally ignored me. Mills got up on my desk and continued to dance.

"Turn off the goddamned radio, you twerp!" I yelled. Someone, imitating me, yelled back, "No swearing, Mr. Mariotti." I grabbed the radio and went to the front of the room. To my relief, Mills got off my desk and sat back down in his seat, cursing me as he went. I could feel my face twitching. "Look, Mariotti's having a nervous breakdown!" said another troublemaker. "You can't control this class, Mariotti, because you don't have juice," shouted Mills. "Shut up and sit!" I shouted back. "Continue with the assignment."

I was shaking as Nicole came up to my desk and asked, "Can you show me how to do this problem?" I began to show her when all of a sudden I was hit in the eye with a spitball. I felt another wave of anger. "Who threw that?" I yelled. The class was again in total chaos. Mills ran up to the front of the room, grabbed the American flag off the wall, and, holding it like a spear, started to pretend to poke me with it. He then raised it up as if to throw it. "Put the flag down," I demanded. Abbott, a Bermudian boy, came up from behind and grabbed Mills around the chest. I moved forward, took the flag, and put it back on the wall. I walked out of the class and, as I did so, was hit in the back with a wad of paper.

I didn't know how to deal with the situation. I wanted to walk out of the school and call it quits. After a minute or two, I realized that I couldn't do that. As I stepped into the hallway to regain my composure, I thought about my dinner with the young men from my third-period class. They had said I was boring—except when I talked about business, about money.

After about three minutes, I walked back into the classroom and, with no introductory comments, started a mock sales pitch, hypothetically selling the class my own watch. I enumerated the benefits of the watch, explaining why the students should purchase it from me at the low price of only six dollars. I noticed immediately that as soon as I started to talk about money, and how to make money by selling something, they actually quieted down and became interested. I didn't know it at the time, but this incident, born of desperation, pointed me toward my real vocation—teaching entrepreneurship to inner-city kids.

When I had their attention, I moved from the sales talk into a conventional arithmetic lesson: if you buy a watch at three dollars and sell it for six, you make three dollars of profit, or 100 percent. Without realizing it, I was touching on the business fundamental of buy low/sell high, and on the more advanced concept of return on investment.

Developing Strength

That evening, I realized I would have to start getting tough—no more Mr. Nice Guy. I even practiced my expression in the mirror. I decided I had to come to my classes ready to be instantly angry. I knew I had to stay very alert. I had the courage and awareness of a man with his back to the wall. I couldn't let a few of these students make me feel like a failure. I kept thinking of Samuel Johnson's remark: "Nothing focuses a man's mind so much as when he's about to be hanged." Unless I could bring my classes under control, I was of little value to students who were actually there to learn—and many of them were. Not only would I be tough, I decided, but I would begin to develop a curriculum around my students' obvious interest in business.

They noticed the difference right away.

Wanda: "What's wrong with you today?"

Tanya: "Why you busting our chops, Mr. Steve?"

Tawana: "Why you no smile, homeboy?" The behavior of all my classes immediately improved. The noise level declined from the roar of Niagara Falls to the murmur of a fashionable café.

Finally, the eighth period arrived. This was the class whose behavior had precipitated my change. I got to the classroom early, cleaned up the debris, and straightened the chairs. By the time I'd finished, there were still no students. I stood at the door, awaiting their arrival. They sensed immediately that something was different, that I had been pushed too far. Some said a quiet "Hi," as they walked in. On the blackboard, I had written:

DO NOW: SIT DOWN.
TAKE OUT A PIECE OF PAPER. PREPARE FOR QUIZ.

The late bell rang, and I locked the door and passed out the daily assignment. About five minutes later, I heard the telltale profanity from down the hall. The students looked at me; I could sense their apprehension. The gang that had humiliated me on the previous day had arrived. They kicked at the closed door and I felt a sudden burst of adrenalin. It was them or me.

I opened the door. Mills tried to come into the room but I put my hand on his shoulder and pushed him back. Had I assaulted him? At that moment, I didn't care. I felt the elation of being right.

"Hey, man, what you doin' pushing me?"

I said nothing.

"What's wrong with you?" Braddock asked with genuine curiosity.

"We didn't mean nothing yesterday," Morrow muttered. Mills was just watching intently. I knew I was going to win.

"I want an apology. I want a *written* apology."

"We didn't do nothing to you."

Morrow tried unsuccessfully to get past me into the room. "I want an apology and it must be written," I said calmly and coldly.

Braddock's protest, "Nobody hurt you," was followed by a stream of profanity.

"You swear at me again and you'll be thrown out of this school so fast you won't even know it, you little twerp," I said, with no emotion.

"What's wrong, Mariotti? No one touched you."

I changed strategies and began to speak more forcefully. "You jerks ruined the class last Thursday. You kept your own people from learning anything. What kind of idiots are you?"

"Mariotti, chill, man," someone said. "No one wants to hurt you, man."

"Shut up, you little wimp," I continued over their noises of astonishment. "Understand this: I'm here to help you learn. If you aren't interested, don't come to class. I'm trying to teach math here. Don't get in my way."

"Mr. Mariotti, are you all right?" It was Lorraine, one of the students in the classroom. The whole class was now listening to this exchange. I ignored her.

"If you don't know basic mathematics. . . ." I caught myself; I was ruining it with syrup. "If you ever disrupt my class again, you'll never get in this room again and not in this school either. Do you understand me?"

No one spoke.

"All right," Mills said. They started to come into the room.

"No, I want a written apology from each of you. Here's paper and a pencil. Write apologies, and when you're finished, slide them under the door." I closed the door and walked back to my desk. The whole exchange had taken only five or six minutes. The class had obviously overhead everything. They were awaiting the outcome, just as I was. "Please get back to work," I said.

I could hardly believe it: One by one, the four pieces of paper were slipped under the door. I waited a minute and then went over to pick them up. I felt the elation of victory as I read the apologies, but by now I'd learned to show no emotion. I went to the door, opened it, and said: "Please take your seats."

The behavior of all my classes improved markedly after this episode. Mills and Braddock, particularly, showed improved conduct. I had them sit in the front of the class with me while I did problems on the blackboard. At first, they were embarrassed by the special treatment; Braddock asked me to keep my voice down as I was explaining to him what "percentage" meant. As I'd suspected, these two kids knew *no* math and their embarrassment had prompted much of their behavior.

TEACHING ENTREPRENEURSHIP

Over the next several weeks, the classes were orderly enough to give me time to think about how I might teach better, and how I could get these kids to learn basic mathematics. When I went to class one day, I had the students make change in a retailer/customer scenario. The "retailer" had to make ten correct transactions—or lose the turn if he or she made a mistake. Nobody wanted to make a mistake.

This game treated math as a practical reality rather than an abstraction. More subtly, it put the students in the position of a shopkeeper—an entrepreneur. What had begun as an intuition slowly developed into a certainty: Whenever I could manage to focus a lesson on some phase of entrepreneurial business, I had the students' attention. I began to do this consciously, using all my ingenuity to get across the bedrock principles of business: buy low, sell high, keep good records, and satisfy consumer needs. I wanted these young people to appreciate the principles of free enterprise: (1) ownership and (2) honest relations with other human beings through the rational self-interest of voluntary trade.

Next, I had the students make mock sales calls (later, when I had the funds, the sales calls were videotaped for peer review). This game taught them that, to sell something to somebody, they had to be civil and polite. They had to *convince* the customers to buy from them; they could not coerce them.

I found *The Wall Street Journal* to be an important teaching tool. When I was teaching at Boys & Girls, I had to remind myself that I was discussing the *Journal* in the most infamous high school in New York. In one class, I ended up supplying each student with a daily copy at my own expense. I held contests in which each kid would pick a stock and track it, and I offered prizes for the biggest gain. I also pointed out that the CEOs of America's largest companies, and indeed everybody who was anybody in the business world, was reading, that morning, the very same newspaper that they were.

Other teachers, and administrators, were constantly urging me to stress reading, writing, math, communications skills, and "good citizenship." I found that approach to be nonproductive, even counterproductive. When these young people got interested in starting their own businesses, they *wanted* to know how to write and add; they knew they needed these skills to conduct business effectively. They also knew that politeness and respect for the people with whom they were doing business were essential.

THE IMPACT OF ENTREPRENEURSHIP EDUCATION

Knowledge of the principles of business modified the behavior of these kids. Entrepreneurship changed the structure of their psyches. Maurice, one of my students at Boys & Girls, although not one of the worst behaved in my classes, was still angry, belligerent, mean, and threatening. He took to salesmanship, however, which he first learned about through role-playing games in class. He became so good that I encouraged him to make actual sales. He invested a small sum in a dozen pairs of sunglasses, which I helped him to buy wholesale. As he began to make a small profit through selling the glasses, his whole facial demeanor changed. Instead of being angry, he was conversational and polite. He had learned to assert himself nonaggressively through the selling process. He had a unique knowledge of his own community, and his familiarity with his local "market" led him to pick those styles of sunglasses his peers would want to buy. By the end of the school year, he was making about $60 a week in his spare time through sales. The increase in his confidence and self-esteem was incalculable.

It became apparent to me that many of these young people had a natural aptitude for entrepreneurship. Their challenging lives encouraged independence of spirit, toughness, unselfconsciousness, and a natural ability in salesmanship. They were comfortable with risk and ambiguity. These same qualities—along with difficulty in doing well in a traditional, structured environment—characterized many great American entrepreneurs such as Henry Ford and Conrad Hilton. I found that the negative characteristics of my students, when channeled into entrepreneurial activities, became positives. The benefits they reaped went far beyond the areas of education and business and academic subjects.

Tawana, for example, had incredibly low self-esteem—until she started her own manicuring business at home after school. She was a little half-hearted about it at first, but as she began giving out the flyers and business cards we had made in class, she could see that she had a real business. She did manicures in her home for seven dollars a session. As her business increased, her behavior changed. Previously, Tawana had rarely changed her clothes. Now, she showed a marked improvement in personal hygiene and in her ability to make friends. Her school attendance rose from an average of one and a half days a week to the whole week. School was where her potential clients were, but she also became a better student.

Tawana went from being a social outcast to having a strong and healthy ego. For Tawana, entrepreneurship was an avenue, a link to other human beings. Like Maurice, she knew her local market intimately. She knew which girls would be likely customers. The $40 or so a week she earned was her lifeline to interacting with other human beings in a mutual bond of self-interest. For Tawana and Maurice, business skills had also, imperceptibly, become social skills.

Other social behavior could change, too. I eventually observed that of the girls in my classes who became interested in entrepreneurship, fewer became pregnant or got married and dropped out of school. When the female students became economically literate, they were not so quick to tie themselves down with children at an early age.

I gave the girls in one of my classes a pre- and post-test on their estimates of the yearly cost of being a mother. Pre-test, they thought, on average, that a baby cost $142 a year. Post-test, the average estimate was $5,600. One of my students, Sonya, seemed to have *only* sexual relationships with other human beings, particularly the boys in the school. When she developed her own little business doing her classmates' hair (both boys and girls), it enabled her to communicate in a nonsexual way. She had something else to talk about, something that permitted her to have relationships without necessarily becoming sexually involved.

Running their own businesses helped my students make better decisions in their personal lives because it taught them about delayed gratification. The primary act of business—buying or making something, and selling it for a higher price than it cost you—takes place over time, with money as a reward. In general, people seem to make better decisions after starting a business. Many times, I saw a student's time preference (i.e., how he or she looked at the future) expand right before my eyes.

I was eager to test my entrepreneurial theories in a new environment, so even though I had survived my baptism by fire, so to speak, at Boys & Girls (which is a much better school these days, due to the efforts of Principal Frank Mickens, among others), I put in for an end-of-term transfer. I wanted to experience other schools in the system. I also wanted to test my entrepreneurial theories in a new environment. My eighth-period class and I had been through hell together—an experience I would never forget. Yet, when I made the announcement that I would be leaving soon, there was no noticeable reaction.

But when I walked into my last class, there was food waiting for me in the front of the room, including a basket of fried chicken. On my desk were two wrapped gifts: a bottle of cologne and a record, *The Best of the Temptations*. Covering the entire blackboard in huge chalk letters was the message:

GOODBYE HOMEBOY.
FROM THE ENTREPRENEURS OF BOYS AND GIRLS HIGH SCHOOL.

Underneath were the signatures of my students.

My last day at Boys & Girls was more affecting than I would have thought possible just a short time before. I was touched by the outpouring of emotion. My class gave me a card saying I was the best teacher they'd ever had. In my business math class, they applauded and made so much noise that my supervisor came in, thinking there was a fight. Three more students came up and said that I was the best teacher they had ever had. I was particularly gratified when Braddock told me: "I've decided to start my own business."

SPREADING THE MESSAGE

In the series of schools I was subsequently assigned to, spreading my "entrepreneurial message" began to require more and more subterfuge. I was teaching the kids the subjects I was supposed to teach, but it took all my ingenuity to use an entrepreneurial or business context—which was the only way to keep up their interest. It wasn't until I was assigned to Jane Addams Vocational High School, in the "Fort Apache" section of the South Bronx, that a principal, Pat Black, understood the potential value of what I was talking about. She gave me permission to teach a class in entrepreneurship. It was an immediate success and soon became the South Bronx Entrepreneurial Project. This allowed me to be out in the open. Instead of disguising entrepreneurial principles, I could offer what I considered to be a crash course in capitalism and free enterprise to young people who didn't even know that the United States operated in a free-market economic system. One-third of the kids in my class at Jane Addams did not know that the United States was a capitalist society; they thought it was communist!

Concepts such as the free-market system aside, what my students could see clearly was that if they had their own businesses, the amount of money they could make would depend on their own hard work and how they conducted themselves. In other words, they realized that information they might have formerly considered irrelevant (reading and math), abstract (economics), or facile (advice on how to dress or behave) could profoundly affect their lives.

Entrepreneurship gave them a sense of importance and a seriousness of purpose—after all, they were the presidents of their own companies, however modest. Their companies gave them something to talk about with other people. They felt more interesting and became much more sociable. I found that there were virtually no business concepts that could not be made comprehensible to my students.

Even such "dry" business topics as the income statement provided unexpected insights. My students seemed to think that the local retailers, who were mostly Asian, made somewhere between fifty and ninety cents profit on every dollar. This notion contributed greatly to a resentment based on race. When they discovered that these retailers, who worked long hours, made closer to four or five cents per sale, my students looked at such businesses, and the people who ran them, very differently.

THE CORE CURRICULUM

Eventually, my core curriculum came to include such subjects as: supply and demand; entrepreneurship as the fulfilling of consumer needs; the invention process, including patents, copyrights, and trademarks; cost/benefit analysis; business ethics; record keeping; the present and future value of money; business communication, with an emphasis on concise memo writing and speaking on the phone; debt-versus-equity financing; venture capital; balance sheets and income statements; franchising; the advantages and disadvantages of sole proprietorships, partnerships, and corporations; the production/distribution chain; how to register one's business; time management and goal setting; quality and customer service; negotiation strategies; advertising and marketing; and, of course, how to make a sales call.

I approached basic writing skills through the business memo. My students were put at ease because I was teaching them simple business communication, not literary or academic writing. I would assign memos that were due the next day, on a wide variety of topics. The main thrust was conciseness. I refused to accept any memo that had more than 300 words, and I announced that I would give an A or F grade after only one reading. The memo had to be clear. If I didn't understand it, it got the F.

Several years later, three of my students were in the wrong place at the wrong time (near a youth who was shooting off a gun) and were picked up by the police. While being held in a detention cell together, out of desperation, they composed a memo that was so simple and so convincing that they were released! I was both proud and horrified. The incident reminded me of what my pupils were exposed to when they weren't in school. However, if they had dealt with the police in their previous verbal style of monosyllables and profanity, the unfortunate event would not have had a happy ending.

Class trips and outside activities were important. Field trips helped demystify the world outside their neighborhoods. When I took my eighth-period students to a flea market in Greenwich Village, a new world opened up. The trip inspired them to want to sell their own merchandise. This led me to develop a two-part activity: My classes negotiated for inexpensive merchandise with wholesalers, and resold it a day or two later at a local flea market. Careful records were kept, the students designed their own posters for the flea market, and I made sure that everyone got business cards.

Later, I took my classes to the New York Stock Exchange, a trip made more meaningful by their familiarity with *The Wall Street Journal.* I found a willing banker and took classes to the bank, where every student opened an account. We toured local businesses owned by entrepreneurs from the same ethnic background as that of the majority of the class, and we registered the students' businesses at the County Clerk's office.

I discovered another important inspirational tool: emphasis on inventions as a route to entrepreneurial financial independence. I was able to tell the students about many overlooked inventions by African Americans, such as the automatic shoe-lasting machine, the gas mask, and the toggle harpoon. Invention contests set their imagination free and were a lot of fun.

A few years ago, one of our students, age thirteen, designed a device to protect the ears from being burned when using curling irons. Her invention was presented in conjunction with a contest held during an NFTE entrepreneurship course she was taking at the Boys' and Girls' Clubs of Newark. She had a patent pending for several years. At Jane Addams Vocational High School, another student came up with a less-than-practical idea for a kind of metal detector that could be worn while walking on the street and provide a warning that someone might be carrying a gun. Inventions are often inspired by real problems. He was trying to devise a way to survive in the ghetto, but his idea didn't work. Years later, I heard he had been shot.

The culmination of the curriculum was the writing of a brief but realistic business plan for a real business. I had each student present his or her plan before the rest of the class. Later, I learned that by bringing in outside judges—a local businessperson, an academic, someone from the media—I could get great publicity for the program and our mission. This coverage gave the kids a further sense that what they were doing could matter to the outside world. During this period, I worked really hard at being a good teacher. Every day I spent six to seven hours preparing to teach. I also traveled to study the techniques of famous teachers. The best was Jamie Escalante, the legendary calculus teacher from East Los Angeles. I watched him teach for hours and adapted many of his techniques. On my last day in his class, he challenged me, saying, "You're a fine teacher. Maybe one day you'll be a great one."

By 1986, even though the principal at Jane Addams was amenable to my programs, I had realized that even the best public school systems can be fundamentally bureaucratic and anti-entrepreneurial. This attitude was underscored one day when an evaluator came to observe my class of eighteen dropouts. The fact that, a week before the end of the school year, I had a class of sixteen students—and one of the absentees was legitimately out sick—was unusual in itself. The evaluation focused, however, on "excessive role playing." The evaluator said the class had "too much emphasis" on entrepreneurship, and class discussions were "too money-oriented."

With each passing year, it became clearer to me that my mission was not just to teach in the inner cities, but to teach entrepreneurship there. I came to believe, very strongly, that entrepreneurship was a more promising way out of the economic dead end of these neighborhoods than entry-level jobs, or more welfare, or other wasteful and unproductive government spending. Although I had reached about 1,800 inner-city kids between 1982 and 1986, in a number of schools in Brooklyn, Manhattan, and the Bronx, it seemed that to continue this work on the scale these programs deserved, I would have to become an entrepreneur again. My "product" would be entrepreneurship itself.

The NFTE Mission

I left the public school system in 1988 and founded NFTE. NFTE's goal is to make entrepreneurship education an integral component of the youth development field, so that every child becomes business-literate. Today, in fourteen American cities, as well as in Europe and South America, we operate programs that have served 28,000 students so far. Based on our empirical observations, we believe our students have, on average, a business formation rate of about 10 percent, and weekly sales of $60. Considering that the adult African American business-formation rate is 1.5 percent, the Hispanic average is 1.0 percent, and the Caucasian American rate is 6 percent, our students are doing extraordinarily well.

We were thrilled when the empirical results of our programs—improved business and entrepreneurial knowledge, improved attitude toward business, and increased business formation rates—were recently confirmed by a follow-up study of NFTE students begun by Dr. Andrew Hahn of Brandeis University in 1993. (To see this research, please visit our Web site at www.nfte.com.) More recent research conducted by the David H. Koch Charitable Foundation, following up with NFTE graduates from six years ago, reaffirms that NFTE's programs are having a significant and positive impact on at-risk youth.

In addition to our year-round entrepreneurship courses, we run a combination business camp for youth/training camp for teachers: NFTE University at Babson College, the nation's leading entrepreneurship education institution, in Babson Park, Massachusetts. We also have co-founded business camps at Wharton School of Business, Columbia University, Stanford, U.C. Berkeley, Georgetown, Tulane, and numerous other colleges.

From 1986 to 1988, on Sundays, I personally taught entrepreneurship to incarcerated youth at Rikers Island prison in New York. I was amazed to see how fascinated they were by the idea of learning to sell legal products. I'm convinced that incarcerated youth are eager to learn about entrepreneurship, and I hope we can be the leaders in this area of youth development, as well.

Perhaps our most exciting new project is BizTech, the state-of-the art on-line learning site we have developed in partnership with Microsoft, under the direction of Jeff Raikes, group vice president of Microsoft. Recently, the State University of New York (SUNY) at Empire State has agreed to grant three college credits to students who complete A NFTE course, on- or off-line, and pass an exam.[2] Soon, students and teachers who don't live near a city with NFTE programs will be able to use BizTech to study entrepreneurship and to interact with other teachers and students around the globe.

I'm very proud of NFTE's leadership role in creating a national movement that is teaching entrepreneurship to youth, particularly at-risk youth. Dozens of nationally known foundations and hundreds of major corporations and entrepreneurs are now funding youth entrepreneurship programs based on our paradigm. I am more convinced than ever that the way to turn around the economic decay of America's inner cities is through teaching its young people entrepreneurship. I think we should recognize that a significant portion of the standard curriculum, as it is taught in most public school systems, could be improved by the addition of entrepreneurship education.

Not all entrepreneurship students will end up owning their own businesses as a lifelong vocation, but one of our most significant findings over the years is that graduates of our programs do make better employees. They are better qualified for anything they eventually do, because they have a broad understanding and knowledge of business in general. They understand how the economic system works. They are better able to join the mainstream because they know how to be participants in our society instead of feeling they are merely some of its victims.

There are *many* NFTE success stories, some of which you'll read in this book, but we've had some terrible losses, too. Fourteen of our students have been murdered, and I've personally attended too many funerals of NFTE students. This has been heartbreaking, but it has also strengthened my commitment to teaching entrepreneurship as an alternative to poverty and the frustration and violence it causes.

I have also been cheered by the success of some of my students from my first year of teaching. I kept in touch with Maurice until about 1990. The last I heard, he was a sales representative for a computer company and was moving to the Midwest. Tawana, who was probably on her way to having children out of wedlock and going on welfare before she learned about entrepreneurship, was still operating her hairstyling business in 1989. Mills and I stayed in contact. He was able to graduate from high school and credited this to his interest in entrepreneurship. He had become very good at math and could do spreadsheets better than I could. After graduation, he got a job as an assistant manager at a flea market, married, and was raising a family. His personal hygiene, which had been outrageously bad, was now very good and he had excellent self-esteem.

Around 1991, I also ran into Therese. I was on my way to the subway. Therese, now twenty-four, was vending, on the street (she had a city license), clothes that she had purchased wholesale. She said that when she had enough money she was going to rent a storefront and would eventually own several stores. She was attending Bronx Community College at night and had even gotten her mother interested in business. She had kept the handouts I used to distribute in my classes, and she used these to help her run her business. "Thanks to you, Mr. Mariotti," she said, "I have always been able to take care of myself and make a living." I have never received a higher compliment.

Chapter 1

EVERYONE LIVES BY SELLING SOMETHING

WHY AMERICA NEEDS ENTREPRENEURS

> **Everyone lives by selling something.**
> —**Robert Louis Stevenson (1850–1894)**
> **Scottish author**

THE DIFFERENCE BETWEEN AN ENTREPRENEUR AND AN EMPLOYEE

Many people dream of owning their own business, being their own boss, and enjoying the reward of unlimited earnings. Entrepreneurship *is* the American dream. But most people hesitate to take the plunge. Like them, you may worry that you don't have enough money, time, or experience to start and operate your own small business.

Michelle insists that there is always time to start your own business, even if you're a single mother *and* a full-time college student.° Michelle should know; at age nineteen, she started her own business while attending college and caring for her daughters—Angela, three years old, and Erica, age eighteen months—and her newborn son, Kristian. Before she started her clothing resale company, À La Mode, Michelle knew nothing about running a business and had very little money. When I met Michelle, I thought she had tremendous natural elegance and poise, but it was clear that she was living a difficult ife as a single mother of three children. Today, she's a successful **entrepreneur.**

° All stories are the experiences of actual NFTE students.

Like Michelle, most Americans earn money by working in business. **Business** is the buying and selling of products and services in order to make money. Someone who earns a living by working for someone else's business is an **employee** of that business.

There are many different kinds of employees. At Ford Motor Company, for instance, some employees build the vehicles, some sell them, and some manage the company. But they all have one thing in common—they do not *own* the business, they *work* for others who do.

Entrepreneurs, in contrast, are both owners and employees. An entrepreneur is responsible for the success or failure of his or her business.

Sell Something for More Than It Costs You to Buy (or Make) It

Michelle loved fashionable clothes, but she lived in New Bedford, Massachusetts. The stores in New Bedford didn't always sell the latest fashions, and, when they did, they charged high prices. During an entrepreneurship class conducted by the National Foundation for Teaching Entrepreneurship, Inc. (NFTE), Michelle took a trip to Manhattan's wholesale clothing district. This visit gave Michelle her business idea. A **wholesaler** is a business that purchases products in bulk from the manufacturer and sells smaller quantities to **retailers.** Retailers buy small quantities from wholesalers and sell single items to customers. At each step along the road from the manufacturer to the customer, the price of the product increases.

Michelle was surprised that wholesale prices were *much* lower than the prices of clothing in stores. Michelle knew there were, in her hometown, many young women like herself who would love to buy the latest fashions at reasonable prices. During her visit to the wholesale district, Michelle learned that all she needed to do to be able to buy from a wholesaler was to apply for a sales tax identification number. Anyone can apply for a sales tax number by calling the state sales tax office and requesting an application for a sales tax number. After the application is filled out and returned, the number will be assigned.

Michelle decided to buy clothes wholesale and sell them for higher prices to her neighbors. She invited a dozen friends to her house for a clothes-buying party. If she sold them out of her home, Michelle reasoned, she could offer the latest styles at lower prices than the stores in her town were charging. Michelle had stumbled on the key to business success: Buy (or make) something for less than someone else is willing to pay to buy it from you! Before she visited the wholesale district again, she collected size information from her twelve friends and asked them whether they had any special requests. Michelle's customers are happy to pay the difference between the wholesale cost and the prices she charges. They know they are getting a great value.

Today, Michelle visits the wholesale district once a month and buys several hundred dollars' worth of clothes. There are many wholesalers in Manhattan, but Michelle has developed good relationships with a few whose products she really likes.

Michelle was afraid she would have to buy bulk quantities in order to get the wholesalers to sell to her, but she found that most of them are comfortable selling her as few as two or three items. They like dealing with Michelle because she doesn't ask for credit. She pays in full when she makes her purchases.

Michelle resells the clothes for around twice the wholesale price she paid. Sales are made from her home or on visits to customers' houses. Michelle's friends and neighbors are delighted to have a less expensive alternative to the local mall. Her customers also enjoy shopping in a more intimate setting.

As Michelle says, "Who would ever think a teenage mother with three children could ever own her own business and graduate from college?" After she finishes college, Michelle plans to open her own clothing boutique. She hopes her success will spark a revival of small businesses in her community.

Chart 1 shows four basic principles that are key to your business success.

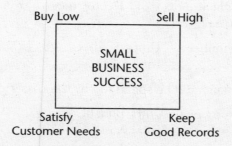

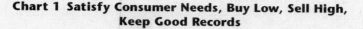

Chart 1 Satisfy Consumer Needs, Buy Low, Sell High, Keep Good Records

KEYSTONING

In her entrepreneurship class, Michelle learned about **keystoning**—buying a product wholesale and then selling it for double the wholesale price. For a simple business, keystoning is a good rule of thumb for covering your costs and making a nice profit. Like Michelle, many young entrepreneurs buy products such as lingerie, cologne, or watches from a wholesaler. You might buy T-shirts from a wholesaler for $3 each, for example, and sell each shirt to your customers for $6.

HECTOR'S SMALL BUSINESS

Hector, a high school student living in the South Bronx, needed to earn money to help support his mother and sister. He tried several fast-food restaurant jobs, but because his right leg had been injured in an accident, he had trouble standing up for hours at a time.

During an entrepreneurship class offered by NFTE, Hector learned about wholesalers and keystoning. On a visit to the wholesale district, he noticed a new type of portable cassette player. He bought ten and, in a brilliant move, *gave* five of them to the "cool" kids in school. Within days, he had sold the other five. The wholesale unit price had been $15; Hector's price to his classmates and friends was $30. (The store's retail price was $45.) Hector eventually sold eighty of these cassette players! Then he moved on to other products. Selling was easier on his leg than restaurant work, and he was making much more money than the minimum wage paid at the fast-food restaurants. To figure Hector's profit on his sales, do the calculations below. (The answers are on page 35).

1. How much money did Hector receive from his sales of eighty cassette players?

   80 (Number of Units Sold) × _____ (Selling Price of One Unit) = _____ (Total Sales)

2. How much did he spend to buy the cassette players?

   80 (Number of Units Bought) × _____ (Wholesale Cost per Unit) = _____ (Total Cost)

3. Profit equals Total Sales minus Total Cost. What is Hector's profit?

   _____ (Total Sales) − _____ (Total Cost) = _____ (Profit)

Ask yourself another good question: How many hours would Hector have had to work, at a job paying him $5 an hour, to earn as much as his profit from selling eighty cassette players?

Hector buys wholesale, keystones, and keeps careful track of his money. You will make a profit in business if you do the same, as long as you are selling something people want to buy.

EVERY BIG BUSINESS STARTED SMALL

The public often thinks of business only in terms of "big" business—companies such as Ford, General Motors, IBM, McDonald's, and Nike. A "big" business is typically defined as having more than 100 employees and selling more than a million dollars' worth of products or services in a year. A "small" business employs fewer than 100 employees and has yearly sales of less than a million dollars.

Surprisingly, the principles involved in running General Motors or owning a corner hot-dog stand are very similar. In fact, most of the big corporations in this country started out as small entrepreneurial businesses, or **ventures.** Each venture began as an idea in the mind of an entrepreneur.

YOU HAVE UNIQUE KNOWLEDGE OF YOUR MARKET

The people a business serves are its **market.** Your market, for example, might be your friends, neighbors, classmates at school, or colleagues at your current job. What might these people want to buy? No one knows the answer better than you do.

The beauty of business is that you already have the most important knowledge that you need to succeed. You know your market better than anyone else. Some successful entrepreneurs did not do well in school; some never even had a chance to go to school. Others were born into poverty. But they all used their unique market knowledge to create successful businesses.

ENTREPRENEUR STORY
BERRY GORDY, MOTOWN RECORDS

Berry Gordy, Jr.'s Motown Record Company is one of the music industry's greatest success stories. Among the artists Gordy discovered or promoted are Michael Jackson, Lionel Richie, the Supremes, Marvin Gaye, Stevie Wonder, and the Temptations. By recording the artists he liked and believed his market would like, Gordy created "the Motown Sound." He eventually recorded an astonishing 110 number-one hits. Gordy's market initially was the black urban community. He has described many of his first hit artists as "kids off the street."

Gordy was a kid off the street himself. He was born and raised in the tough Detroit ghetto of the 1930s and 1940s. Determined to escape the grinding poverty around him, Gordy turned to professional boxing. Although he won ten out of fourteen fights as a featherweight, he realized he was not big enough to have a great boxing career.

Gordy loved pop and jazz music, so his next career move was to open a jazz record shop. The shop soon went bankrupt, however, so Gordy took a job on the assembly line at Ford Motor Company. During his spare time, he wrote songs and went to nightclubs.

As his passion for music grew, Gordy became determined to break into the recording industry. He traveled to New York to make contacts with producers and publishers. After a series of rejections, he finally sold a few songs in the mid-1950s. When Gordy was age twenty-eight, Jackie Wilson recorded his song "Reet Petite." This was followed by another hit, "Lonely Teardrops," which sold a million copies. Gordy's share of the proceeds of these sales, however, was so paltry that he was forced to return to Detroit to work at Ford again. The experience made him determined to start his own production company and record label. He was tired of trying to get his foot in the door at someone else's operation.

To pursue his dream, Gordy borrowed $700 from his sister Anna and built a makeshift recording studio in the basement of a rundown house in Detroit in 1958. He began to audition performers. One of the kids who came in off the street was Smokey Robinson. Gordy signed him and a group of teenagers who called themselves the Miracles. Within a year, Smokey and the Miracles had two major hits. Gordy used the profits from their hits to sign more great newcomers such as the Supremes and Marvin Gaye.

Motown's Universal Appeal

Although Gordy started off making records for his market—black urban soul—he had an instinct for polishing his performers' sound and image to make them appealing to white middle America. The Supremes, for example, always had to be impeccably dressed and made-up, and their records were sweetened with string arrangements to make their songs sound more like the mainstream hits already playing on the radio. Producer Michael Gentile, who wrote the "Tears of a Clown" arrangement recorded by Smokey Robinson, has said that Gordy told him to write arrangements that would bring Motown artists "into the living rooms of white America on a Sunday afternoon."

Gordy devoted himself to developing his artists. He listened to every track they cut. If he didn't feel a song was perfect, it was recorded again. Soon, Motown's appeal was universal. Gordy once estimated that African Americans bought only half as many recordings of one of the Miracles' hits, "Shop Around," as white teenagers did.

By the early 1970s, Motown sales exceeded $10 million per year. Gordy branched into film with the movie *Lady Sings the Blues*, starring Diana Ross. By 1983, Motown was the largest black-owned company in America, with annual revenues of $104 million. In mid-1988, Gordy sold his company to MCA Records. He was then free to enjoy the tremendous wealth he had earned by using his unique knowledge to start a successful business.

DEVELOP YOUR UNIQUE KNOWLEDGE

You can develop your own unique market knowledge by applying your creativity and intelligence to your market. What do people in your market need? Want? Enjoy? You know your neighborhood better than someone from another neighborhood ever could. You have had life experiences that no one else has had.

These experiences make up your knowledge of the world. You can use that knowledge to become a successful entrepreneur. Entrepreneurship is about connecting your business ideas to the needs of your market.

The great thing about entrepreneurship is that your success is not limited by your abilities or education. You should never feel that you are not good enough, or creative enough, or smart enough to succeed. In fact, recent research indicates that your creativity and intelligence are limitless, as long as you use them.

BUSINESS IS AN ADVENTURE

Entrepreneurs are constantly discovering new markets and trying to figure out how to supply those markets efficiently and make a **profit.**

A business makes a profit when money from sales is more than money spent paying the bills. Business is very unpredictable—entrepreneurs never know ahead of time how people are going to react to any of their decisions. That's what makes entrepreneurship such an adventure.

I worked in the international financial department of Ford Motor Company before I became an entrepreneur. People sometimes ask me whether it's scary to leave the security of a corporate job and start your own business. Personally, when I started my first little business, I felt nothing but exhilaration. The day I founded my business, my self-esteem soared. I went from being unemployed to being a professional entrepreneur.

Entrepreneurs See Opportunities Where Others See Problems

After I left Ford, I began working as a consultant. My first contract was for a foundation, which paid me to go to the Caribbean and interview entrepreneurs about the problems they were having when they exported their products to the United States. During those interviews, I realized that there was a huge opportunity to solve their problems by starting an import–export business. They needed someone to represent them in the United States and to help them make sales. This could be my business!

When I returned to New York, I began advertising my services as a manufacturer's representative in Chamber of Commerce newsletters. (I had found out that an ad could be placed in the newsletters for free.) I started to get 800 to 900 letters a month from developing countries. Soon, I was representing manufacturers from West Africa, Pakistan, Bangladesh, and other countries.

Business Is a Process of Discovery

I describe business as a process of discovery because a big part of the entrepreneurial experience is trying to forecast the future of consumer needs. Some famous entrepreneurs have gone bankrupt and then succeeded later with a different business. Henry Ford went bankrupt twice before the Ford Motor Company succeeded. It's important to learn from failure or disappointments. Don't let them get you down.

Most successful entrepreneurs open and close many businesses during their lifetimes. A new business usually takes some time to turn a profit. If a new business continues to lose money, however, the entrepreneur may close it. A business that is losing money is **insolvent.** Closing a business is nothing to be ashamed of; it may be the best decision that can be made.

Some entrepreneurs will try very hard to keep a business open even when it is losing money. If money from sales is still not enough to pay bills, however, the business will eventually go **bankrupt.**

A bankrupt business is declared legally unable to pay its bills. A court can force the owner to sell items of value owned by the business, or **assets,** to raise money to pay bills. Sometimes, even the personal possessions of the owner are sold, and the proceeds are given to the **creditors**—the people to whom the business owes money.

THE ENGINE OF THE ECONOMY: ENTREPRENEURSHIP

Entrepreneurship has become the engine of our economy. Most of the new jobs created in this country in the past decade have been created by small, not big, businesses. Jeffry A. Timmons, Professor of Entrepreneurial Studies at Babson College, calls this explosion in entrepreneurship, in America and around the world, "the silent revolution." He notes that today more than one in seven Americans chooses to be self-employed. Meanwhile, the big corporations that used to employ so many Americans have been steadily losing jobs.

According to Professor Timmons, "The vast majority of the nearly 2 million millionaires in the United States in 1993 accumulated their wealth through entrepreneurial acts." Today, some 90 percent of students graduating from MBA programs say they want to start their own businesses, not climb the corporate ladder.[1]

Because starting a business does not require large amounts of time, money, or experience, entrepreneurship has proven to be an effective way for minorities and women to enter the business world. The U.S. Small Business Administration (SBA) reports that 70 percent of all African-American-owned startups, or new ventures, are funded from personal savings or by family and friends. Most are started with less than $5,000.

Presently, almost half of all new products are created by small, entrepreneurial companies. Almost half of the workforce in the United States is employed by small businesses. In 1992, for example, businesses owned by women were employing more of the U.S. population than all the Fortune 500 companies combined.

A Successful Entrepreneur Creates Jobs and Wealth

Entrepreneurs have a powerful impact on society. A successful entrepreneur can create jobs, products, services, and wealth. These come about when the entrepreneur makes good choices about how to use scarce **resources.** Resources are things such as oil, wood, cotton, **capital,** labor, or land that are used by businesspeople to create products and services. Capital is money used as a business resource. Most resources are scarce; that is, the available supply is limited.

As an entrepreneur, your goal is to add value to scarce resources. Let's say you are selling homemade cookies. You buy butter, eggs, flour, sugar, and other ingredients to make your cookies. These ingredients are your resources. You hope that people will like your cookies so much that they will be willing to buy them for a price that covers the cost of the ingredients *and* provides you with a profit. If customers buy your cookies for that price, you can be said to have added value to your resources. They are worth more when you use them to bake cookies. If your cookies taste bad, however, and customers don't want to buy them, you have wasted those resources.

I believe that every person should learn how to start and operate a business. Imagine how a hundred new entrepreneurs could revitalize an impoverished community!

Profit Tells You if You've Made the Right Choices

Entrepreneurs are constantly making choices about how to use scarce resources. Those choices directly affect how much profit a business makes. You might decide this week, for instance, to buy margarine instead of butter because margarine is cheaper, even though your cookies may not taste as good made with margarine. This type of choice is called a **tradeoff.** You are giving up one thing (taste) for another (money).

If your customers don't notice the change and continue to buy your cookies, you have made a good choice. You have conserved a resource (money) and increased your profit by lowering your costs. The increase in profit confirms that you have made the right choice.

If your customers notice the change and stop buying your cookies, your profit will decrease. The decrease in profit signals that you have made a bad choice. Next week, you'll probably buy butter again. The tradeoff wasn't worth it. Every choice an entrepreneur makes is a tradeoff.

THE PROS AND CONS OF BEING AN ENTREPRENEUR

Being an entrepreneur can be a twenty-four-hour-a-day obsession. It can be extremely rewarding or very painful. Being your own boss can be exhilarating one minute and terrifying the next. So can being financially responsible for the success or failure of your enterprise. As you read the pros and cons listed below, think about what you want out of life. What are your priorities? If being independent, working hard, and building your own fortune are goals of yours, and you aren't afraid of taking risks and possibly failing, entrepreneurship may be for you. If you value financial security and the support of colleagues, you'll probably do better as an employee rather than an entrepreneur.

Pros of Entrepreneurship

- **Independence:** Business owners do not have to follow orders or observe working hours set by someone else. Entrepreneurship can even provide an opportunity for someone to prove to society what he or she can accomplish. In the 1960s, Thomas Burrell came to believe that, because he was African American, no matter how good he was at his advertising job, he wasn't going to be promoted any further by the ad agency that employed him. He quit and started his own company, Burrell Communications Group. Today, with annual sales of over $60 million, it is the largest black-owned ad agency in the United States.

- **Satisfaction:** Turning a skill, hobby, or other interest into your own business can be very satisfying. Edwin Land, founder of Polaroid, turned his love of photography into a multimillion-dollar business when he developed and marketed the instant-print camera.

- **Financial Reward:** Through hard work, the sky can be the limit. Most of the great fortunes in this country were built by entrepreneurs. Countless small businesses have grown into large companies that have produced fortunes for their owners. Many entrepreneurs also create wealth by building businesses and selling them when they have become profitable. A successful business can sometimes be sold for a tremendous sum. At the age of forty-eight, for example, Jeno Paulucci sold his Chinese food business, Chun King, to R.J. Reynolds for $63 million in cash.

- **Self-Esteem:** Knowing you created something valuable can give you a strong sense of accomplishment. Oil tycoon Jake Simmons, Jr.'s first job was as a porter on a train. When a white passenger told him, "Boy, come here and get my bags!" Simmons told the man that he resented being called "Boy." The man's response was, "Young man, if you don't want to be called a boy, then don't do a boy's work, because boys carry bags for men." Simmons was so shaken that he left the job as soon as he could and swore to himself that he would be his own boss. He went on to create the world's most successful minority-owned oil conglomerate.

Cons of Entrepreneurship

- **Business Failure:** Many small businesses fail. You risk losing not only your money but also the money invested in your business by others. Henry Ford, the founder of Ford Motor Company, had several small business failures before making it big. He once said, "Failure is a chance to begin again more intelligently. It is just a resting place." He also said, "We learn more from our failures than our successes."

- **Obstacles:** You will run into problems that you will have to solve by yourself. You may face discouragement from family and friends. Liz Claiborne's family was dead set against her becoming a fashion designer and starting her own business. Her father was afraid the business world would be too rough on her. Claiborne proved him wrong by building Liz Claiborne, Inc. into a billion-dollar corporation.

- **Loneliness:** It can be lonely and even a little scary to be completely responsible for the success or failure of your business. In the early 1900s, Madame C.J. Walker traveled all over the United States by herself for two years, promoting her hair care products—a brave move, in those days, for a widowed African American woman with little education.

- **Financial Insecurity:** You are not guaranteed a set salary or any benefits. You may not always have enough money to pay yourself. King C. Gillette invented the disposable razor and started the Gillette Company, which is a billion-dollar business today. In 1901, though, Gillette's fledgling company was $12,500 in debt— a lot of money, back then. As Gillette recalled, "We were backed up to the wall with our creditors lined up in front waiting for the signal to fire." Gillette managed to secure financing from a Boston millionaire and save the company. An entrepreneur may face equally intense financial challenges many times.

- **Long Hours/Hard Work:** You will have to work long hours to get your business off the ground. Some entrepreneurs work six or seven days a week. During the early years of establishing McDonald's restaurants around the country, Ray Kroc worked about eighty hours a week. His simple motto was, "Press on."

As you may have realized while reading these pros and cons, they often represent two sides of the same coin. The hard work of establishing and running your own business can reap great financial rewards and build your self-esteem. Although you may face loneliness, financial insecurity, and other setbacks, as you overcome these obstacles you will become a much stronger person. Even if your business fails, you will have gained valuable business experience. Your next business will be more likely to succeed.

When I was self-employed in the import–export business, for example, I worried more about money than I did when I was working for Ford, but I felt much less stress in my interpersonal relationships. I really enjoyed not being dependent on anyone but myself for my job security. And I was having a lot more fun!

At the end of each chapter of this book, you will find discussion of a business that is ideal for a young or beginning entrepreneur who has limited time, money, and experience. All of the types of businesses described have been successfully run by young people.

CASE STUDY: T-SHIRTS

Herbert and Koung were in one of the first entrepreneurship classes I taught at Wharton School of Business. They sat next to each other and were two of the quietest pupils I'd ever had. I was concerned that they wouldn't do well because they were so quiet. I also thought they probably wouldn't become friends because Herbert is African American and Koung is Cambodian. Within a few days, however, I noticed that they always had their heads together. Next thing I knew, they had decided to go into business together.

Herbert and Koung realized that, between the two of them, they owned dozens of T-shirts imprinted with various logos or designs. Like them, their friends practically lived in T-shirts, so Herbert and Koung started a T-shirt screening business called T-Shirt Designers, in Minneapolis. They began by hand-screening shirts for a local restaurant. Eventually, they saved up enough money to purchase a silkscreening machine. They can now print up to a hundred shirts an hour and use up to four colors per shirt. This has enabled them to take on much larger T-shirt printing jobs and earn more money. One of their clients is the National Foundation for Teaching Entrepreneurship, Inc. Their story shows that business often crosses ethnic and cultural lines and can lower friction between different groups of people.

How many T-shirts do you own with something printed or painted on them? How many do your friends own? Decorated T-shirts are very popular. It's easy to make colorful T-shirts that other people will want to buy from you.

Silkscreening and fabric painting are two easy ways to turn a plain T-shirt into a profitable creation without investing much money.

Silkscreening

Silkscreening is a stencil method of printing. Place the silkscreen, which has your design cut into it, on top of the T-shirt. Next, use a wedge to push the ink through the screen onto the T-shirt. The ink comes through the screen only where your design has been cut into it.

Supplies	Where to Find
Silkscreen	Arts & crafts store
Wedge	Arts & crafts store
Ink	Arts & crafts store
Plain T-shirts	Wholesaler

Fabric Painting

Fabric painting is a good method to use if you want each of your T-shirts to have a unique design. You paint directly onto each shirt. Experiment with gluing decorative jewelry to shirts, too.

Supplies	Where to Find
Fabric paints	Arts & crafts store
Plain T-shirts	Wholesaler

Market Research

Before making your T-shirts, conduct some market research. Ask your friends and other potential customers what size T-shirts they buy. Ask them what designs they might like, and what price they might be willing to pay for your shirts.

Tips

- Wear one of your creations to promote your business.
- Offer to silkscreen T-shirts for a school sports team or a local rock band to sell. They supply the design, you translate it onto the T-shirts.
- NFTE graduates have sold just about anything one can buy from a wholesaler. Typical products purchased for resale have included watches, lingerie, earrings, combs, pens, calculators, and hats.

ANSWERS: HECTOR'S SMALL BUSINESS (SEE P. 24)

1. How much money did Hector receive from his sales of 80 cassette players?

   80 (Number of Units Sold) × $30 (Selling Price of One Unit) = $2,400 (Total Sales)

2. How much did he spend to buy the cassette players?

   80 (Number of Units Bought) × $15 (Wholesale Cost per Unit) = $1,200 (Total Cost)

3. Profit equals Total Sales minus Total Cost. What is Hector's cost?

   $2,400 (Total Sales) − $1,200 (Total Cost) = $1,200 (Total Profit)

4. How many hours would Hector have had to work, at a job paying him $5 per hour, to earn as much as his profit from selling eighty cassette players?

   $1,200 (Total Profit) ÷ $5 per hour = 240 hours

RESOURCES

Books

A Teen's Guide to Business: The Secrets to a Successful Enterprise, by Linda Menzies, Oren S. Jenkins, and Rickell R. Fisher (New York: MasterMedia Limited, 1992).

The authors are successful teen entrepreneurs. The book covers everything from how to dress for different business situations to how to run different types of youth enterprises.

Magazines for Entrepreneurs

Inc. magazine, founded by my friend Bernard Goldhirsh, is the magazine most widely read by entrepreneurs. If you want to know what's happening in entrepreneurship in America, read *Inc.* It's available at newsstands and bookstores and by subscription.

> *Inc.: The Magazine for Growing Companies*
> 38 Commercial Wharf
> Boston, MA 02110
> (800) 842-1343
> www.inc.com

Two other excellent publications for entrepreneurs are *Fast Company* magazine and *Entrepreneur* magazine.

> *Fast Company*
> 77 North Washington Street
> Boston, MA 02114-1927
> (800) 688-1545
> www.fastcompany.com

> *Entrepreneur*
> 2392 Morse Avenue
> Irvine, CA 92614
> (949) 261-2325
> www.entrepreneurmag.com

As entrepreneurship has taken hold among women and minorities, several magazines have sprung up to serve those markets. The best are:

> *Black Enterprise Magazine*
> 130 5th Avenue, 10th Floor
> New York, NY 10011-4399
> (212) 242-8000
> www.blackenterprise.com

> *Hispanic Magazine*
> 331 Madison Avenue
> New York, NY 10010
> (212) 986-4425
> www.hispanic.com

Other Resources

The Small Business Administration (SBA) is a government agency created to support and promote entrepreneurs. The SBA offers free and inexpensive pamphlets on a variety of business subjects. Some local offices offer counseling to small business owners. Contact the SBA at:

Small Business Administration
409 Third Street, SW
Washington, DC 20416
(800) 827-5722
www.sbaonline.sba.gov

To reach the Small Business Answer Desk, which assists entrepreneurs with their questions and can help you locate an SBA office near you, call (800) 368-5855.

The Service Corps of Retired Executives (SCORE) is an organization of retired businesspeople who volunteer as counselors and mentors to entrepreneurs. To locate an office near you; contact:

Service Corps of Retired Executives
26 Federal Plaza
New York, NY 10021
(212) 264-4507

The National Association of Women Business Owners helps female entrepreneurs to network. You can even join a local chapter of female entrepreneurs in your area.

National Association of Women Business Owners
1413 K Street, NW, Suite 637
Washington, DC 20005
(301) 608-2590
www.membrane.com/philanet/key/nawbo.html

Chapter 2

OPPORTUNITY RECOGNITION

TRAIN YOUR MIND TO RECOGNIZE OPPORTUNITIES

Once you shape a company to service the marketplace and your services are necessary, the company develops a compulsion of its own to grow.

—Liz Claiborne
Fashion designer and founder of Liz Claiborne, Inc.

WHAT PROBLEM CAN YOU SOLVE?

What does the word "opportunity" mean to you? Is it a chance to get something for nothing? A chance to do something you've never done before? A job? An education? What about a problem? I'll bet you've never thought of a problem as an opportunity, but it is. Many amazing businesses have been created, in fact, by entrepreneurs who were frustrated by problems and developed businesses to solve them.

Anita Roddick started The Body Shop, Inc. because she was tired of paying for perfume and fancy packaging when she bought makeup. So Roddick created simple, inexpensive packages and even encouraged recycling of containers from her shops. She kept her prices low and her advertising down to earth (Roddick once said it was "immoral" for cosmetics companies to use pictures of glowing sixteen-year-olds to sell antiwrinkle creams to forty-year-old women).

Bill Gates is another problem solver. Before he started Microsoft, most software was so hard to use that it was downright terrifying to the average person. He decided to create software that would be fun and easy to use, and he built a multibillion-dollar business.

For the mental training needed to recognize business opportunities, Roddick suggests entrepreneurs ask themselves the following questions:

- What product or service would make my life easier or more enjoyable?
- What makes me annoyed or angry?
- What product or service would take away my aggravation?

Creating Opportunities from Fantasies

Business opportunities are also created when entrepreneurs fantasize about products or services they would love to have in their lives. Prime your imagination by asking yourself (or your friends) questions like:

- What is the one thing you'd love to have more than anything else?
- What does it look like? Taste like?
- What does it do?

Widen Your World

The best way to train your mind to recognize opportunities is to broaden it with lots of new experiences. Keep an eye out for opportunities, no matter what you are doing. Some great (and fun!) ways to broaden your mind include:

- Traveling.
- Meeting new people.
- Learning a language.
- Reading books you might not normally read.
- Attending lectures, poetry readings, concerts.
- Trying new hobbies.
- Watching the news; reading newspapers and magazines.
- Discussing news events with friends and mentors.

- Internships (nonpaying part- or full-time jobs that give you hands-on experience). Many businesses, from newspapers to charities, offer internships to young people.

Stimulate your brain as much as you can with music, art, dance—input! Research has shown that the more new stuff we try, the smarter and more creative we become.

A Little Background Music, Please

Are you beginning to understand why entrepreneurs are considered the creative force behind this country's huge economy? Some economists call entrepreneurship the engine of the economy. Although entrepreneurship has taken off in the United States in the past 100 years, and has been responsible for creating many of this country's jobs and great fortunes, "entrepreneur" is actually a French word from the 1600s. The French originally used "entrepreneur" to describe someone who undertakes a big project, but it came to mean a businessperson who developed new and improved ways of doing business.

Entrepreneurs Exploit Changes in Our World

Today's business experts have focused the definition of "entrepreneur" even more sharply. Management guru Peter Drucker says that "not every new small business is entrepreneurial or represents entrepreneurship." Drucker believes that for a business to be considered entrepreneurial, it should exploit changes in our world. These changes can be technological, like the explosion in computer technology that led Bill Gates to start Microsoft, or cultural, like the collapse of communism, which has led to all kinds of new business opportunities in Eastern Europe.

Drucker defines an entrepreneur as someone who "always searches for change, responds to it, and exploits it as an opportunity."[1] Could that someone be you?

Where Others See Problems, Entrepreneurs Recognize Opportunities

At NFTE, we've boiled down lots of thoughts about entrepreneurship to one simple definition that we think says it all:

An entrepreneur recognizes opportunities where other people see only problems.

Train your mind to recognize opportunities and you will be a very successful entrepreneur. Try thinking of three problems that annoy you and a business solution for each:

Problems	Business Solutions
1. _____	1. _____
2. _____	2. _____
3. _____	3. _____

An Idea Is Not Necessarily an Opportunity

There's a catch, however. Not every wild business idea you have is an opportunity. *An opportunity is an idea that is based on what consumers want.* Many a small business has failed because the entrepreneur didn't understand this.

How do you recognize when an idea is an opportunity? Professor Jeffry A. Timmons, the author of *Entrepreneurship for the 21st Century,* suggests that you look for these four characteristics:

1. It is attractive to customers.
2. It will work in your business environment.
3. It can be executed in the window of opportunity that exists. (The window of opportunity is the amount of time you have to get your business idea to your market. If competitors have already had the same idea and gotten their product to the market first, that window of opportunity has slammed shut.)
4. You have the resources and skills to create the business, *or* you know someone who does and who might want to work with you.

Four Roots of Entrepreneurial Opportunity

You've probably figured out by now that entrepreneurs are optimists! Where other people see problems, entrepreneurs see potential businesses. Just by changing your attitude whenever you catch yourself in a negative place, you can become a better entrepreneur You can also train your mind to recognize opportunities by thinking about these four roots of opportunity:[2]

1. **Problems:** Could you create a business that would solve a problem for yourself or other people?

2. **Change:** Any change can stir up new business opportunities. Read the newspaper! Look for changing laws, situations, or trends.

3. **Inventions:** Even if you don't invent something, you might find a creative way to sell or market a new invention. Maybe you could be the one to bring a new invention to your community first! Technology is developing at lightning speed. Read the magazines that cover technologies that you find interesting, and think about how to create a business from new advances.

4. **Competition:** If you can find a way to beat the competition, you can create a very successful business with an existing product or service. Look at the businesses in your community. Could you do a better job? Could you be faster? More reliable? Cheaper? If so, you may be looking at a business opportunity.

Internal Opportunities

No matter what business you start, it has to meet a consumer need. But many successful entrepreneurs have started businesses that *initially* did not appear to meet much consumer need. Many entrepreneurs have built on passion alone. An internal opportunity is one that comes from inside you—from a hobby or from some passion that you have.[3] That passion won't ignite a successful business, though, unless you can find a way to make other people share your passion—or find folks who already do.

ENTREPRENEUR STORY
RUSSELL SIMMONS, DEF JAM

In the late 1980s, Russell Simmons was promoting rap concerts at the City University of New York. Most record executives thought rap was a trend that would run its course in a year or two, but Simmons really loved rap and believed it could be huge. For $5,000, Simmons formed

Def Jam Records with fellow student Rick Rubin. They produced hit records by Run DMC and LL Cool J. Simmons eventually bought out Rubin and created the multimillion-dollar Def Jam empire, which has produced the Def Jam comedy television shows, the record label, and a line of clothing.

Simmons took a chance on this internal opportunity because he believed that if you personally know ten people who are eager to buy your product or service, ten million would be eager to buy it if they knew about it. Lucky for him, he was right about rap! But he could have been wrong. That's the problem with internal opportunities. Just because you are passionate about something doesn't mean enough other people will share your passion and sustain your business.

External Opportunities

When you look outside yourself for business ideas, you can find external opportunities. Maybe you notice that people in your neighborhood are complaining about the lack of available day care, so you start a day care center. The business might succeed, but you could burn out quickly if you aren't the type of person who loves to be around screaming toddlers all day long. That's the problem with external opportunities—your business idea may fill a need for the market, but you may not have the interest, skills, or passion to enjoy putting in the time and energy needed to make it a success.

The best business opportunities are both internal and external. Ideally, a business that you are passionate about meets a huge external need in the marketplace. Simmons loved rap and hoped that other people would, too. As it turned out, both white and black audiences were bored with rock and looking for a fresh new sound. And rap fit the bill.

The Team Approach to Opportunity

Simmons and Rubin turned Def Jam into a huge success because they made a good team. Alone, neither of them had enough money to launch a record label, but together they were able to do it. Plus, they each knew different artists and had different contacts in the record industry.

Every person you know is a potential business-formation opportunity. Your friends or family members may have skills, equipment, or contacts that would make them valuable business partners.

Let's say you would love to start a T-shirt business, but you're not an artist. If you have a friend who is an artist, the two of you can start a business together. Or maybe you'd like to form a DJ business, but you only have one turntable. If you form the business with a friend, you can pool equipment and records.

When forming a business team, organize the business so that everyone involved shares in the ownership and profits. People work much harder when they are working for themselves. But no matter how enthused you and another person get about a business idea, please remember that every business idea is not an opportunity. For an idea to be an opportunity, it must lead to the development of a product or service that is of value to customers.

Eco-Opportunities

Entrepreneurs need to stay up-to-date not only on changes in technology, which can lead to business opportunities, but also on environmental and social issues. These can lead to great business opportunities, too.

Cleaning up our land, air, and water, for example, has become an issue in recent years, and the growing concern for the environment is creating lots of opportunities for entrepreneurs. Maria Coler and her former partner started Hydrotechnology Consultants, based in Hoboken, New Jersey. The company brings building sites into compliance with environmental laws. When a contractor wants to build an apartment building on some land that was previously used by a factory, for instance, the land and water must first be tested to make sure they're not too polluted for residences. That's where Maria comes in. She tests the ground and water, and then tells the contractor what needs to be done, if anything, to clean the site. If cleaning has to be done, she hires and supervises crews to do the work, and then retests the site to certify that it complies with all environmental clean-up standards.

It's interesting to note that the three practices recommended by environmentalists are all sound business practices that can increase your profit by helping you lower your costs:

1. **Reducing:** Cutting back or buying less.
2. **Reusing:** Finding another use for a product, or giving it to someone else to use again.

3. **Recycling:** Breaking the product down and reconstituting it as something fresh.

One of the most moral acts an entrepreneur can do is to use resources—land, air, water, and so on—frugally and economically so that future generations can enjoy them, too. Not so coincidentally, using resources as efficiently as possible not only cuts down on pollution but keeps your business competitive.

CASE STUDY: CYBER CAFÉ

Lee Gaddies believes the single biggest opportunity available right now to entrepreneurs—especially minority entrepreneurs—is the Internet. In an article by Ruby L. Bailey in the *Detroit Free Press* (February 11, 1999), Gaddies, the owner of Alphabase A Cyber Café, says of African Americans: "We're constantly playing a game of catch-up, instead of being on the edge. We now have the opportunity to be at the right place, in the right time, with the right tool."

That tool is the computer, according to Gaddies, 32, who took out a $65,000 loan (using his home as collateral) to open Alphabase A Cyber Café. His 3,000-square-foot café has seventeen computers and a staff committed to teaching people how to use them. The café serves coffee and provides computer classes and Internet access.

A Lou Harris survey quoted by Bailey found that African Americans account for one quarter of all spending on the Internet. About 24 percent of African Americans use the Internet, compared to 30 percent of whites, the survey found. Gaddies argues that African Americans can use the Internet to substantially increase their access to business opportunities—in part because skin color is a lot harder to determine on the Web. Consider that retailers made some $2.3 billion in Internet sales last year, and that amount is expected to climb to $108 billion by 2003. African Americans who have felt shut out of business opportunities by discrimination, or by not having much capital, have a striking opportunity here to transcend both those problems and capture some of that e-commerce for themselves.

The only discrimination that exists on the Web is based on how good your Web site is, Gaddies says. "It [the Web] allows you to have a presence equal to a multimillion-dollar company. Never before in history has every single citizen been able to have access to this kind of information and power at their fingertips. It becomes the great equalizer." Sounds like opportunity knocking, doesn't it?

RESOURCES

Books

Setting up a store on-line is getting easier every day. For business ideas, check out *101 Businesses You Can Start on the Internet*, by Daniel S. Janal (International Thompson Publishing, Inc., 1996).

Other Resources

On-line business is called "e-commerce." Check out the following Web sites for e-commerce opportunity updates:

E-commerce News, www.internetnews.com/ec-news
Electronic Commerce Guide, e-comm.internet.com
Sell It On The Web, www.sellitontheweb.com

Chapter **3**

A Successful Venture Satisfies a Consumer Need

And You Know What the Consumers in Your Market Need

No nation was ever ruined by trade.
—Benjamin Franklin (1706–1790)
American statesman, writer, and inventor

Satisfying a Consumer Need

What could you sell that consumers you can reach would want to buy? To be successful, you need a clear vision of what those consumers need.

Five Ways to Satisfy a Consumer Need

For a business to be successful, it must satisfy a need of enough **consumers** to generate a profit. There are five basic ways an entrepreneur can satisfy a consumer need:[1]

1. Develop a new **product** or **service.**
2. Uncover new resources or technologies.
3. Apply existing resources or technologies in new ways.
4. Find new markets for an existing product or service.
5. Improve an existing business.

Filling a consumer need generates **revenue,** or money from sales.

ENTREPRENEUR STORIES
STEVE JOBS AND STEPHEN WOZNIAK, APPLE COMPUTER; BILL GATES, MICROSOFT

Some entrepreneurs recognize a consumer need that consumers themselves don't see immediately. Henry Ford imagined an automobile in front of every home long before most consumers ever thought of owning their own cars. Stephen Wozniak saw a computer inside every home at a time when computers were used only by universities, labs, and corporations. "The Woz" and his close buddy, Steve Jobs, founded Apple Computer when they were barely out of high school, and Apple became a leader in the development of personal home and office computers. Bill Gates, inspired by Apple's success with selling computer hardware, started Microsoft, a company that would become the world leader in computer software.

How Apple Developed the Personal Computer

Apple Computer was founded by Wozniak and Jobs in a garage in 1975, when the two friends were only in their early twenties.

Wozniak had a natural aptitude for electronics. His father was an outstanding engineer who worked for the Lockheed Corporation in California. Wozniak started reading his father's technical literature when he was only nine years old. He built his own radio receiver and transmitter and got into ham radio operation when he was only eleven. "The Woz," as he was nicknamed, became fascinated with computers as an eighth-grader. His room was filled with pictures of them. He designed and built a computer that won first prize at the Bay Area Science Fair.

Wozniak had a playful side, as well. He loved to play baseball and was big on practical jokes. In fact, he spent most of his first year at the University of Colorado playing practical jokes on his dorm mates. That summer, he met Steve Jobs, a high-strung, enterprising young man. He and Jobs became best friends.

Jobs encouraged Wozniak to go into the business of selling to college students a "blue box" he had built. The blue box was an illegal electronic device that could be used to make free long-distance telephone calls. The boxes cost $60 to make. Jobs and Wozniak sold them wholesale for $80. After selling about 200 boxes in 1973, they decided the business was too risky and closed shop.

Wozniak dropped out of college and landed a job with Hewlett-Packard, a major computer company. Jobs dropped out too, and traveled to India. He shaved his head and made a determined effort to study Buddhism. He soon tired of meditating and returned to Cupertino, California, where he got a job with Atari and hooked up again with Wozniak.

Wozniak was a member of the Homebrew Club, a group of computer enthusiasts. He was determined to build a small "personal" computer to show the Club.

When Wozniak finally succeeded, Jobs saw its market potential. They agreed to go into business together. First, however, Wozniak offered Hewlett-Packard a chance to develop his small computer. Hewlett-Packard failed to see the potential of the personal computer and turned him down. So, with $1,300, Jobs and Wozniak started Apple Computer in Wozniak's parents' garage in Cupertino, California.

At first, business was very slow. Jobs and Wozniak knew they needed to build a better computer. Wozniak worked on his design until he created the Apple II, which is considered one of the great achievements of the computer industry.

Jobs, meanwhile, searched for someone willing to invest in the company. After being turned down by friends and family, he found Mike Markklula. Markklula invested $91,000 in the company in return for a share of the profits. Within three years, Apple's sales grew to over $100 million.

In 1994, Apple set a record with net sales of $9.19 billion, up 15 percent over 1993. Apple was successful because Jobs and Wozniak filled a consumer need that the giants of the computer industry had failed to notice. The company continues to succeed by producing new products, such as the colorful iMac, that consumers want. In 1999 it sold almost $2 billion worth of computers per quarter.

Apple's Success and New Consumer Needs: Bill Gates Founds Microsoft

Because consumer needs constantly change, new business opportunities are always developing. Bill Gates, the founder of Microsoft, was, like Stephen Wozniak, supersmart and obsessed with computers. A few years younger than Wozniak and Jobs, Gates grew up hearing about Apple's efforts to place a computer on every office desk and in every home. Gates quickly realized that because Apple had developed a new product and was applying existing resources or technologies in new ways, new consumer needs were developing.

Owners of Apple computers needed software to run them. Gates decided that he would fill that consumer need by applying the resources and technologies he knew and by uncovering new resources and technologies. He was also determined to find new markets by making his software so easy and so much fun to use that people who had never dreamed they could operate a computer would realize that they could.

Jobs and Wozniak were the hardware kings, so Gates resolved to be the software king. In those days, software—the programs that made computers *do* things—was not considered an important business. Software was boring. It was more often given away or traded than sold.

Gates's great insight was to commercialize software. He hired brilliant young people like himself to design software that made computers do things ordinary working people wanted them to do—calculate and display budgets, edit manuscripts, add graphics. Gates made his software colorful and easy to use. He packaged it attractively. Gates made software fun, and consumers kept coming back for more. By 1992, Microsoft was worth $22 billion, and Bill Gates was worth over $7 billion. At age thirty-six, he was the richest person in America.

How Did Gates Do It?

The best entrepreneurs love risk and adventure, and they possess great vision and drive. Bill Gates has these qualities in spades. He has used them, along with his formidable brainpower, to build Microsoft Corporation into one of the most powerful players in the computer industry, and to make himself the richest person in America. He even replaced Steve Jobs as the media's designated personal computer visionary.

In 1976, Gates and his friend Paul Allen hired several other talented programmers and began writing the software for two corporate customers' hardware. National Cash Register and General Electric were the customers.

By the end of 1982, however, the age of the personal computer had arrived, and millions of people wanted software to run their new gadgets. Revenues at Microsoft were up to $34 million; over 200 people were working for the company. Gates developed a reputation for hiring the best and the brightest, and running them ragged. The press called his employees "Micro-kids." The youthful employees, dressed in jeans and sneakers, conducted plastic sword fights in the hallways.

Gates himself was developing a reputation as intense, driven, and work-addicted. He had bought a high-performance Porsche that enabled him to speed between his home and Microsoft. Despite his hectic schedule, Gates kept his vision in mind: People want easy-to-use software. This vision led to the development of Windows, a software program whose graphics were so easy to understand that someone with no experience on a computer could figure out how to use it by trial and error.

Gates Rolls Out Windows

Gates rolled out Microsoft Windows on May 22, 1990, before a throng of reporters, analysts, and industry watchers. He was just thirty-four years old, and a multibillionaire. He was also taking on IBM, one of the world's most powerful corporations. Gates had tried to sell Windows to IBM, with whom he had a partnership, but IBM had turned him down and was developing its own competitive software, an operating system called OS/2.

Like many of Gates's pet projects, Windows was enormously risky, but the reward was great. Gates used his company's power to try to make Windows the industry standard. His competitors responded with a price war. As profits on software sales fell, Gates expanded into other computer-related developments, such as faxing and the information highway. Microsoft programmers continue to hack out new or improved programs to help consumers use the latest advances in the fast-moving digital universe. The 1995 version of Windows, for example, includes software for running a modem and getting on-line.

Today, Gates recognizes the impact entrepreneurship education can have on young people. Microsoft is sponsoring a NFTE program in Seattle, as well as a BizTech online curriculum and summer Biz Camps. One of my goals is to get successful entrepreneurs more involved with entrepreneurship education so that more young people can gain a basic knowledge of how to create wealth.

PRODUCTS AND SERVICES

Along with their products, both Apple and Microsoft provide their consumers with services, such as consulting and technological assistance.

Products (also called "goods") are *tangible*—they can be seen and touched. Some examples of products a young entrepreneur might sell are ties, candy, baked goods, T-shirts, or watches.

Services are *intangible*—they can't be touched. Some examples of services a young entrepreneur might sell are baby-sitting, pet care, house painting, or word processing. Gates made his megafortune by anticipating the needs of consumers as computer technology developed. Today, many people are using their computers to go "on-line" and gain access to the information highway. Where there are consumers, entrepreneurs follow.

RIDING THE INFORMATION HIGHWAY

As more people invest in fax machines and use modems to get on-line, the opportunities to promote your business are expanding. Instead of mailing ads or coupons to prospective customers, for instance, why not fax them? If you have a modem hooked up to your computer and fax machine, you can save time by programming your computer to fax your flyer to a list of fax numbers. The computer will automatically send your promotional piece to the numbers on the list, leaving you free to do something else.

At one time, an account at a university or government agency and a working knowledge of a difficult programming language were needed to hook into the information highway. Now, all you need is a modem and an account with America Online, CompuServe, or any of the Internet access providers around the country. Microsoft and IBM are building Internet software into the latest versions of Windows and OS/2. Numerous books are available to guide you. Two of the best are *The Whole Internet User's Guide and Catalog* (O'Reilly & Associates, Sebastopol, California, 1992) and *New Riders Official Internet Yellow Pages* (New Riders, Indianapolis, 1994).

Your access provider will give you software that your computer will use to browse the Internet (the Net) and to send and receive electronic mail (e-mail). Once you're on the Net, you can send and receive e-mail from an estimated 30 million users. You can use e-mail to communicate with suppliers and customers.

You can also keep in touch with thousands of special-interest newsgroups. No matter what your business, your potential customers will be talking about their needs in a Net newsgroup. Once you are exploring the Net, you will be able to find lists of newsgroups that discuss every subject imaginable. Newsgroups are excellent sources of information about markets for your business, too.

THE WORLD WIDE WEB

When you're comfortable with being on-line via your server, you'll be ready to explore deeper levels of the Internet. The World Wide Web (the Web) is a subsection of the Internet. Documents on the Web can include images and sound. These documents are also called home pages. Establishing a home page on the Web is the most exciting approach to making your presence known.

Designing a Web page for your business isn't simple, but where there's a consumer need, there's usually an entrepreneur. You should be able to find someone offering a Web page design service. Try the computer department of a local college. One of the students might be the entrepreneur you need.

The Internet Business Center offers many business resources, including examples of commercial Web pages, or sites. Another source of information about putting your business on the Web is a site called Commercial Use. To learn more about technology and what it can do for your business, check out Chapter 15, "Technology Is Your Generation's Competitive Advantage."

VOLUNTARY EXCHANGE

All business, whether conducted on-line or off-line, is made up of **voluntary exchange.** Voluntary exchange is a trade between two people who agree to trade money for a product or service. When you buy new software for your computer, no one is forcing you to trade. You and the seller of the software agree to the exchange because you both benefit from the trade.

The opposite of voluntary exchange is **involuntary exchange.** A mugging is an involuntary exchange. One person forces the other person to give up something and get nothing of value in return. Involuntary exchange requires force. Only one person benefits from an involuntary exchange. To start a successful business, you will need to sell a product or service for which someone will *want* to exchange money.

THE DESIRE FOR MONEY IS NOT A STRONG ENOUGH REASON TO START A BUSINESS

Any business, large or small, needs to make money to survive and grow. Some of the most successful entrepreneurs in the world, however, have said that the desire to make money is not a good enough reason to start one's own business.

I heard Steve Jobs make that point during a speech he gave in the mid-1980s. He talked about how important it is to follow your heart and do something that you love. Focusing on the money, he said, does not get you very far. An entrepreneur needs a vision.

The financial rewards of owning your own business may not appear until after many years of very hard work. The desire to make money may not be enough to keep you going through the difficult early period of your business.

Most successful companies are founded by someone who has a dream. Henry Ford dreamed of a "horseless carriage" that the average American could afford. Jobs and Wozniak imagined a computer on every desk. Gates imagined his software in every computer. A vision provides the motivation to succeed.

When Wozniak and Jobs envisioned a computer in every home, computers were very large, expensive appliances. They were available only to universities, scientists, and large companies. What product or service is available today to only a few select consumers? Can you envision how it might meet a need for many consumers in the future? Let your imagination run wild. You just might come up with the vision for a successful business.

SUCCESS STARTS WITH IDEAS— NEW OR REPACKAGED

Profitable businesses are all based on good ideas, but don't be discouraged if you haven't come up with a brand new idea for a business that has never been imagined before. Very few ideas are actually new. Most new companies are started by repackaging old ideas and concepts or combining them with new technology. Computer dating, for example, combined existing computer technology and personal dating services.

To be an entrepreneur, you don't have to come up with a new invention or product. *It is necessary, though, to provide a product or service that fills a consumer need.*

CASE STUDY: BABY-SITTING SERVICE

Providing baby-sitting service is the first business of many young people. Most baby-sitters go to the home of the children, but Tanya had a different idea. She decided to offer a baby-sitting service based in her own home, for four children in her South Bronx neighborhood. In that way, the children could play together.

Like many NFTE students, Tanya had grown up under the tremendous stress of living in a harsh urban environment. I constantly told her that because she had overcome all the things she had faced already, she was certainly strong enough to run a small business. That's a point I'd like to stress: Any pain or difficulty you've had in your life will actually make you a stronger, more resilient entrepreneur.

> **Out of every adversity comes an equal or greater benefit.**
> **—Napoleon Hill**

On two evenings a week, the parents of the four children brought them to Tanya's house for two hours. This gave the parents time to go out to dinner or do errands. The children enjoyed going to Tanya's house because they got to play together.

Tanya charged $5.00 per child for the two-hour period. For each baby-sitting evening, therefore, she earned:

$$\$5.00 \times 4 \text{ children} = \$20.00$$

Each week, Tanya earned $40.00 from her business. Her cost per child for each week was around $.50 for juice and milk. Her total weekly costs were $2.00. Her weekly profit, therefore, was $38.00. Tanya realized that she could easily double her profit by caring for another set of four children on two other weekday evenings. She also began offering weekend baby-sitting services for the same rate.

As Tanya learned, parents of young children are always searching for responsible baby-sitters. You probably have friends who baby-sit. Think about starting a service like Tanya's, or serving as a baby-sitter *finder* for busy parents.

Each week, have the baby-sitters who work for your service call to tell you when they can work. In return for matching baby-sitters with jobs, you can charge a commission. A commission is a percentage of each sale. You could charge 10 percent, for example.

Let's say the Smith family needs a baby-sitter on Friday night for four hours. You look on your list and see that your friend Sara can work Friday night and lives near the Smiths. Mrs. Smith agrees to pay Sara $5.00 per hour. That means Sara will earn:

$$\$5.00 \text{ per hour} \times 4 \text{ hours} = \$20.00$$

Sara pays *you* 10 percent of $20.00 because you got her the job. To figure your commission, you need to express the percentage as a decimal.

1. "Percentage" means "out of a hundred." Ten out of a hundred is stated as 10 percent, or 10%.

$$\frac{10.00}{100} = .10$$

2. Another way to express any percentage as a number is to move the decimal point two places to the left (this is the same as dividing the percentage by 100):

   20% becomes .20   45% becomes .45   10.5% becomes .105

3. To figure your commission, multiply the percentage, expressed in decimal form, by the total sale:

   Commission on Sara's job = $20.00 × .10 = $2.00

Your commission is $2.00. That may not sound like much, but it will add up as your service expands.

What You'll Need to Get Started

- Babysitters and parents must be able to contact you. You'll need to circulate a phone number (call-waiting service is a good idea) *where they can reach you,* and buy an answering machine. Record on the machine a message that reassures your callers that you're a responsible person.

- Set up a simple **filing system** (a grocery box and some folders will do) to keep track of:

  Parents: phone numbers, addresses, directions to their homes, number of children, ages of children, any special problems or needs

  Sitters: phone numbers, times and days they can work, allergies or other special problems or needs (you can't send someone who is allergic to cats to baby-sit in a home where there are cats, for example)

  Jobs: when and for what family each baby-sitter worked, how much money he or she made, whether he or she paid you your commission

- A large month-by-month **calendar** with day-boxes, to mark the dates and baby-sitters you've booked. Day books and calendars are often sold at a discount in January each year.

- **Flyers** advertising your business. A flyer is a one-page advertisement of the service you're offering. From one neat, dark-inked original, you can photocopy countless copies.

- **Business cards** that give basic facts about your service and how to contact you.

- **Marketing ideas.** Place flyers on local grocery store bulletin boards, in laundromats, and in other neighborhood places that busy parents frequent. Give a flyer and a business card to any parents you meet. Make **T-shirts, headbands,** or **hats** advertising your service, and give one to each baby-sitter you sign up.

THE ENTREPRENEUR AS PROBLEM SOLVER

Where other people see problems, entrepreneurs see opportunities for creating new businesses. Countless businesses, great and small, have been started because an entrepreneur was annoyed by a problem.

Anita Roddick started The Body Shop, Inc.—a skin care and cosmetics company that uses natural ingredients—because she was tired of paying for perfume and fancy packaging when she bought makeup. Before her, Georgette Klinger founded her self-named skin care company because she had terrible acne.

I. Try thinking of three problems that annoy you and a business solution for each:

Problem	Business Solution
1. _____	1. _____
2. _____	2. _____
3. _____	3. _____

II. Now think about where you live. Are there any problems you could solve for your community? List five business opportunities in your community and the need(s) each would satisfy:

Business Opportunity	Need(s) Satisfied
1. _____	1. _____
2. _____	2. _____
3. _____	3. _____
4. _____	4. _____
5. _____	5. _____

III. One good way to start thinking like an entrepreneur is to imagine how you would respond to a challenge or an opportunity, or even to some information about consumers. Given the following hypothetical situations, what business would you consider starting?

Situation	Business Opportunities
1. A 100 percent increase in the price of gasoline is announced.	_____
2. A going-out-of-business sign is placed in the window of the local grocery store.	_____
3. A new airport is being built near your home.	_____
4. The number of women entering the workforce is dramatically increasing.	_____
5. Three new families with children are moving into your neighborhood.	_____

6. You know a lot of people who are planning to get married. _____

7. You live near a college. _____

THE ENTREPRENEUR AS PROBLEM SOLVER

Sample Answers

I. List three problems that annoy you and a business solution for each.

Problem	Business Solution
1. Many neighborhood pet cats are having kittens.	1. Provide a "Kitten Giveaway" service.
2. Delivery people have a hard time reading addresses on houses.	2. Offer to paint addresses on curbs.
3. It snows a lot each winter where you live.	3. Start a snow removal service.

II. Think about where you live. List five business opportunities in your community and the need(s) each would satisfy.

Business Opportunity	Need(s) Satisfied
1. After-school day care	1. Need for working parents to have children cared for until parents come home.
2. Party clown service	2. Need for entertainment for children's parties and other events.
3. Garage cleaning	3. Need for someone to take care of a messy and time-consuming job.
4. Car wash and wax	4. Need to have car cleaned regularly.
5. Resell used clothing and toys	5. Families need inexpensive clothes and toys for growing children.

III. Given these hypothetical situations, what business would you consider starting? Remember, every problem offers an opportunity to solve it and make a profit.

Situation	Business Opportunities
1. A 100 percent increase in the price of gasoline is announced.	1. Start a carpool service.
2. A going-out-of-business sign is placed in the window of the local grocery store.	2. Offer delivery service from a grocery store near the neighborhood.
3. A new airport is being built near your home.	3. Start a car service.
4. The number of women entering the workforce is dramatically increasing.	4. Open a day care center.
5. Three new families with children are moving into your neighborhood.	5. Start a baby-sitting service or a playgroup.
6. You know a lot of people who are planning to get married.	6. Start a bridal shower planning service.
7. You live near a college.	7. Provide word processing and research assistance for term papers.

RESOURCES

Books

Gates by Stephen Manes and Paul Andrews (New York: Touchstone, 1994), a national bestseller, is a fast-paced biography of Bill Gates.

Insanely Great by Steven Levy (New York: Viking, 1994) tells the story of how Apple grew.

Accidental Empires: How the Boys of Silicon Valley Make Their Millions, Battle Foreign Competition, and Still Can't Get a Date by Robert X. Cringely (New York: Harper Business, 1992) is a hugely entertaining story of the development of the computer industry.

Two books that will help you navigate the Internet are:

The Whole Internet User's Guide and Catalog (Sebastopol, California: O'Reilly and Associates, 1992).

New Riders Official Internet Yellow Pages (Indianapolis: New Riders, 1994).

For a thorough discussion of the role of the entrepreneur in satisfying consumer needs, see:

Master Curriculum Guide: Economics and Entrepreneurship, edited by John Clow et al. (Joint Council on Economic Education, 1991). Contact:

> National Council on Economic Education
> 1140 Avenue of the Americas
> New York, NY 10036
> (212) 730-7007

Other Resources

The Young Entrepreneurs' Organization (YEO) is a nonprofit organization whose mission is to assist entrepreneurs under age 35. YEO was founded by my friend and NFTE board member Verne Harnish in 1987. Contact YEO at:

> The Young Entrepreneurs' Organization
> 10101 North Glebe Road
> Arlington, VA 22207
> (703) 527-4500

Junior Achievement (JA) is one of the leading youth educators in the fields of economics and business. For information on a JA program near you, contact:

> Junior Achievement
> National Headquarters
> 1 Education Way
> Colorado Springs, CO 80906
> (719) 540-8016

If you want to start a Web site for your business, check out InterNIC, www.internic.com, where you can register the name you want for your Web site.

Chapter 4

ECONOMICS 101

LEARNING ABOUT MARKETS WILL
GIVE YOU AN EDGE

There's no such thing as a free lunch.
—Milton Friedman (b. 1912)
American economist

HOW ENTREPRENEURS RESPOND TO DEMAND

Choosing a business was easy for nine-year-old Darryl of Newark, New Jersey. He loved video games and electronics more than anything. More importantly, though, Darryl had a great ability to think about what people would buy. A lot of kids don't think that way; they buy what *they* want. Darryl tried to figure out what *his customers* wanted.

Darryl started selling electronic games to his family and friends. He soon realized, though, that he and his customers craved variety. Darryl noticed that video clubs were renting a variety of movies to members, but no one was renting out video *games*. Darryl decided to start a video game club. His customers can rent lots of different games for the price of buying one.

Without realizing it, Darryl was responding to a demand for rental electronic games. This was a demand that the local stores had not recognized. Darryl noticed it because he—being a kid who loves video games—had unique knowledge of the market.

By renting cartridges to customers at 25 cents per night, Darryl's Electronics boasts profits of $15 per week. Not bad, considering he is only open for business on Friday and Saturday!

Supply is the business (entrepreneurial) response to consumer demand. Supply is the amount of a product or service businesses are willing to provide at various prices.

Demand is the amount of a product or service that consumers are willing and able to buy at various prices.

How Prices Communicate Information

In a **free-enterprise** (or free-market) system, what is produced, the price, and the quantity bought and sold are determined by supply and demand. In a free market, anyone—even a nine-year-old!—may start a business.

Price relays information between the consumer and the entrepreneur. The entrepreneur knows quickly when the price of a product is too high: Most consumers refuse to buy the product. The entrepreneur knows when the price is too low because the product sells out very quickly and consumers want more. The price of the product is being determined by the laws of supply and demand.

Filling Prescriptions at a Lower Price[1]

Jane C. I. Hirsh has used the power of pricing to build her business, Copley Pharmaceuticals, from a $500 loan from a friend into a billion-dollar company. Copley produces generic drugs, in response to consumer demand for cheaper prescription drugs.

Hirsh worked as a hospital pharmacist for eight years after college. She learned that many drug companies were making a substantial profit. Hirsh realized that part of the amount the consumer was charged was related to the use of the brand name of the product. She reasoned that if she produced generic versions of common drugs, she could sell her drugs at lower prices and draw consumers away from brand-name drugs.

In 1972, Copley and her husband started Copley Pharmaceuticals, Inc., in Canton, Massachusetts. Although the company initially had some close brushes with failure, as it developed the strength to get its products placed in more pharmacies, sales began increasing at a steady rate of 30 percent per year.

Today, Copley makes generic versions of fourteen over-the-counter drugs and fifty-six prescription drugs. Its biggest sellers are Miconazole Nitrate (which treats yeast infections) and Procainamide (a heart drug). Of her business, Hirsh says, "I'm not a high-finance person, I'm a pharmacist. I care about people, product development equipment, and manufacturing. It isn't sexy, but it sure is profitable."

LAW OF DEMAND[2]

Hirsh knew only one thing about business or economics when she started her business: Lower prices would attract customers. She was instinctively relying on the law of demand.

According to the law of demand, as price goes up, the quantity demanded by consumers goes down. As the price falls, the quantity demanded by consumers rises.

Let's say you get permission to sell soda at a Little League baseball game. During the first half of the game, you charge $2.00 per can of soda and sell two dozen cans. During the second half of the game, you try lowering your price to $1.00 per can. You sell five dozen cans.

The people attending the game have "obeyed" the **Law of Demand:** If everything else remains the same, people will demand more of something at a *lower* price than they will at a *higher* price.

LAW OF SUPPLY

On the other side of every market is a supplier. The supplier also reacts to price changes.

If your small business is baking and selling cookies, for example, how many cookies would you be willing to make if you thought that the cookies would sell for $.25 each? What if people were willing to pay $1.00 each? You would probably work harder and try to supply more cookies at that price.

The entrepreneur who acts this way is obeying the **Law of Supply:** If everything else remains the same, businesses will supply more of a product or service at a *higher* price than they will at a *lower* price.

ENTREPRENEUR STORY
WILLIAM HEWLETT, HEWLETT PACKARD

William R. Hewlett was obeying the laws of supply and demand in 1972 when he had his electronics company, Hewlett-Packard, start manufacturing scientific calculators that were to sell for around $400. At the time, most scientists used slide rules to make their calculations. Slide rules cost only $20. As a supplier, Hewlett was attracted to producing the higher-priced calculators. As a brilliant engineer, Hewlett believed that other scientists were probably as sick as he was of using slide rules and would buy the expensive calculators as a substitute, despite their higher price. He was eager to start supplying the high-priced calculators.

The calculators became the hottest product in the electronics industry and quickly rendered the slide rule obsolete. Hewlett-Packard's sales tripled to $1.8 billion by 1978. In 1994, Hewlett-Packard's sales were $25 billion.

ENTREPRENEUR STORY
WILLIAM MCGOWAN, MCI[3]

AT&T's monopoly of the long-distance telephone business was largely broken up by the dogged determination of one man, William McGowan. He founded MCI Communications Corporation, which destroyed AT&T's monopoly by offering an alternative service using radio microwaves. The price to consumers was as much as 50 percent cheaper.

Breaking AT&T's Monopoly: How McGowan Started MCI

William McGowan took on AT&T with a company he had purchased in 1968 for only $50,000. McGowan had been contacted by John Goeken, who was trying to build a microwave system between Chicago and St. Louis to expand his mobile-radio business. For five years, AT&T had used its might to prevent Goeken from receiving Federal Communications Commission (FCC) approval for his operation. Goeken was driven close to bankruptcy.

As McGowan told *Money* magazine in 1982 ("Six Who Succeeded," December 1982), he bought Goeken's company because "the fact that it [taking on AT&T's monopoly of communication] had never been done before made the idea all the more irresistible." After the FCC finally approved the Chicago–St. Louis link in 1969, McGowan went on a fund-raising crusade for his new venture. He raised over $100 million in four years and got the FCC to agree to support nationwide long-distance phone competition.

AT&T, meanwhile, fought MCI at the FCC, in Congress, and by filing numerous harassing lawsuits. Although conducting the fight was expensive for McGowan, the results were worth it many times over. In 1980, a federal jury in Chicago found AT&T guilty of antitrust violations and awarded $1.8 billion in damages to MCI. Although the award amount was reduced when AT&T appealed the case, the damage had been done. MCI was in business as a viable alternative long-distance service provider. Other competitors, such as Sprint, jumped into the market as well.

Today, MCI has over a million customers. MCI, Sprint, and AT&T still duke it out with television commercials and price wars. The biggest winner is the consumer.

USING THE LAWS OF SUPPLY AND DEMAND TO PREDICT MARKET BEHAVIOR

Knowing the laws of supply and demand will help you make good business decisions. If you believe the demand for a product is going to rise, for instance, it would be wise to start selling that product, because the price that people are willing to pay for it is going to rise, too.

For example, what can you expect will happen to the demand for air conditioners in the summer? Why? What is likely to happen, therefore, to the price of air conditioners in the summer?

The demand for air conditioners will probably rise in the summer because more people will want air conditioners to cool their homes and offices. At first, therefore, the price of air conditioners will probably rise. Suppliers of air conditioners will be able to raise their prices because more people will be demanding air conditioners. The higher prices of air conditioners, in turn, will encourage more suppliers to supply air conditioners. Eventually, the price of air conditioners will come down again.

If you suspect that the demand for a product is going to drop, it would make sense to get out of that market and start producing something else. What do you think would happen to the price of gasoline, for example, if many people were to begin using electric cars? Why?

If everyone were to begin using electric cars, the demand for gasoline would fall. Suppliers would be forced to sell gasoline at a lower price, to try to attract consumers away from electric cars. Many suppliers would probably stop selling gasoline and move into another market.

SETTING THE PRICE

Together, demand and supply determine how much will be bought and sold and what the price will be in a market. Remember, a market is a group of people buying and selling a product or service. Businesses would like to charge high prices for their products and services.

Consumers seek low prices. The market price is a compromise between what the buyer wants to pay and the entrepreneur wants to charge.

There is a price at which the amount that producers want to sell equals the amount that consumers are willing to spend. This is the **market clearing price.**

SUPPLY AND DEMAND SCHEDULES

Let's say you go to a record store to check out some CDs. Whether you will purchase anything will depend on the price of CDs at the store. If there is a sale and all CDs are discounted from $16 to $14, you might buy more CDs than you would if they were $16 each.

In contrast, the owners of the store would prefer to sell the CDs at the highest price they can get. The forces of supply and demand are at work on both you (the consumer) and the owners of the store (the suppliers). You will buy more CDs if the price of a CD decreases. They will supply more CDs if the price of a CD increases.

A list of how many units of a product consumers are willing to buy at different prices is called a **demand schedule.** Here is a demand schedule for a customer at a record store. Every individual has a different demand schedule. Your demand schedule reflects how you feel about money and CDs.

Price of One CD	DEMAND SCHEDULE (Number of CDs Customer Is Willing to Buy at That Price)
$20	0
18	1
16	2
14	3
12	4
10	5
8	6

You can see from the demand schedule that as the price of CDs declines, the customer is willing to buy more of them.

A list of how many units of a product sellers are willing to supply at different prices is called a **supply schedule.** Here is a supply schedule for the record store owner.

| SUPPLY SCHEDULE | |
Price of One CD	Number of CDs Owner Is Willing to Supply at That Price
$ 8	0
10	1
12	2
14	3
16	4
18	5
20	6

You can see from the supply schedule that as the price of CDs rises, the record store owner is willing to supply more of them.

THE MARKET CLEARING PRICE

The supply and demand schedules for the CDs have been plotted on Chart 2. The point at which the supply and demand curves cross is the **market clearing price.** This is the price at which the number of CDs the customer is willing to buy and the number the record store owner is willing to supply are the same.

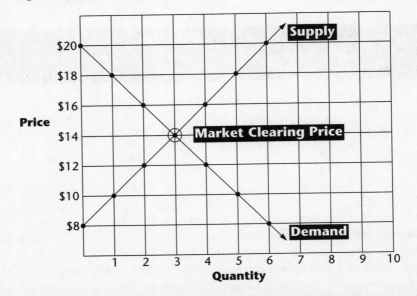

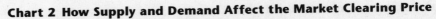

Chart 2 How Supply and Demand Affect the Market Clearing Price

According to the chart, the market clearing price is $14. For $14, the customer wants to take home three CDs. For that price, the record store owner is willing to sell three CDs.

Supply, demand, and price information are communicated quickly and clearly between consumers and entrepreneurs in the free-market system. Learning to forecast supply and demand in your market is a key to success.

COMPETITION KEEPS PRICES DOWN AND QUALITY HIGH

The laws of supply and demand work best in competitive markets. When businesses are competing with each other, they try to attract consumers by lowering prices, improving quality, and developing new products and services.

Government regulations, or anything else that keeps entrepreneurs from entering a market, will make it less competitive. Less competition leads to higher prices, poorer quality, and fewer new products and services.

MONOPOLY

When a market has only one supplier of a product or service, that supplier is commonly said to have a monopoly. The word **monopoly** comes from two Greek words—*monos,* which means "single," and *polien,* which means "to sell."

If there is only one grocery store in your neighborhood, there is less incentive, or encouragement, for that store to lower its prices or improve quality to attract customers. If you are the only seller of T-shirts in your market, there is less incentive for you to create new designs.

A monopoly is the opposite of competition and has the opposite effect. In a monopoly, the supplier has no incentive to lower prices or improve quality to attract the consumer. The consumer has no choice but to go to that supplier. Monopolies generally keep prices high and quality low.

In free markets, monopolies seldom last long. Other entrepreneurs will enter the same market with the same or similar products, and will compete for the same customers. If you ever find yourself in a monopoly position, you should behave as if you have many competitors:

offer the lowest possible price with the highest possible quality. If you don't, you will soon find yourself with many competitors and fewer customers.

The best ways to prevent monopolies are: keep markets free, make it easy for people to start businesses, and encourage as many people as possible to learn the basics of entrepreneurship.

GOVERNMENT-OWNED OR GOVERNMENT-ENCOURAGED MONOPOLIES

Most of the monopolies that exist today in the United States are owned and operated by some level of government. The United States Postal Service is one example, fire departments are another.

Some people believe the government should not own and operate these monopolies but should allow postal, educational, and other services to be supplied by private businesses. These people argue that private businesses, competing with each other, would provide better and cheaper service than the government monopolies do.

Monopolies that arise in the private sector tend to be the result of government interference in the marketplace. Such monopolies tend to be destroyed by competition once the government interference is removed. One example is AT&T, which virtually monopolized long-distance phone service until certain government regulations concerning licensing for long-distance phone service providers were removed in the 1980s. Since then, MCI, Sprint, and other competitors have been able to grab shares of the market away from AT&T by offering cheaper phone service rates. AT&T has responded by lowering its rates and by improving the quality of its service with its True Voice® system. Consumers of phone service have benefited greatly from the increased competition in the market.

COMPETITION ENCOURAGES CHANGE

Like McGowan, every entrepreneur is trying to fill a consumer need more cheaply and effectively than the competition.

Suppose you have a T-shirt business. Everybody at your school wants to wear one of your custom-made designs. They pay a relatively high price that allows you to make a large profit. Your T-shirt business is a monopoly. You are the single seller of custom T-shirts in your market.

But then a friend of yours also goes into the T-shirt business. Many of the students like her designs, too. Now you have competition. The supply of custom T-shirts in your market has just increased. What's more, your friend decides to sell her T-shirts for three dollars less than yours. Now she's getting all your customers. To compete with her and win back your customers, you will have to lower your prices and perhaps bring out new designs as well.

You may decide that rather than compete with your friend for T-shirt customers, you are going to sell jewelry. The famous economist Joseph Schumpeter called this process of constantly changing businesses "creative destruction."[4]

COMPETITION KEEPS BUSINESS EXCITING

Entrepreneurship is never boring. The market is always changing, and competition is always around the corner. Risk and uncertainty are two elements that make small business so exciting.

Entrepreneurship is a discovery process. Each time you make any choice regarding your business, you will quickly get feedback from your market: The demand for your product or service will rise or fall. If the demand for your product or service falls, the market is telling you to move on to a different product or service. If the supply of your product or service rises, the price will start to fall. You might find that you can't sell enough of your product or service to make a profit. If you are in the marketplace as a competitor, don't be ashamed if you lose a business. The market is just telling you to move on to a new enterprise.

CASE STUDY: HOME AND OFFICE PLANT CARE

Do your friends say you have a green thumb? People like to have plants in their homes and offices, but they don't always have time to care for them. Home and office plant care is a business that is inexpensive to start and doesn't require a lot of time. Most plants need attention only once or twice a week, so plant care is a great small business for a busy student or parent.

Make a flyer and ask permission to put it up in the lobbies of office buildings near your home or school. To recognize and learn how to care for different types of plants, visit your local plant nursery or shop. Ask the owner to recommend some books you can read, or look up some titles in the book index at your library.

Supplies	Where to Find Them
Watering can (a long, narrow spout is best)	Hardware store or nursery
Plant food	Nursery or flower shop
Rag for dusting plant leaves	Make from old shirts or towels
Notebook for instructions on how to care for plants	Stationery store
Calendar to keep track of visits	Stationery store

Tips

- Ask customers for detailed instructions on how they care for each plant. Write them down!
- Offer customers a discount on your service if they refer you to a new customer.

Fresh Produce or Flowers

If you have a *really* green thumb, try a fresh produce or flower business, like James did. At age ten, James grew a row of watermelons and cantaloupes. He made $150 selling some of the fruit to friends and relatives. James was so excited that he kept increasing his crop a little bit each year.

By the time he was age fifteen, James was planting two-and-a-half acres and supplying three local grocery stores with produce. He named his business Fresh-Pik Produce and had business cards printed. He used custom-made stickers to label his boxes of produce.

At age sixteen, James had enough money saved to build a large greenhouse for starter plants. He rented ten acres, a tractor, a sprayer, and a plow. From that year's planting, James supplied eight local stores and several wholesalers. He plans to major in horticulture and make farming his life's work.

RESOURCES

An engaging overview of economic thinkers, from Adam Smith to present experts, is *The Worldly Philosophers,* 6th Edition, by Robert Heilbroner (New York: Simon & Schuster, 1986).

For a very readable explanation of the principles of economics, try *The Economic Way of Thinking* by Paul Heyne (Otappan, NJ: Macmillan, 1994). One of the classics on the subject is *Capitalism and Freedom* by Milton Friedman (Chicago: University of Chicago Press, 1963).

A groundbreaking recent discussion is *Black Economics: Solutions for Economic and Community Empowerment* by Jawanza Kunjufu (Chicago: African American Images, 1991).

For a great discussion of supply and demand, see: *Master Curriculum Guide in Economics, Part II, Strategies for Teaching Economics,* which is available from:

National Council on Economic Education
1140 Avenue of the Americas
New York, NY 10036
(212) 730-7007

Other Resources

If you are curious about what the competition is charging for a product or service you intend to sell, visit the Company Lookup site, www.companylink.com, for info on 100,000 companies. Another site with this kind of data is Companies Online, www.companiesonline.com.

Chapter 5

What It Takes to Be an Entrepreneur

. . . And How to Strengthen What You've Got

Entrepreneurship is personal.
It is what you can do almost by yourself.
—John H. Johnson (b. 1918)
American publisher of *Ebony* and *Jet* magazines

What Kinds of People Become Entrepreneurs?

Many successful entrepreneurs started life with very little money or education. Some had really rough childhoods—in fact, facing challenges early in life can actually prepare you to become an entrepreneur!

Entrepreneurs tend to be risk takers who are good at adapting to change and developing their personal strengths. This may be why a fair share of great American entrepreneurs have been **immigrants.** Immigrants are people who move away from their homeland to settle in a new country. They face many challenges that exercise their minds, including learning a new language and new customs. In a sense, they are forced by circumstances to become entrepreneurial. Immigrants may also see market opportunities that people already living in a community have overlooked. Perhaps this is why so many immigrants to the United States have started their own small businesses.

HOW A YOUNG IMMIGRANT BECAME A SUCCESSFUL ENTREPRENEUR

A national winner of NFTE's Entrepreneurial Spirit Award in 1994 was a sixteen-year-old whose family had immigrated to California from China after living for a while in Vietnam. When Linh's family arrived in San Francisco, she quickly learned that business was an important part of American life. She never thought of herself as the entrepreneurial type, though.

Linh came from a culture that valued quiet, respectful behavior. She was somewhat suspicious of salespeople. "Acquiring the knowledge of business made me understand that salespeople are not scam artists," she says, "[and] this allowed me to be open to the concept of selling products."

Linh originally sold candy through her company, Sensational Sweets Unlimited, but when she found candy to be a slow seller, she switched to wholesale jewelry. Perhaps because she was sensitive to the negative reaction some people might have to a strong verbal sales pitch, Linh decided to create a catalog for her business. Linh took color photographs of each style of costume jewelry she was offering and combined them with descriptions, prices, and order forms to create her own product catalog. Her catalog has been a big hit and a great sales tool for her expanding business. Linh has recently added hair bands and stationery to her product line.

CHILDHOOD CHALLENGES CAN INSPIRE GREATNESS

Linh's childhood was very challenging. Her family left China because of the political repression there, but when they moved to Vietnam they found it wasn't much safer. When Linh moved to San Francisco, she faced both culture shock and the challenge of learning a new language.

Like Linh, many successful entrepreneurs have come from challenging backgrounds. Growing up in a tough environment required them to become driven and competitive just to survive.

Entrepreneur Story
Dave Thomas, Wendy's

Dave Thomas, the founder of the Wendy's restaurant chain, was only five years old when his adoptive mother died. Dave was raised by his adoptive grandmother until his adoptive father remarried. His grandmother's husband was killed working on a railroad, and she had worked very hard to support four children. Thomas says he got most of his down-to-earth family values from her.

Thomas's adoptive father remarried three times, so Dave was bounced around a lot from home to home. In his biography, *Dave's Way,* Thomas says these childhood traumas taught him some important lessons that helped him become successful in business. These lessons were:[1]

1. Look for people who care about you, and learn from them.
2. Dream early, and build your goals on your dream.
3. Learn to rely on yourself early.
4. If there are things you don't like in the world you grow up in, make your own world different.
5. Take a step every day.
6. Be yourself.

Entrepreneur Story
Tom Monaghan, Domino's Pizza

Tom Monaghan, the founder of Domino's Pizza, had a tough childhood. He was raised in orphanages and foster homes; his father had died when he was four. He lived with his mother for a couple of years, but she sent him to a foster home when they could not get along. Monaghan struggled in school—he graduated last in his high school class and was expelled from a Catholic seminary. He tried college six times but never got past his freshman year.

In 1960, Monaghan and his brother Jim borrowed $900 and bought a foundering pizzeria in Ypsilanti, Michigan. Jim left within the year, but Tom hung on, surviving two near-bankruptcies and a fire. Slowly, he opened new stores. In 1979, he was sued by the Amstar Corporation for infringing on the name of Domino sugar. Amstar won the first round, but Monaghan won on appeal. Through entrepreneurship, Monaghan—who had never succeeded at anything—discovered that he had perseverance and drive. He enjoyed making pizza and was committed wholeheartedly to making Domino's Pizza a household name.

During these years, Monaghan worked eighteen hours a day, seven days a week. He traveled all over the Midwest visiting other pizzerias to check out their operations. By the time the lawsuit with Amstar was settled, Domino's had grown to 290 stores. Only a year later, Monaghan opened his 500th store. Today, Domino's has almost 5,000 stores in the United States and about 300 in other countries.

In 1983, Monaghan realized a boyhood dream when he purchased the Detroit Tigers baseball club for $54 million. A year later, the Tigers won the World Series.

Many other great entrepreneurs have overcome poverty, racism, and language and cultural barriers. For example:

- The most successful African American in the oil industry, Jake Simmons, Jr., was raised on a ranch in Oklahoma in the early 1900s. At that time, the state government was openly racist. Some blacks were even lynched, but Simmons and other black Oklahomans fought hard for their freedom. Simmons went on to build a great fortune from oil and land deals.

- The owner of the Chun King Chinese food company, Jeno Paulucci, was born to a very poor Italian family in Minnesota. His father was a coal miner. To make extra money, the Paulucci family ran a grocery store out of their home. Paulucci had a knack for making different kinds of food attractive to the consumer. He sensed the American consumer would buy canned versions of popular Chinese foods, like chow mein. He used funny commercials to make Chun King foods very popular.

- Shipping tycoon Aristotle Onassis was one of the richest people in the world in the 1960s. As a youngster, Onassis had immigrated to Argentina from Greece. He learned Spanish at night and sold tobacco by day. When he was only fifteen, he landed a big tobacco order and used his earnings to invest in more tobacco to sell. As he accumulated more money, he started the small businesses that he eventually built into his great financial empire. Onassis married Jacqueline Kennedy after her husband, President John F. Kennedy, was assassinated.

CHARACTERISTICS OF THE SUCCESSFUL ENTREPRENEUR[2]

No one is born with all the characteristics needed for success. Think about the traits represented in Chart 3. Which of these characteristics do you already possess?

Adaptability

Persuasiveness

Risk Taking

Honesty

Confidence

Vision

Competitiveness

Perseverance

**Chart 3 Do You Have What It Takes to Be a Successful Entrepreneur?
(Artist: Al Stern)**

If you are lacking some characteristics but have energy and motivation, the other traits can be developed. Listed below are a dozen of the traits generally considered most important for an entrepreneur to develop. Which ones do you think you could develop with a little effort?

1. Adaptability—the ability to cope with new situations and find creative solutions to problems.

2. Competitiveness—the willingness to compete with and test oneself against others.

3. Confidence—the belief that you can do what you set out to do.

4. Discipline—the ability to stay focused and stick to a schedule and deadlines.

5. Drive—the desire to work hard to accomplish one's goals.

6. Honesty—the commitment to tell the truth and deal with people fairly.

7. Organization—the ability to structure one's life and keep tasks and information in order.

8. Perseverance—the refusal to quit; the willingness to keep goals in sight and work toward them despite obstacles.

9. Persuasiveness—the knack for convincing people to see your point of view and to get them interested in your ideas.

10. Risk Taking—the courage to expose oneself to possible losses.

11. Understanding—the ability to listen to and empathize with other people.

12. Vision—the ability to see the end results of your goals while working to achieve them.

From the list above, list four traits that you think you have:

1. _____

2. _____

3. _____

4. _____

Now list four traits that you think you could develop:

1. _____

2. _____

3. _____

4. _____

THE POWER OF A POSITIVE MENTAL ATTITUDE

No matter how many entrepreneurial characteristics you have or develop, they won't do you any good unless you combine them with a positive attitude. Numerous entrepreneurs have cited "a positive attitude" as a key to their success ever since Napoleon Hill coined the phrase in his inspirational books.

A man who knew the meaning of "the power of positive thinking" was W. Clement Stone. He turned a positive attitude into a $500 million fortune by building one of the largest insurance companies in America, Combined Insurance Company.

When he was only fifteen, Stone began selling insurance policies to help his mother pay the bills. His first assignment was a large office building. He was so afraid to even enter the building that, to get up his courage, he made up optimistic phrases like "When there's nothing to lose and much to gain by trying, try." Once inside the building, he actually *ran* from office to office trying to sell his policies before his fear of rejection could overwhelm him.

Stone discovered that people responded to his positive attitude by buying insurance policies. While still in high school, Stone was selling forty insurance policies a day. He went on to revolutionize the sales profession with the idea that it was the attitude of the salesperson that sold the product.

Entrepreneurs are optimists—they *have* to be, in order to see opportunities where others see only problems. At NFTE, we've learned to think of the brain as hardware and thoughts as software. Essentially, your thoughts program your brain.

MADAME C. J. WALKER: THE ENTREPRENEUR AS A FORCE FOR SOCIAL GOOD

When I was still teaching, I took some students on a field trip in Harlem. We went into a beauty shop and asked the woman who owned it how she got started in business. She said she would ask her mother. Her mother, who was a wonderful elderly lady, said she had gotten her start in the business through Madame C. J. Walker. That's how I first heard of this influential African American entrepreneur.

Some people don't realize they have what it takes to be entrepreneurs until later in life. Madame C. J. Walker didn't start her own business until she was age thirty-eight. She became one of the first African American millionaires. Her success had a tremendous positive impact on her community. Not only did she employ many black women, she set them up in business for themselves.

Madame Walker was orphaned in early childhood and raised by her married sister in Louisiana farm country. When Madame Walker was age twenty, her husband died. She moved to St. Louis and worked as a washerwoman for eighteen years to support herself and her daughter.

Walker Starts Her Business at Age Thirty-Eight

When she was thirty-eight years old, Walker developed a formula for a new hair product for African American women. In addition, she created a compound specially suited to the complexion needs of black women. In 1906, Walker remarried and moved to Denver, Colorado. She began selling her products door-to-door. This sales method allowed her to demonstrate their benefits. Soon, Walker was training other women to sell her products. She also set up a thriving mail-order business.

At the peak of her career, Walker employed over 3,000 people. Most of her employees were women who sold the products door-to-door as "Walker Agents," much like today's Avon Ladies sell makeup and personal care products.

Walker organized her agents into clubs that promoted not only their business, but also social and charitable causes. Walker gave cash prizes to the clubs that did the most charitable and educational work for African Americans.

The attention drawn to the Madame C. J. Walker Manufacturing Company by the charitable work of Walker and her agents was considerable. Walker became one of the most famous women in America. She made large contributions to the National Association for the Advancement of Colored People (NAACP), as well as to homes for the aged and needy, and to scholarships for African American students.

When Walker died in 1919, she left two-thirds of her fortune to educational institutions and charities. She also left behind many Walker Agents who started their own businesses. Her legacy of

African American women owning small businesses is still strong in many urban areas today.

HOW MUCH OF AN ENTREPRENEUR ARE YOU?[3]

This survey, developed by The National Federation of Independent Business, is a great way to assess your character. Read each of the qualities and explanations listed. Rate the degree to which you believe you possess that quality by circling a number from 1 to 10. After six months, you can mark the survey again, using a different color pen or pencil, and see how you've grown.

Quality	Explanation	Range
Drive	Highly motivated	1 2 3 4 5 6 7 8 9 10
Perseverance	Sticking to task or goal	1 2 3 4 5 6 7 8 9 10
Risk Taking	Willing to take chances	1 2 3 4 5 6 7 8 9 10
Organization	Life and work in order	1 2 3 4 5 6 7 8 9 10
Confidence	Sure of yourself	1 2 3 4 5 6 7 8 9 10
Persuasiveness	Able to convince others	1 2 3 4 5 6 7 8 9 10
Honesty	Open, truthful	1 2 3 4 5 6 7 8 9 10
Competitiveness	Eager to win	1 2 3 4 5 6 7 8 9 10
Adaptability	Coping with new situations	1 2 3 4 5 6 7 8 9 10
Understanding	Empathy with others	1 2 3 4 5 6 7 8 9 10
Discipline	Able to stick to schedule	1 2 3 4 5 6 7 8 9 10
Vision	Able to think of long-term goals	1 2 3 4 5 6 7 8 9 10
		(low ⟶ high)

Date of first self-rating _____   Total Score _____

Date of second self-rating_____   Total Score _____

CASE STUDY: HOUSE CLEANING

When Maria's husband was sentenced to four years in prison for selling drugs, she didn't know how she was going to support herself and her two young children. Fortunately, she had taken a NFTE course in high school, so she decided to start her own business.

Today, Maria has an apartment-cleaning business in Manhattan. She cleans for four customers per week. Maria charges $64.00 per cleaning job, so her gross income per week is $256.00 (4 clients × $64.00 per client).

Maria's only expense is travel, which costs her around $15.00 per week. All the cleaning supplies are provided by the customers, and Maria does no advertising of her business. Instead, she asks each satisfied customer to recommend her to a friend. Maria's net income is $241.00 per week ($256.00 gross income per week − $15.00 weekly expenses).

It's hard for working mothers and fathers to keep up with housework. This could be a great money-making opportunity for you.

You probably have already had some "on-the-job training" if you've done chores at home. Make flyers to advertise your services. A flyer is a one-page advertisement that you hand out to potential customers and post on bulletin boards. You can draw a flyer by hand or design it on a computer. It can be simple or fancy, but should be eye-catching and include your name, the name of your business, and your phone number. List on your flyer the following jobs that you can do: sweeping, mopping, dusting, emptying garbage, doing dishes, cleaning bathrooms, doing laundry.

Put up your flyers in grocery stores and laundromats, and on community bulletin boards. You could offer your customers the choice of having you use their cleaning supplies at their house, or, for a higher fee, having you bring your own supplies.

Tips

- Do a great job so you can build a base of repeat customers.
- Write on an index card the name, address, and phone number of each customer, and list the exact chores you did. Review the list if you're called back for additional cleaning sessions.
- Offer a discount to any customer who hooks you up with a new customer.
- If the service grows, think about expanding into office cleaning.

RESOURCES

Here are some books about how to develop success characteristics, including the W. Clement Stone classic and an update by an African American author Napoleon Hill's famous *Think and Grow Rich*.

Have You Got What It Takes? How To Tell If You Should Start Your Own Business by Joseph Mancuso (New York: Prentice-Hall Press, 1982). This short and funny book is still a bestseller today.

Success Through a Positive Mental Attitude by W. Clement Stone (Englewood Cliffs, NJ: Prentice-Hall, 1962).

Think and Grow Rich by Napoleon Hill (New York: Harper & Row, 1989).

Think and Grow Rich by Dennis Paul Kimbro (New York: Fawcett Columbine, 1991).

My own self-published book, *Homeboys,* is an account of my teaching days in the New York City public schools and how I came to realize that many of my students possessed entrepreneurial characteristics as a result of their urban experiences. For a copy, write to me at:

Steve Mariotti
NFTE
120 Wall Street, 29th Floor
New York, NY 10005

Chapter 6

YOU GET WHAT YOU NEGOTIATE!

HOW TO MAKE WIN–WIN AGREEMENTS

You don't get what you deserve, you get what you negotiate.
—Chester L. Karrass
American negotiation expert and author

NEGOTIATION IS ABOUT COMPROMISE, NOT WINNING

In his best-selling book, *You Can Negotiate Anything,* Herb Cohen tells the story of a brother and sister squabbling over how to divide the last quarter of a pie. Just as the boy gains control of the knife, their mother arrives on the scene. "Hold it!" she says. "I don't care who cuts the pie, but whoever does cut it has to give the *other* person the right to select the piece they want."

To protect himself, the boy cuts the pie into two pieces of equal size. The moral of the story is that if two people shift their focus *from defeating each other to defeating the problem,* everyone benefits.

The best negotiators live by this idea. **Negotiation** is the art of achieving your goals through discussion and bargaining with another person. An example of negotiation is a buyer and a seller discussing the price of an item until an agreement is reached.

A big part of my job at NFTE is negotiating with our funders. Even though I'm running a nonprofit organization, I do as much negotiating as I would if I were the president of a for-profit corporation. In your personal life, you are probably continually involved with negotiations. The better you get at negotiating, the better you will become at getting what you want by helping the other person to get what he or she wants.

Negotiation is about **compromise,** not about winning. Compromise is sacrificing something you want so that an agreement can be reached that is acceptable to you *and* the person with whom you are negotiating. In the example above, the brother and sister were more interested in beating each other to a bigger slice of pie than they were in satisfying their appetites.

The two siblings forgot the most important principle of negotiation: The other person is not your enemy! The best negotiations are those in which both parties are satisfied—they have reached a "win–win" agreement. Conduct your negotiations as if you will be dealing with that person again very soon.

ENTREPRENEUR STORY
BILL GATES, MICROSOFT

In 1980, when Bill Gates was only twenty-four years old, he conducted one of the most important negotiations of his life with one of the most powerful companies in the world, IBM.[1] IBM was interested in having Microsoft work with it on IBM's top-secret effort to develop a personal computer. No doubt, "Big Blue," as IBM was known, expected little Microsoft, which was a $7 million company with fewer than forty employees at the time, to be a pushover. After all, IBM's annual revenues were hitting $30 billion.

The Early Years: Before Negotiations

Before his negotiations with IBM, however, Gates had set his goals and organized his thoughts. He knew exactly what he wanted to achieve and just what his boundaries were. IBM offered to pay Microsoft $175,000 for an operating system, called MS DOS, for IBM's new personal computers. Gates wasn't willing to sell his company's program code for that price, however, because he knew IBM would want to use the code on a variety of future machines. Gates decided he would hold out for royalties and retain ownership of MS DOS. He also wanted to retain the right to license copies of the program's code to other parties. Later, IBM was to regret its failure to purchase MS DOS outright. The licensing deal ended up costing Big Blue a lot of money.

The principles of negotiation that Gates used before entering this important negotiation with IBM were the same ones you should use before any negotiation. They are:

1. Set your goals and organize your thoughts. What do you want to achieve in the negotiation? Write down your goals and thoughts on note cards, and keep them with you during the discussion.

2. Decide what your boundaries are. Think about what the best deal *for you* would be. Then think about what the worst deal would be. What is the minimum you would be willing to accept? What is the maximum you are seeking? Knowing these limits ahead of time will prevent you from getting carried away and giving up too much of one thing in order to get something else.

3. Put yourself in the other person's shoes. What does he or she want from the negotiation? What is his or her minimum? Maximum? Things that aren't very important to you could be very important to the other person. You could give up these to get what you want.

During Negotiations

During the negotiations with IBM, Gates stuck to his plan. Despite the nervousness he felt inside about negotiating with IBM, Gates gave clear, calm presentations to IBM executives regarding the operating system that Microsoft proposed to supply to IBM. In the past, Gates had jeopardized deals with customers and suppliers by being too intense and too eager to win. This time, he knew he would have to make a worthwhile offer for the deal with IBM to succeed.

IBM's representative, Sandy Meade, was surprised by Gates's boldness on the royalty issue. Meade recalled, in the book *Gates,* by Stephen Manes and Paul Andrews (Touchstone, 1994), that, unlike other software companies with which IBM had negotiated, "I never felt they [Microsoft] needed the money."

Meade's negotiating tactic was to remind Gates that his relationship with IBM was a "long-term relationship with the potential for big business." Gates had guessed correctly that IBM would be willing to pay royalties to use Microsoft's program code in IBM's personal computers. In return for IBM's agreement to pay royalties, Microsoft committed to a brutal delivery schedule. Gates was in the habit of having dinner at his parents' home on Sunday nights. After he signed the deal with IBM, Gates told his mother not to expect him for at least six months.

During negotiations, Gates and his team used all of the tactics listed below. Memorize them and practice using them during your negotiations.

1. Let the other person name a price first. When discussing a price, try to let the other person make an offer first. This will reveal his or her position.

2. Try extremes. If the person won't reveal his or her position, throw out an extreme figure—very high or very low. This will force the other person to come forward with some type of response that will guide you.

3. Show a willingness to bargain. As negotiations proceed, respond to each counteroffer by giving up something you already decided in advance that you could afford to give up.

4. Use silence as a tool. After you have initially stated your case, don't say anything for a few moments. Your silence can prompt the other person to say something that you can turn to your advantage.

5. Always ask for more than you are offered. When the other person wants you to pay back a loan in ten days, for instance, ask for fifteen. You may have to settle for twelve, but that's better than the original demand.

As a small business owner, you will have to negotiate frequently—with suppliers, with customers, and with employees. How well you negotiate will greatly affect the success of your business.

NEGOTIATION IN ACTION

Here's an example of how the techniques listed above can be used in a simple negotiation. A young entrepreneur who wants to sell his product at a flea market is ready to negotiate with the flea market manager. Before the negotiation, the entrepreneur has determined his goals:

1. To be excused from paying the entrance fee.
2. To be allowed to set up early.

He has also thought about the flea market manager's needs. The key to a successful negotiation is similar to the key to a successful business: Figure out the other person's needs and how you can satisfy them.

As you read the dialogue below, notice that the entrepreneur is careful to make sure the manager understands how the negotiation can benefit him and the flea market. See if you can spot the negotiation techniques in action.

ENTREPRENEUR: Hi, I'm Steve, and I'd like to sell here on Saturday. I was wondering if I could talk to you about it.

MANAGER: Sure, go ahead.

ENTREPRENEUR: I think there are three good reasons for having young people like me get involved with the flea market. It's good for community relations, you can probably get some publicity out of it, and it will attract more young people to the flea market as customers.

MANAGER: Well, that sounds great, do you want to sign up now?

ENTREPRENEUR: I do, but as a young entrepreneur I don't have the money to cover the fee. As I develop my business here, though, I could begin to pay you.

MANAGER: I don't know if I'm willing to waive the fee.

ENTREPRENEUR: (Doesn't say anything.)

MANAGER: How about $50 instead of $100?

ENTREPRENEUR: (Doesn't say anything.)

MANAGER: How about $25?

ENTREPRENEUR: I understand what you do here, I think it has value. But my position is that I would be bringing a lot of value to the flea market, and I need to put my initial capital into building my business, which will benefit you in the long run.

MANAGER: All right, I'll waive the fee.

ENTREPRENEUR: I have something else that would really help me. Could I come in an hour early to set up?

MANAGER: No. No way.

ENTREPRENEUR: I need to do this because I feel I'm at a disadvantage with the more experienced vendors.

MANAGER: (Doesn't say anything.)

ENTREPRENEUR: When do you get here?

MANAGER: This Saturday I won't get here until a half hour before we open.

ENTREPRENEUR: That would be great. Could I meet you here and come in with you? That way I won't inconvenience you.

MANAGER: OK.

NEGOTIATION IN ACTION II

Here's a negotiation between Jack, who's selling a used stereo, and Sara, who wants to buy it. Before the negotiation, Sara determines her goals:

1. To be able to return the stereo if it stops working within two months.
2. To pay one-third what it would cost in the store.

The essence of negotiation is figuring out how to meet the other person's needs, so Sara thinks about what she has to offer in return. The stereo has been advertised in the paper for a couple of weeks, so she figures that the seller would like to get rid of it and not have to pay for more ads or worry about selling it anymore. She can offer:

1. To pay immediately in cash.
2. To take the stereo away that day.

Next, she sets her boundaries:

1. Not to spend more than $250.
2. Not to accept less than one month for return if the stereo stops working.

SARA: Are you still interested in selling the stereo?

JACK: Yes, I am.

SARA: What price were you looking for?

JACK: I'd like $500.

SARA: (Doesn't say anything and shows frustration on her face.)

JACK: Well, I'm willing to negotiate down to $400 but that's my final offer.

SARA: I know you've had the ad in for a couple of weeks. I'm willing to pay cash and take the stereo today. I feel $150 would be fair.

JACK: $150 is ridiculous. I'm willing to go down to $300.

SARA: (After remaining silent for a few moments) I'm willing to go up to $200 but I want two months to return it if something goes wrong, and I'd like to try it today.

JACK: All right, you can try it. Here it is.

SARA: I still want to be covered in case it breaks in two months.

JACK: Two months is unreasonable.

SARA: I'm willing to negotiate on that. What can you offer as a price and money-back guarantee?

JACK: (After a moment of silence) I'll go $250 and give you one month.

SARA: OK. How about $225 and a month and a half.

JACK: You've got a deal.

DON'T LET "MAYBE" WASTE YOUR TIME[2]

The most frustrating negotiations are not the ones that end in a firm No but those that end with a Maybe.

Maybes feel encouraging, but they waste your time and keep you from pursuing other options. When someone can't seem to give you an answer, say something like, "I know you can't say Yes right away, but I think it's fair for me to ask you to give me a No by the end of the week."

If he or she says No at the end of the week, fine; now you can move on to a new person. Don't forget to ask the person who says No: "If you can't do it, whom can you recommend who might?"

CASE STUDY: SOUND AND LIGHTING COMPANY

When Harold was sixteen, he started spinning records for parties in his Philadelphia neighborhood. His first gig was at an aunt's wedding reception, for which he was paid $125 for five hours. Harold recalls, "It would have taken me a full week of working at my fast-food restaurant job to make that kind of money."

As a student in the University Community Outreach Program's (UCOP/NFTE) entrepreneurship course at the Wharton School of Business, Harold had learned how to use flyers and business cards to promote a business. He used his initial earnings to buy business cards, and he posted flyers around town. Soon, Harold was taking home as much as $400 after spinning records all weekend. In 1991, when Harold was twenty-two, he formed the Nu X-Perience Sound and Lighting Company with a friend, Jeffrey, who invested in the business the $50,000 he had inherited from his father's estate.

Jeffrey's investment put the company in the big leagues. After a year of doing sound and lights for fraternity parties, the partners began to attract major clients, including the United Negro College Fund and the Philadelphia Labor Day parade. The company now earns as much as $2,000 on weekends.

Eventually, Harold hopes to provide sound and lights for concert headliners. "That's where the money is," Harold says, adding, "there are few African American companies doing that."

Harold started his business because he enjoyed playing music for people. If you're the kind of person who keeps up with the latest musical trends, you'd probably make a great DJ, too. People hire DJs for a variety of events, including parties, weddings, and sales. This is a more expensive business to start than some—unless you already own one or two turntables and lots of records.

Some DJs join or form record pools. These are clubs that let DJs rotate or share records, so they always have new records to play at parties. Ask at your local record store about DJ clubs. DJs also get records by getting on mailing lists for record labels. Do you know of any local record labels trying to get more attention for their artists? Call them and ask about getting free records in return for exposing the artists to a wider audience by playing the records at parties.

What You'll Need to Get Started

- One or two turntables. If you use two turntables, you'll also need a mixer.
- Speakers and amplifier.
- Records.
- Flyers. Advertise your service by handing out flyers at parties and school events.

RESOURCES

Books

The following books are among the best written on negotiating. Cohen's book is filled with humorous anecdotes and is easy to read. Karrass's book is a classic by the father of negotiation theory, and Jandt's book provides an in-depth look at the win–win philosophy.

You Can Negotiate Anything by Herb Cohen (New York: Bantam Books, 1993).

The Negotiating Game: How to Get What You Want by Chester L. Karrass (New York: Harper Business, 1992).

Win–Win Negotiation: Turning Conflict into Agreement by Fred Jandt (New York: John Wiley & Sons, Inc., 1987).

Field Guide to Negotiation by Gavin Kennedy (Cambridge, MA: Harvard Business School Press, 1994).

Chapter 7

FINANCIAL RECORDS THAT WILL HELP YOUR BUSINESS FLOURISH

STEP-BY-STEP INSTRUCTIONS FOR EASY BOOKKEEPING

The second half of a man's life is made up of nothing but the habits he has acquired during the first half.
—Fyodor Dostoevsky (1821–1881)
Russian novelist

John D. Rockefeller reportedly kept track of every penny he spent from age sixteen until his death in 1937 at the age of ninety-eight. His children said that he never paid a bill without examining it and making sure he understood each item. His ledgers became an important source of information about him to his biographers.

A NECESSARY HABIT

Most entrepreneurs aren't as enamored of keeping good records as Rockefeller was. I've personally had a hard time paying attention to my own record keeping. I finally made a deal with NFTE's financial manager. When I'm late turning in my personal expense accounts to him, I pay him twenty dollars! This motivates me to do it on time. I've found that being up-to-date with my personal financial records gives me a great feeling of organization and self-confidence.

NFTE students are required to keep daily records of their personal spending while they are taking our course. Getting in the habit of keeping good records helps them run their businesses more effectively.

After graduating from high school, Tokunbo took a summer entrepreneurship course with the UCOP program run by NFTE at Columbia University. During the course, she learned how to keep good records. "Bookkeeping and record keeping became major priorities," she says.

Tokunbo has her own nail-care business. She uses nail enamel and paste-on gems to create elaborate custom fingernail designs for her customers. Her prices range from $6.50 for regular manicures to $25 for a full set of tips and wraps.

At first, Tokunbo didn't think she needed to worry about accounting. After a while, though, she realized that "Keeping good records enables you to be smart about money."

"With basic accounting skills," she adds, "I have been able to expand my business and gradually able to see a profit." Tokunbo has even shown other people in her family how to start their own businesses.

How to Set Up Your Financial Records

By the time you've finished this chapter, you will have an easy, yet effective, system for keeping your business's financial records straight.

Start by keeping a record of all your income and expenses on *ledger sheets* or in an *accounting journal*. (These are sold at stationery stores or office supply stores.) Set up your records to look like Chart 4A–4D (pages 96–99).

Income is recorded as a **credit** entry. Income is money received from the sale of products or services, or from your job or an allowance. **Expenses** are recorded as **debit** entries. Expenses are the costs of doing business.

Record Cash Transactions on the Left Page of Your Ledger

Income is recorded on this page as cash received. Expenses are recorded as cash disbursed. Label each column of the page as follows:

1. Date
2. Explanation
3. (Paid) To/(Received) From
4. Cash Received
5. Cash Disbursed
6. Cash Balance

BUSINESS LEDGER					
Date	Explanation	To/From	Cash Received	Cash Disbursed	Cash Bal.

Chart 4A Business Ledger, Left Page

BUSINESS LEDGER				
Startup/Invest.	Revenue (1)	C.O.G.S. (2)*	Op. Costs (3)**	
				Income Statement
				Revenue (1):　　$
				Less C.O.G.S. (2):　$
				Gross Profit:　　$
				Less Op. Costs (3):　$
				Profit:　　　$
				Taxes:　　　$
				Net Profit:　　$
				Return on Investment =
				(Net Profit ÷ Startup/Inv. × 100)

*Cost of Goods Sold
**Operating Costs

Chart 4B Business Ledger, Right Page

PERSONAL LEDGER					
Date	Explanation	To/From	Cash Received	Cash Disbursed	Cash Bal.

Chart 4C Personal Ledger, Left Page

PERSONAL LEDGER						
Revenue		Cost				
Business/Work	Allowance/Gift	Food	Clothing	Travel	Entertainment	Other

Chart 4D Personal Ledger, Right Page

When you sell your product or service to a customer, always give the customer a bill **(invoice).** You will need to purchase a receipt/invoice book with two-part, carbon-copy receipts/invoices. When you make a sale, give the top copy to the customer as his or her receipt (or record of expense). Keep the second copy as your invoice (or record of income).

When your customer has paid the bill, mark the invoice "paid." It represents your customer's receipt. Keep a record of each invoice, usually in numbered order or organized by customer name. Each invoice that is prepared and sent (or given) to a customer is recorded as a credit entry when the invoice is paid by the customer.

EXPLAIN THE TYPE OF INCOME OR EXPENSE ON THE RIGHT PAGE OF YOUR JOURNAL

This kind of bookkeeping is called "double-entry bookkeeping" because each transaction is entered twice—once on the left page, and once on the right. If you receive cash from making a sale, for example, you enter the amount of the sale under "Cash Received" on the left page (Chart 4A). You *also* enter it under "Revenue" on the right page (Chart 4B). If you spend money on an operating cost like making flyers, you enter the amount of the cost under "Cash Disbursed" in Chart 4A. You also enter it under "Operating Costs" on the right page. Label the right page as shown in Chart 4B:

1. Startup (Costs)/Investment
2. Revenue
3. Cost of Goods Sold
4. Operating Costs

Always get a **receipt** for every purchase you make. A receipt is a slip of paper with the date and amount of your purchase printed on it. You can refer to the receipt to fill out your journal.

Save your receipts until tax time, when they will literally be worth money. The U.S. tax laws allow business owners to deduct many of their expenses from their taxable income. These **deductions** can save you money, but you must keep the receipts to prove that you actually had the expenses.

Keep your receipts in a shoebox or file. In another shoebox or file, keep all your invoices.

USING YOUR DAILY RECORDS

If you start with a balance of zero, the ledger or journal **balance** is determined by subtracting total cash disbursed from total cash receipts. The actual physical amount of money you have in your hand after a day of business will match the balance in your ledger if you have been keeping good records.

Keeping good records is really very simple, as long as you do it every business day. If you start skipping days, or trying to keep numbers in your head, maintaining reliable records will be hard. There will be times when you will be too busy to record a credit or debit at the moment it occurs. But if you follow the rules below, you will always have a written record that you can use to fill in your journal later.

Keeping track of the flow of money in and out of your business will teach you how to adjust your efforts to make your business successful. The business ledger or journal shows you how you are spending your money. You can try to improve your balance by lowering certain expenses or increasing income.

As you can see from Chart 4B, your income statement falls out of your business ledger or accounting journal. Simply total each column and put the totals from the columns labeled (1), (2), and (3) in the appropriate places in the Income Statement column. When you know your Net Profit, shown in the Income Statement column, you can determine your business's Return on Investment: Divide your Startup Costs or Investment into your Net Profit, and multiply by 100.

CASH FLOW

You can use your ledger or journal to keep track of the money your business earns and spends each business day. Keeping receipts for every purchase you make will help you get in the habit of keeping track of your **cash flow.** Cash flow is the cash receipts less the cash disbursements for a business over a period of time. One measure of your cash flow at a point in time is the cash balance in your journal.

You can be running a profitable business but still be insolvent if your cash balance becomes negative. To avoid getting caught without enough cash to pay your bills, follow these three rules:

1. Collect cash as soon as possible. When you make a sale, try to get paid in cash at the time of the sale.
2. Delay paying bills as long as possible without irritating the supplier. Most bills come with a due date. The phone bill, for instance, is typically due within thirty days. That means you can take up to thirty days to pay it without irritating the phone company and having them come after you for the money. *Never* pay a bill after the due date, however, without getting permission from the supplier first.
3. Always know your cash balance.

> **Collect your cash and postpone your bills!**

KEEPING GOOD RECORDS

Jason has a T-shirt silkscreening business. Listed below are his transactions for the month of July. Study how Jason recorded each transaction on his ledger pages (Chart 5A and 5B on pp. 104–105), and how he calculated his income and return on investment for the month. Assume an opening cash balance of $1,000.

1. To start his business, Jason buys a silkscreen frame, ink, a wedge, and other basic supplies on July 1. These cost him $250.
2. On July 2, he buys four dozen T-shirts from a wholesaler for $240.
3. On July 6, Jason registers to sell his T-shirts each weekend in July at a local flea market. Registration costs him $100. He then goes to a print shop and spends $20 on business cards and $10 on flyers.
4. On July 7, Jason goes to the flea market. He sells all his T-shirts at $12 each.

5. On July 10, Jason goes back to the wholesaler and buys five dozen T-shirts for $300.

6. On July 14, he sells four dozen T-shirts at $12. To get rid of the last dozen, he drops his price to $10 each.

7. On July 16, Jason buys five dozen T-shirts for $300. He spends $50 on ink and prints another $10 worth of flyers.

8. Jason is back at the flea market on July 21, but it rains in the afternoon and he sells only three dozen shirts at $12 each.

9. On July 25, he buys and screens two dozen more shirts for $120. During the final flea market on July 28, Jason sells all his remaining shirts (four dozen) for $12 each.

Using Jason's records as a model, make ledger entries of separate transactions—purchases and sales—on at least eight business days for the business you would like to start (or have started) as an entrepreneur. Be sure to track your cash balance carefully.

CASE STUDY: PERSONAL GROOMING SERVICE

Tokunbo took her high school business with her to college. At school, she does the nails of about four customers a week. Her costs are minimal, since she conducts her service either in her room or in her customers' rooms. Tokunbo advertises her business through flyers.

Monique is another young woman who started a personal grooming business—African hair braiding. Unfortunately, the state of Kansas shut the fifteen-year-old down for operating without a cosmetology license. Ironically, Monique was forced to close her business because an official at the Kansas Cosmetology Board read about an entrepreneurship award she had won.

Monique's business, A Touch of Class, had been earning her a profit of about $100.00 a month. The Board informed her that she could not braid hair for profit without taking a year of classes at a cosmetology school. Monique says few schools even teach braiding and none will take her until she turns seventeen.

Monique's plight caught the interest of *The Wall Street Journal,* which published an article critical of the Kansas Board. "The Board won't let me earn my own money," Monique says in the article, "and won't let kids like me learn how to take care of ourselves."

JASON'S BUSINESS LEDGER					
Date	Explanation	To/From	Cash Received	Cash Disbursed	Cash Bal.
6/30/00					$1,000
7/1/00	Silkscreen start-up supplies	Ace Arts		$250	750
7/2/00	4 dozen T-shirts	Joe Wholesale		240	510
7/6/00	Monthly registration fee	Flea market		100	410
7/6/00	Business cards	Print shop		20	390
7/6/00	Flyers	Print shop		10	380
7/7/00	Sold 4 dozen T-shirts @ $12	Flea market	$576		956
7/10/00	5 dozen T-shirts	Joe Wholesale		300	656
7/14/00	Sold 4 doz. @ $12, 1 doz. @ $10	Flea market	696		1,352
7/16/00	5 dozen T-shirts	Joe Wholesale		300	1,052
7/16/00	Silkscreen ink	Print shop		50	1,002
7/16/00	Flyers	Print shop		10	992
7/21/00	Sold 3 doz. @ $12 (rained)	Flea market	432		1,424
7/25/00	2 dozen T-shirts	Joe Wholesale		120	1,304
7/28/00	4 dozen T-shirts @ $12		576		1,880
Totals			$2,280	$1,400	$1,880

Chart 5A Jason's Business Ledger, Left Page

JASON'S BUSINESS LEDGER				
Startup/Invest.	Revenue (1)	C.O.G.S. (2)*	Op. Costs (3)**	
$250				
		$240		
			$100	Income Statement
			20	
			10	Revenue (1): $2,280.00
	$576			Less C.O.G.S. (2): $ 960.00
		300		Gross Profit: $1,320.00
	696			Less Op. Costs (3): $ 190.00
		300		Profit: $1,130.00
			50	Taxes: $ 282.50
			10	Net Profit: $ 847.50
	432			
		120		
	576			Return on Investment
				Net Profit ÷ Startup/Inv.
$250	$2,280	$960	$190	$847.50 ÷ $250 = 339%
				Instructions
				1. Record transactions as
				they occur.
				2. Keep all receipts and invoices.
				3. Estimate taxes as 25%, or
				profit × .25. In this case,
				$1,130 × .25.

*Cost of Goods Sold
**Operating Costs

Chart 5B Jason's Business Ledger, Right Page

Monique's story illustrates the importance of researching all state and local laws before starting your own small business. To learn what licenses you may need, contact your local Chamber of Commerce. You should also check with your state or local Board of Health.

Tips

- When providing personal grooming services, always keep your equipment very clean. Many states require manicurists to sterilize all nail-care instruments.
- Be friendly to your customers. Getting one's hair or nails "done" should be relaxing and enjoyable.

RESOURCES

Books

The Complete Guide to Money and Your Business by Robert E. Butler and Donald Rappaport (Englewood Cliffs, NJ: Prentice-Hall, Inc., 1989).

Accounting the Easy Way, 3rd Edition, by Peter J. Eisen (New York: Barron's Educational Series, Inc., 1995).

Other Resources

Kid's Business Software
Homeland Publications
2615 Calder Road
League City, TX 77573
(713) 332-9764

Send a self-addressed stamped envelope to receive more information on computer software Bonnie Drew has developed to help you print business cards, keep track of appointments, and manage money for your business. The software is for IBM PCs and costs $14.95. (Site licenses are available for schools.)

When your business is up and running, you should have your financial records checked at least once a year by a certified public accountant—probably around tax time. To find a CPA in your area, try CPA Finder at www.cpafinder.com.

Chapter 8

GETTING A GRIP ON YOUR COSTS

A SIMPLE SYSTEM FOR TRACKING COSTS AND PROFITS

If I see something I like, I buy it; then I try to sell it.
—Lord Grade (b. 1906)
British film and TV entrepreneur

Keeping good records helps you keep track of the costs of running your business. Finding creative ways to cut costs often means the difference between having a struggling business and a thriving one. Anyone can spend unlimited amounts of money and create a great product, but then he or she has used up more resources than the product is worth. The entrepreneur's goal is to create a product for *less* than the consumer is willing to pay for it.

At NFTE, we've lowered our programs' cost per child by 30 percent in the past two years. Keeping careful records showed us that one cost we could attempt to reduce was the cost of our BizBag™. The BizBag™ is a book bag filled with our books and with receipt books, calculators, and other items students need to run their businesses. We've been able to lower the cost of the BizBag™, while still improving its contents, by finding cheaper suppliers and ordering in bulk.

ENTREPRENEUR STORY
LEONARD JACOBY AND STEPHEN MEYERS, JACOBY AND MEYERS[1]

Cutting overhead costs can make the difference between a profitable and an insolvent business. Cutting costs can also help a company break into a new market by enabling it to offer its products or services at a lower price than the competition. In 1976, entrepreneur and lawyer Gail Koff teamed with lawyers Leonard Jacoby and Stephen Meyers to use this strategy to develop an untapped market for legal services.

Koff and her partners realized that wealthy people could afford to pay for lawyers, and poor people had access to legal aid. Middle- and working-class people were left in the lurch. Indeed, the American Bar Association had estimated that nearly 70 percent of the population did not have adequate access to the legal system.

Jacoby & Meyers' solution was the retail legal clinic—a neighborhood law office that would provide quality legal services to average-income people at a reasonable cost.

Instead of the lush suite of law offices that visitors to a law firm typically encounter, customers of Jacoby & Meyers can visit any one of 110 small storefront offices around the country. Koff and her partners developed an office management system to be followed by all their branch offices. Improving office efficiency was another way to cut costs.

To keep fees low, though, would also require a high volume of cases, so Jacoby & Meyers became the first law firm to advertise. In its television commercials, Jacoby & Meyers offers very inexpensive consultations, and guarantees that customers will receive a written estimate of potential fees.

Today, Jacoby & Meyers serves over 10,000 people a month. The Federal Trade Commission has noted that legal clinics have stimulated the legal services industry to become more competitive, leading to lower prices and better service for consumers.

ENTREPRENEUR STORY
HENRY FORD, FORD MOTOR COMPANY

When Henry Ford was trying to make his vision of an automobile in front of every house in America a reality, the cost of building a "horseless carriage" stood in his way. The automobile had just been invented and was very expensive to produce. It was considered a plaything for rich people. But Ford was determined to build an automobile that many consumers could afford.

In those days, cars were manufactured one at a time. It was a slow, expensive process. To cut manufacturing costs, Ford invented the assembly line. The cars were assembled, or built, as they rolled past the workers on a conveyer belt. The concept of the assembly line was adopted by many companies and helped develop many industries.

Ford's idea cut costs enough to be able to sell an affordable automobile to the average American and still make a profit. His Ford Motor Company became one of the biggest car manufacturers in the world. He also revolutionized industry by introducing the concept of mass production on a grand scale.

COSTS

The costs of starting and operating a business are divided into the following categories:

1. Startup costs
2. Cost of goods sold
3. Operating costs, including fixed costs and variable costs

Startup costs are the one-time expenses of starting a business. Startup costs are also called the "original investment" or "seed money." In a restaurant, for example, startup costs would include stoves, food processors, tables, chairs, silverware, and other items that are not replaced on a regular basis. Also included might be the one-time cost of buying land and constructing a building.

For a hot-dog stand, startup costs might look like this:

Hot-dog cart	$1,500.00
License from the city	200.00
Starting supply of hot dogs, buns, mustard	300.00
Business cards and flyers	50.00
Telephone answering machine	100.00
Total startup costs	$2,150.00

OPERATING COSTS

The **operating costs** of a business are those costs that are necessary to operate the business, not including the cost of goods sold. Operating costs can almost always be divided into six categories. An easy way to remember the six operating costs that most businesses will have is to memorize the code word USAIIR. It stands for:

1. **U**tilities (gas, electric, telephone)
2. **S**alaries
3. **A**dvertising
4. **I**nsurance
5. **I**nterest
6. **R**ent

Operating costs are also called **overhead**.

Overhead Is Divided into Fixed Costs and Variable Costs

Operating costs are divided into two types of costs: fixed costs and variable costs. **Fixed costs** are operating costs that stay the same, regardless of the range of sales the business is making. Rent can be an example of a fixed cost. Whether a shoe store sells 200 or 300 pairs of shoes in a month, it still pays the same rent on the store, so the rent is considered a fixed cost.

Variable costs are operating costs that change, depending on the volume of sales, but cannot be assigned directly to the unit of sale. If a cost can be assigned directly to a unit of sale, it should be viewed as part of the cost of goods sold.

An example of a variable cost might be electricity. A flower shop, for example, stores many more flowers in its refrigerators around Easter or Mother's Day. The refrigerators require more electricity to cool all the flowers. Electricity, therefore, is an operating cost that is higher when the store is selling more flowers. In a small business, those operating costs that stay constant are fixed costs. Those that fluctuate with sales, but cannot be assigned to a specific unit of sale, should be viewed as variable costs.

Cost of Goods or Services Sold

The **cost of goods sold** can be thought of as the cost of selling *one additional unit* of a product. The **cost of services sold** is the cost of serving one additional customer. For Jacoby & Meyers, the cost of goods sold is the cost of providing legal services for one customer. The cost of goods sold in a restaurant is the cost of the food served to a customer. The *total* cost of goods sold increases as the number of customers served increases.

An example of the cost of goods sold of a turkey sandwich is shown in the following table.

Item	Analysis	Cost per Sandwich
Turkey (4 oz.)	$ 2.60 per pound ÷ 4	$0.65
Bread (large roll)	.32 per roll × 1/2	0.16
Mayonnaise (1 oz.)	1.60 per 32-oz. jar ÷ 32	0.05
Lettuce (1 oz.)	0.80 per pound ÷ 16	0.05
Tomato (4 oz.)	2.20 per pound ÷ 1/8	0.28
Pickle (1/4)	0.20 per pickle ÷ 4	0.05
Wrapper	10.00 per 1,000 ÷ 1,000	0.01
Cost of goods sold		$1.25

GROSS PROFIT PER UNIT

Once you know your cost of goods sold and have defined your unit, you can calculate your gross profit per unit.

The cost of goods sold of the sandwich, subtracted from the price customers pay for the sandwich, equals the **gross profit per unit** for the sandwich.

Selling Price – Cost of Goods Sold = Gross Profit per Unit

In this case:

Price of sandwich	$4.00
Cost of goods sold	−1.25
Gross profit per sandwich	$2.75

As an entrepreneur, you must keep the cost of goods sold secret. If customers learn your cost of goods sold, they'll use that information to try to negotiate a lower selling price. If someone tries to sell you a sandwich for $4.00 and you know it costs only $2.75 to make it, would you be willing to buy it? Or would you try to negotiate the seller down to $3.00? What if you knew it cost $1.25 to make it?

> **Never reveal your cost of goods sold. If you do, customers will try to negotiate a lower selling price.**

Gross profit can be figured per unit, as in the turkey sandwich example. To get an idea of how a business is doing as a whole, however, you'll need to figure total gross profit. This is done by subtracting total cost of goods sold from total revenue, as in the following example.

Yolanda has a business selling designer watches. She buys the watches from a wholesaler for $15.00 each. Her cost of goods sold for each watch, therefore, is $15.00. She sells them for $30.00 each. What is her gross profit when she sells ten watches?

$$\text{Total Revenue} = 10 \text{ watches} \times \$30.00 = \$300.00$$
$$\text{(Selling Price)}$$

$$\text{Total Cost of Goods Sold} = 10 \text{ watches} \times \$15.00 = \$150.00$$

$$\text{Total Gross Profit} = \$300.00 - \$150.00 = \$150.00$$
$$\text{(Revenue)} \quad \text{(Cost of Goods Sold)}$$

> **Total Revenue – Total Cost of Goods Sold = Total Gross Profit**

PROFIT

Gross profit only subtracts cost of goods sold (for a "product" business) from revenue. It does not take into account the operating costs of running a business. To figure profit, the entrepreneur must subtract operating costs from gross profit. In other words, Yolanda does not actually keep $150.00 from the sale of ten watches. She still has operating costs to cover.

Yolanda spends $25.00 per week on flyers that she puts up all over town to let people know what styles of watches she has available and how to contact her. Her profit, therefore, is:

$$\underset{\text{(Gross Profit)}}{\$150.00} - \underset{\text{(Operating Costs)}}{\$25.00} = \underset{\text{(Profit)}}{\$125.00}$$

Gross Profit – Operating Costs = Profit

PROFIT PER UNIT

Sometimes, an entrepreneur wants to know how much of the sale of each unit is profit. An easy way to calculate profit per unit is to divide total units sold into profit. If Yolanda wants to know how much profit she makes each time she sells a watch, she would divide the number of watches she sells into the profit.

Profit per Unit = $125.00 ÷ 10 watches = $12.50 per watch

For every watch she sells, Yolanda is earning a profit of $12.50.

Profit ÷ Units Sold = Profit per Unit

TRACKING YOUR CASH FLOW

Despite all the good information and guidance a monthly income statement provides to you as an entrepreneur, you can't guide your business's daily operation using the income statement alone. You also need to use a monthly cash flow statement to track the cash going in and out of the business. Cash flow is, simply, the difference between the money you take in and the money you spend.

Remember, cash is the lifeblood of your business. Run out of cash and you're dead. Without cash on hand, you can find yourself unable to pay important bills, even when your income statement says you are earning a profit. This can happen because there's often a time lag between when you make a sale and when you receive the cash for that sale. That time lag can be a dangerous period for your business. William Stolze, author of one of the best books on starting a business, *Start Up: An Entrepreneur's Guide to Launching and Managing a*

New Business (Career Press, 1994), calls the cash flow statement "by far the most important financial control in a startup venture."

Noncash Expenses Can Distort Your Cash Picture

The income statement can also distort your cash picture because it may include noncash expenses like depreciation. When you depreciate an asset, you deduct a portion of its cost from your income statement. But you aren't actually physically spending that amount of cash. You don't hand anyone cash when you record a depreciation expense on your income statement.

Depreciation is a noncash expense because there's no cash going out of the business. If depreciation is deducted from an income statement, therefore, the income statement no longer accurately reflects how much cash the business is really holding. On your cash flow statement, therefore, you will need to add back the amount you deducted from the income statement as a depreciation expense.

Your Cash Position

As an entrepreneur, you need a cash flow statement to depict the cash position of your business at specified points in time. A cash flow statement records inflows and outflows of cash when they occur. If a sale is made in June, but the customer doesn't pay until August, the income statement will show the sale in June, but the cash flow statement won't show the sale until August, when the cash actually flows into the business.

Lola, owner of Lola's Custom Draperies, had the monthly cash flow statement shown on page 115. The first section of a cash flow statement records all sources of cash that come into the business and the dates they are received. Lola recorded her total cash inflows, or receipts, for the month of March.

The next section reports cash outflows that occurred that month—cost of goods sold, rent and utilities, monthly salaries, and sales commissions. Your costs may include insurance payments and interest on a loan.

The last section shows the net change in cash flow, before and after taxes. This tells you whether the business had a positive or negative cash flow that month. You can have all the sales in the world and still go out of business if you don't have enough cash flowing in to cover your monthly cash outflows. The cash flow statement is, essentially, your business's cash budget.

**Cash Flow Statement for Lola's
Custom Draperies, Inc., March 1999**

Cash Inflows

Sales, 3/1–3/31	$65,400	
Total Cash Inflows	**$65,400**	

Cash Outflows

Costs of Goods Sold	$29,360	
Factory Rent and Utilities	8,000	
Salaries and Administrative	12,000	
Sales Commissions	6,540	
Total Cash Outflows	**$53,900**	

Net Cash Flow Before Taxes	**$11,500**	($65,400 – $53,900)
Taxes	2,875	($11,500 × .25)
Net Cash Flow	**$ 8,625**	

Risking Your Cash on Inventory

As discussed previously in this book, an entrepreneur takes a risk every time he or she spends cash. If you buy inventory, for example, you take the risk that no one will buy it or that no one will be willing to spend what you paid for it—or more, so that you can make a profit.

There are two other risks with inventory: storage costs and pilferage. You have to make sure you can sell the inventory at a price that will cover any of the costs of storing it. You also need to be able to sell it at a price that will cover pilfering, which is stealing of inventory by employees or customers. Barney's, the famous New York clothing store, had a 7 percent pilferage rate, which contributed to driving it out of business.

There's also the danger that you'll invest in inventory because you expect to receive cash from customers who owe you money (accounts receivables). Be aware that a percentage of your accounts receivables will probably never be collected. If you aren't keeping track of cash by updating your cash flow statement, you can get caught in a squeeze between your suppliers—who want you to pay for inventory you've purchased—and customers who haven't paid you for product they bought.

And here's the catch: If you can't pay your creditors, you could lose ownership of your business. That's what happened to Donald Trump when he built the Taj Mahal in Atlantic City. He couldn't pay his bank loans, so he had to give the banks 80 percent ownership in the Taj Mahal.

These are all reasons to keep an ongoing cash flow statement for your business. Check it every day, and calculate your burn rate. In the next chapter, you'll learn how to use your balance sheet to keep an eye constantly on two ratios—quick and current—that tell you whether your cash on hand is getting too low to cover your debts.

Forecasting Cash Flow

As you get your business off the ground, you'll need to prepare monthly cash flow projections to make sure you'll have enough cash coming in to pay your bills.

You can forecast cash flow in two steps:

1. Project your cash receipts from all possible sources. Remember, orders are not cash receipts because you can't guarantee that every order will yield cash. Some orders may be canceled, some customers may not pay up. Cash receipts are checks that you are *sure* are going to clear.
2. Subtract from these projected cash receipts any expenses you expect to have. Cash expenses are only those expenses you will actually have to pay during the projected time period.

How can you be sure that these projections will be accurate? You can't be sure, but do them anyway. And review and update them constantly.

Here's an example:

Cumulative Cash Flow Graph

Stolze suggests plotting your business's cumulative cash flow on a simple graph. This is a great way to see how you're doing. The goal is for your cash flow to eventually head north! The graph on page 117 shows that this business needs to raise financing to meet its negative cash flow.

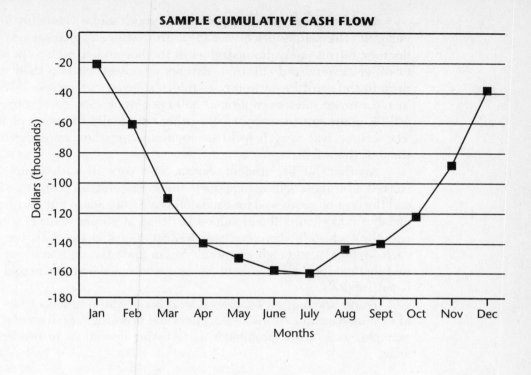

SAMPLE CUMULATIVE CASH FLOW

CASE STUDY: HANDMADE CRAFTS

Do you like to work with wood? Or to sew? If making things comes easy to you, consider making a simple product to sell. People enjoy buying handmade products. Some products you could make include: decorative pillows, stuffed animals, puppets, bird cages, jewelry, and candles.

Think of something that you will enjoy making *and* that people in your market will want to buy!

A great place to sell handmade crafts is at a flea market. You can obtain a list of flea markets from the Chamber of Commerce in your town or city. Contact the flea market management office to find out how to rent a booth or table.

Some of our students have sold their handmade items in unusual places—like hospitals. One of our most successful students, Kathleen, spent 90 percent of the last year of her life in a hospital, but that didn't stop her from running a successful business from her bed.

Kathleen made jewelry. Her cost of goods sold was roughly $1.50 per unit. Her selling price was $5 or $6. Kathleen's market was the doctors, nurses, and administrators in the hospital, as well as parents of other hospitalized children. Parents who were visiting their children in the ward loved to buy Kathleen's jewelry as presents. Kathleen's average sales were around $300 per week. She even started a NFTE course in the hospital for other terminally ill young people. The course was very helpful in counteracting the depression that some of them felt.

Another NFTE student, Susan, was very ill with lupus, but started a business selling handmade dolls. Her startup cost was $200, and the cost of goods sold for each doll was $7.50. Susan put four hours of labor into each doll and valued her time at $5 per hour. Her total cost for each doll, therefore, was $27.50. She sold the dolls for $45 each, and sold about eight per week. Susan made the dolls at home and sold them at local flea markets. Several stores in the area also sold her beautiful dolls.

Before starting any business in your home, call your local Chamber of Commerce and look into zoning laws and licensing requirements. For example, some towns prohibit manufacturing operations in residential areas.

What to Bring to the Flea Market

- Colorful flyers
- Business cards to give to customers
- A receipt book; give each customer a receipt
- Lots of change

RESOURCES

Books

For a thorough treatment of costs, see Chapter 2, "Cost, Volume and Profit Analysis," in *The Portable MBA in Finance and Accounting,* edited by John Leslie Livingstone (New York: John Wiley & Sons, Inc., 1992).

Another great reference is *The Complete Guide to Financial Management for Small and Medium-Sized Companies* by Donald Brightly (Englewood Cliffs, NJ: Prentice-Hall, 1995).

Other Resources

A *Handbook of Small Business Finance* is available from the Small Business Administration for a small fee. To order it, call your local SBA office or contact:

Small Business Administration
409 Third Street, N.W.
Washington, DC 20416
(800) 827-5722

If you have a service business, you will need to track the time and expense you spend on each client. Check out *Timeslips* software from Timeslips Corporation and *Buy the Hour* software from Austin Computer Resources.

Chapter

Using Financial Statements to Steer Your Business

Easy Income, Cash Flow, and Balance Sheet Statements

Money is better than poverty, if only for financial reasons.
—Woody Allen (b. 1935)
American filmmaker

And the Three Financial Statements Are . . .

Even a really small business can get complicated pretty fast if the entrepreneur isn't tracking its income and expenses. That's why entrepreneurs use three financial statements to steer their businesses: (1) an income statement, (2) a cash flow statement, and (3) a balance sheet. *Please,* don't skip this chapter because you think learning to prepare financial statements is going to be complicated or difficult. My special ed students have learned to prepare them! You can, too.

1. **Income statement.** Entrepreneurs draw up a monthly income statement to track income and expenses and see whether their businesses are profitable. Monthly income statements

are like scorecards that show the financial condition of your business at the end of each month. They show the sales (income) and the costs (expenses) you recorded during the month. If your sales are greater than your costs, your income statement balance will be positive; your business earned a profit. If your sales are less than your costs, your income statement balance will be negative; your business operated at a loss during that month. The income statement is also called a **profit and loss statement.**

2. **Cash flow statement.** Despite all the guidance a monthly income statement provides, you can't guide your business's daily operation using the income statement alone. You also need to prepare a monthly cash flow statement to track the cash going in and out of the business. The cash flow statement records inflows and outflows of cash *when they occur.* If a sale is made in June, but the customer doesn't pay until August, the income statement will show the sale in June, but the cash flow statement won't show the sale until August, when the cash actually flows into the business. Even when your income statement shows a profit, you may run out of cash and have to shut down because you can't pay your phone bill.

3. **Balance sheet.** The balance sheet is typically prepared once a year. It shows the **assets, liabilities** (debts), and **net worth** of a business. The net worth, the difference between assets and liabilities, is also called the **owner's equity.** Monthly income statements track a business's performance over a year's time. The balance sheet is more like a snapshot of the business's condition at the end of the business year.

THE SEVEN PARTS OF AN INCOME STATEMENT*

An income statement is an entrepreneur's scorecard. It answers the question: "How'm I doin'?" If your business is not making a profit, examining the income statement can tell you what may be causing the

---

* This statement is simplified, but is useful for a small business.

loss. You can then take steps to correct the problems before your net losses run you out of business.

Preparing monthly income statements will encourage you to keep your ledger up-to-date and accurate. You will use the information in your ledger to prepare your income statement at the end of each month.

Income statements are made up of the following parts (we'll be using their call letters, A through G, when we place these parts in equations):

A. Sales: How much money the company will be receiving for selling a product.

B. Total Cost of Goods Sold: The cost of making one unit times the number of units sold. *Never disclose your Cost of Goods Sold.* Keep secret how much you are paying to make your product so you can sell it for a profit.

C. Gross Profit: Sales minus Cost of Goods Sold.

D. Operating Costs: Items that must be paid to operate a business, including:

D1. Fixed Costs.

D2. Variable Costs.

These items include Utilities, Salaries, Advertising, Insurance, Interest, and Rent (referred to as USAIIR).

E. Profit Before Taxes: A business's profit before paying taxes but after all other costs have been paid.

F. Taxes: Payments required by federal, state, and local governments, based on a business's profit. A business must pay sales, income, and other business taxes.

G. Net Profit or Loss: A business's profit or loss after taxes have been paid.

Remember Hector's small business, described in Chapter 1? Let's say Hector finds a wholesaler looking to unload some ties. Hector buys twenty-five ties at $2.00 each and sells them all at $4.00 each. His revenue is $100.00. He spent $24.00 on flyers to advertise his ties. The income statement quickly shows whether Hector is making a profit.

Hector's Income Statement		The Math
A. Sales	$100	(25 ties × $4 per tie = $100)
B. Less Total Cost of Goods Sold	$ 50	(25 ties × $2 per tie = $50)
C. Gross Profit	$ 50	(A – B = C)
D. Less Operating Costs		
D1. Fixed Costs $ 24		
D2. Variable Costs +0	$ 24	($24 for flyers)
E. Profit Before Taxes	$ 26	(C – D = E)
F. Taxes	$ 6	(Taxes = $6)
G. Net Profit/(Loss)	$ 20	(E – F = G)

Hector's business is profitable.

BREAK-EVEN ANALYSIS

When sales and costs are equal, the income statement shows no net profit or net loss. The total at the bottom of the income statement is zero. This condition is called the **break-even point.** Many new businesses lose money in the beginning, but, to survive, a business must at least break even. It is vital for you to know how many units the business must sell during a month to cover costs and break even. Break-even analysis allows you to determine this number.

Unit of Sale

First, though, you must define your **unit of sale.** If you are selling ties, one unit of sale can be defined as one tie. If you are selling word processing, you can define one unit of sale as one hour of word processing. It's up to you.

Once you've defined a unit of sale, figure your **gross profit per unit.** This is the first step toward determining how many units you will have to sell to break even. Gross profit per unit is the selling price of the unit minus its cost of goods sold.

Selling Price per Unit − Cost of Goods Sold per Unit = Gross Profit per Unit

Let's look at Hector's income statement again. Assuming his unit of sale is one tie, what is Hector's gross profit per unit?

Hector sells each tie for $4. His cost of goods sold for each tie is $2. His gross profit per unit, therefore, is $4 − $2 = $2.

Calculating Break-Even Units

Because many small business operating costs are fixed, break-even is typically calculated by assuming that *all* operating costs are fixed. Using his gross profit per unit, Hector can calculate how many ties he will have to sell each month to cover his fixed costs. This simple formula divides gross profit per unit into monthly fixed costs to determine break-even units:

$$\frac{\text{Monthly Fixed Costs}}{\text{Gross Profit per Unit}} = \text{Break-Even Units}$$

$$\frac{\$24 \text{ (Monthly Fixed Costs)}}{\$2 \text{ (Gross Profit per Unit)}} = 12 \text{ Break-Even Units}$$

Hector has to sell twelve ties each month to stay in business. If he sells fewer than twelve ties, he will suffer a net loss. If he sells more than twelve ties, he will earn a net profit.

Including Variable Cost in Break-Even Analysis

Most young entrepreneurs' businesses don't have variable costs, but if you want to calculate break-even units including variable costs, you must first determine your variable cost per unit. Then, use this formula to figure your break-even units:

$$\frac{\text{Monthly Fixed Costs}}{\substack{\text{Gross Profit per Unit} - \\ \text{Variable Cost per Unit}}} = \text{Break-Even Units}$$

A shoe store has the following costs:

Variable Cost per Unit: $1 (sales commission per pair of shoes sold)

Monthly Fixed Costs: $1,100
Gross Profit per Unit: $12

The break-even point would be $1,100 ÷ ($12 − $1) = $1,100 ÷ $11 = 100 pairs of shoes. The store needs to sell 100 pairs of shoes a month (a little more than three pairs of shoes per day) to stay in business.

Including Depreciation on an Income Statement

If you buy expensive, long-lasting assets, such as a computer, you will want to include **depreciation** in your income statement. Depreciation is a certain portion of the cost of an asset that is subtracted each year until the asset's value reaches zero; it reflects the wear and tear on an asset over time.

This wear and tear reduces the value of the asset, so it's a cost of doing business. Depreciation is typically shown as an operating fixed cost on the income statement. Hector doesn't include depreciation on his income statement because his business doesn't have any assets—such as a computer, a car, or manufacturing machinery—that would have their worth reduced over time by wear and tear.

But let's say you open your own Hometown Restaurant. You buy $3,000 worth of tables and chairs. You know that those tables and chairs will have to be replaced in about five years because they will be worn out. If you subtract $600 a year from your income statement and put that money into a bank account, in five years you will have saved $3,000—enough to replace your tables and chairs. That's the point of depreciation—to help you save now so you can replace your assets as they need to be replaced. Many business owners forget that depreciation is a real yearly cost of using an asset. To forget about depreciation is to grossly overstate your profit.

Lola's Custom Draperies, Inc. is a more complex business than Hector's, but the income statement follows the same format as the income statement for Hector's business, and its goal is still the same—to show whether the business is profitable. Lola's income statement on page 126 includes depreciation.

Financial Ratio Analysis

Entrepreneurs don't just look at their income statements; they analyze them by dividing sales into each line item. Each item can then be expressed as a **percentage,** or share, of sales. Percentages express

Income Statement for Lola's Custom Draperies, Inc.
March 1999

Sales	$ 85,456	
Cost of Goods Sold		
Materials	11,550	
Labor	17,810	
Less Total Cost of Goods Sold	$ 29,360	($11,550 + $17,810)
Gross Profit	**$56,096**	**($85,456 − $29,360)**
Operating Costs		
Fixed Costs		
Factory Rent & Utilities	$ 8,000	
Salaries & Administrative	12,000	
Depreciation	2,000	
Variable Costs		
Sales Commissions	8,000	
Less Total Operating Costs	$ 30,000	($8,000 + $12,000 + $2,000 + $8,000)
Profit Before Taxes	$ 26,096	($56,096 − $28,000)
Taxes (25%)	6,524	($26,096 × .25)
Net Profit/(Loss)	**$19,572**	**($26,096 − $6,524)**

numbers as part of a whole, with the whole represented as 100 percent. Relating each element of the income statement to sales by stating the element as a percentage will help you notice changes in your costs from month to month.

You probably know that half (½) of something can be expressed as 50 percent, but here's how that percentage is actually figured:

1. Divide the numerator (top number) by the denominator (bottom number) of the fraction. To do that, add two decimal places to each number:

$$\frac{1}{2} = 1.00 \div 2.00 = .50$$

2. Multiply that result by 100 to express it as a percentage:

$$.50 \times 100 = 50 \text{ percent } (50\%)$$

By expressing each item on the income statement as a percentage of sales, you'll start to see the relationships between the items. A dollar is made up of 100 pennies, so a percentage also helps you express each item as part of a dollar. For example, suppose that 40 cents of every dollar of your sales was spent on cost of goods sold. Your gross profit per dollar of sales would then be 60 cents (60 percent). Your net profit, after 30 cents were spent on operating costs and 10 cents on taxes, would be 20 cents (20 percent). These percentages are referred to as a business's **financial ratios.**

By analyzing your income statement items as percentages of sales, you can see how costs are affecting your net profit. Apple Computer, Inc. noted, in its financial overview for 1994, for example, that it reduced operating costs that year to 21.2 percent of net sales, down from 28.8 percent in 1993. Net profit rose 15 percent in 1994, and a portion of that increase was probably due to a 7.6 percent reduction in operating costs. (P.S. Talk like this and you'll definitely impress a few people!)

A Fast-Food Restaurant's Income Statement

Given below is an income statement for one year, for a fast-food restaurant in New York City. Successful entrepreneurs know it's important to keep track of costs *each month* in order to make sure profits aren't getting eaten up. For a real challenge, cover the last column and try doing the financial ratio analysis of this income statement. (*Hint:* Divide sales into each line item.)

Income Statement		1 Year	Ratio Analysis
Sales		$2,600,000	100%
Cost of Goods Sold:			
Food	$792,000		
Paper	108,000		
	$900,000		
Less: Total Cost of Goods Sold		900,000	35%
Gross Profit		$1,700,000	65%
Less: Operating Costs		1,000,000	38%
Profit		$ 700,000	27%
Less: Taxes		233,000	9%
Net Profit/(Loss)		$ 467,000	18%

Creating Wealth by Selling a Profitable Business

If your business is successful, your income statements will prove it by continually showing a net profit. A successful small business can usually be sold for between three and five times its yearly net profit. If your net profit for one year is $10,000, for example, you might be able to sell your business for at least $30,000 (3 × $10,000).

ENTREPRENEUR STORY
CHARLES SCHWAB, CHARLES SCHWAB & COMPANY

Charles Schwab opened his own brokerage firm in 1971, when he was thirty-four years old.[1] Schwab uncovered a market niche when he began offering discount pricing to informed investors who were tired of paying hefty commissions to stockbrokers. Investors who didn't need someone else to do their research and make their decisions flocked to Charles Schwab & Company. By 1981, the company's earnings were $5 million. In 1982, BankAmerica Corporation bought Charles Schwab & Company for $53 million but left Schwab in place as CEO. Today, Schwab has offices across the United States and is expanding overseas.

Investing at a Discount

We tend to think that only companies involved with social activism or progressive politics are "doing good," but, in fact, most successful entrepreneurs are improving society simply by finding a more efficient way to use scarce resources. Charles Schwab, for instance, offers stock trading at commissions that are 30 to 40 percent below average. On a $1,000 trade, therefore, the consumer saves $30 to $40 that he or she can spend elsewhere. Schwab's company has also created 1,500 jobs.

THE CASH FLOW STATEMENT

Before you can sell your business for lots of cash, though, you'll need to run it for at least a few months! And to do that, you'll come to rely on your cash flow statement.

The cash flow statement records inflows and outflows of cash *when they actually occur.* If a sale is made in the Christmas rush but the customer doesn't pay until March, the income statement will show the sale in December but the cash flow statement won't show the sale until March, when the cash flows into the business.

Depreciation, as you've learned, is a non-cash-flow expense—no cash is actually going out. If depreciation is deducted from an income statement, therefore, the income statement no longer accurately reflects how much cash the business is holding. On your cash flow statement, therefore, you will need to add back the amount you deducted from the income statement as a depreciation expense.

The cash flow statement is divided into three sections:

- The first section records all sources of cash that come into the business and indicates the actual dates when they are received. These are cash inflows, or receipts.
- The second section reports cash outflows that must be made within that month—insurance payments, interest payments, cost of goods sold, monthly salaries, and the like.
- The third section shows the net change in cash flow before and after taxes. The entrepreneur can see whether the business had a positive or negative cash flow that month.

Cash flow is the lifeblood of your business. Run out of cash and you're dead.

Next, you'll learn how to use a balance sheet to keep an eye constantly on two ratios—quick and current—that tell you whether your cash on hand is getting too low to cover your debts.

THE BALANCE SHEET: A SNAPSHOT OF THE BUSINESS

Unlike the income statement and the cash flow statement, which entrepreneurs prepare monthly, the balance sheet is typically prepared at the end of the business's fiscal year. The fiscal year is the twelve-month accounting period chosen by the business. The fiscal year may differ from the calendar year (January 1 to December 31). Many businesses use a fiscal year that runs from October 1 to September 30. A business that uses the calendar year would prepare its balance sheet in

December. Once a business chooses its fiscal year, it cannot change it without approval from the Internal Revenue Service.

The balance sheet has three sections:

1. **Assets.** All items of worth owned by the business, such as cash, inventory, furniture, land, machinery, and so on.
   - Current assets are assets that can be sold for cash (liquidated) within one year.
   - Long-term assets are those that would take more than one year to liquidate.
2. **Liabilities.** All debts owed by the business, such as bank loans, mortgages, lines of credit, and loans from family or friends.
   - Current liabilities are those that must be paid within one year.
   - Long-term liabilities are those that are paid over a period longer than one year.
3. **Owner's Equity.** Also called capital or net worth, this is the amount that is left over after liabilities are subtracted from assets. Owner's equity is the stated value of the business to the owner.

The Financial Equation

The balance sheet is divided into two columns. On the left, or *assets,* side are listed all the business's assets. On the right, or *liabilities,* side are listed all the business's debt and equity.

Assets – Liabilities = Net Work (or Owner's Equity or Capital

- If assets are greater than liabilities, net worth is positive.
- If assets are less than liabilities, net worth is negative.

Every item in a business is financed with either debt or equity. All items that are owned are assets, but if an item was financed with debt, the loan is a liability. Liabilities are listed on the right side of the balance sheet.

If an item was purchased with the owner's own money, it was financed with equity. Equity is listed on the right side of the balance sheet. Depreciation hits both sides of the balance sheet—it is subtracted from the value of an asset on the left side of the balance sheet and from the value of the owner's equity on the right side.

Say your Hometown Restaurant owns its tables and chairs and has $10,000 in cash, but you took out a $5,000 loan to buy a new stove. The tables and chairs are worth $3,000 and will need to be replaced in five years, so you are deducting $600 yearly for depreciation. But the $5,000 stove will need to be replaced in ten years, so you need to set aside yearly depreciation of $500 toward a new stove. The total depreciation expense of $1,100 ($600 + $500) is subtracted from the value of the assets on the left side of the balance sheet. Depreciation is also subtracted from the owner's equity on the right side of the balance sheet, because it represents a decline in the worth of the assets due to wear and tear.

Hometown Restaurant—Balance Sheet, January 1999

Assets		Liabilities	
Cash	$ 10,000	Loan (for Stove)	$ 5,000
Tables and Chairs	3,000	Owner's Equity	11,900
Stove	5,000	($10,000 cash	
Subtotal	$ 18,000	+3,000 tables and chairs	
Less Depreciation	1,100	−$1,100 depreciation)	
Total Assets	**$16,900**	**Total Liabilities**	**$16,900**

> **The Financial Equation:**
> **Total Assets = Total Liabilities + Owner's Equity**

Notice how total assets equals total liabilities on the balance sheet? *On any balance sheet, both sides must show the same total.* If your balance sheet total on the asset side doesn't equal the total on the liability side, you've goofed somewhere.

FINANCIAL ANALYSIS

When you get to Chapter 19, "Financing Strategies That Work for Young Entrepreneurs," you'll learn that the balance sheet is an especially good tool for looking at how a business is financed. At a glance, you can see how much debt a company is carrying.

For now, though, all you need to know is that you can also analyze your business's **liquidity** (the ability to convert assets into cash), using the balance sheet and the following ratios:

$$\text{Quick:} \quad \frac{\text{Cash plus Marketable Securities}}{\text{Current Liabilities}}$$

$$\text{Current:} \quad \frac{\text{Current Assets}}{\text{Current Liabilities}}$$

The quick ratio tells you whether you have enough cash (plus any stocks or bonds you could sell quickly to raise cash) to cover your current debts. If it's greater than one, you are in excellent shape. With the current ratio, a number greater than one indicates that if you had to, you could sell some assets to pay off your debts and avoid bankruptcy.

CASE STUDY: TRANSCRIPTION SERVICE

Barbara, who has multiple sclerosis, was transcribing documents as a home worker for companies that provide transcription. She took a NFTE course at Queensborough College, where physically challenged people were being trained to start businesses in their homes. Barbara became convinced that she could make more money and be more independent working for herself. Her company, Barrett Unlimited, now earns revenues of around $2,500 a month providing legal and medical transcriptions.

Not only is Barbara pleased with her success and independence, she believes starting a home business "will be an important part of the future for disabled workers."

According to a January 26, 1993, article in *The Wall Street Journal*, more and more physically challenged people like Barbara are turning to entrepreneurship. Gregory, who is paralyzed below the neck and breathes with the aid of a respirator, started Jireh Medical Supply Company from his St. Louis home. He supplies medical equipment to the disabled via mail order. Gregory says his market niche is disabled people who are overcharged by medical equipment suppliers.

Other home-based businesses started by disabled entrepreneurs include phone services such as tarot-card readings, and handmade merchandise. Zully started making shoes for people who, like herself, suffer from misshapen or odd-sized feet due to polio or other illness. She originally sold the shoes from her Chicago home, but the demand for them became so great that she opened a store called "Zully's." Her store's annual revenue was $55,000 in 1993, according to the *Journal.*

Tips

- Disabled people who receive federal disability assistance of any kind should investigate whether earnings from a home-based business could jeopardize their payments. Inquiries should be addressed to the local office of the Social Security Administration.

RESOURCES

Books

For a very clear, entrepreneur-oriented discussion of the income statement, see Chapter 10, "Accounting and Management Decision Making," in *The New Portable MBA,* edited by Eliza G.C. Collins and Mary Anne Devanna (New York: John Wiley & Sons, Inc., 1995).

How to Start, Expand & Sell a Business by James C. Comiskey is a guide to the creation of wealth through entrepreneurship (Santa Barbara, CA: Venture Perspective Press, 1985).

Other Resources

The *Small Business Reporter* is a series of over 100 pamphlets on entrepreneurial subjects, including financial statements. Each pamphlet is available for a small postage and handling charge. For a free index, write to:

Small Business Reporter
Bank of America
P.O. Box 3700, Dept. 36361
San Francisco, CA 94317

Chapter

Am I Doing the Right Thing?

Return on Investment: A Great Decision-Making Tool

All our records had to be hits because we couldn't afford any flops.
—Berry Gordy (b. 1929)
American founder of Motown Record Company

INVESTMENT

"To invest" means to put your personal resources of money, time, and energy into something from which you expect to gain financial profit or personal satisfaction in return. Starting your own business is a big **investment** of your resources. How do you decide whether starting a business is the best possible investment of your money, time, and energy? In this chapter, we'll explore the methods top businesspeople use to make such decisions.

RATE OF RETURN

When you start a business, you commit to a long-term, day-after-day investment of your own time, energy, and money. You do this because you believe that someday your business will return more than the present value of the time, energy, and money you put into it. Without realizing it, you have calculated the **rate of return** on your investment and have found it to be acceptable.

134

Businesspeople need to know what the rate of return will be on their investments. Rate of return is often called **return on investment** (ROI). ("Return" means "profit," and "on" means "divided by.") It is expressed as a percentage of the original investment.

I have found that any young person can learn to calculate rate of return. In my own business, I discovered that rate of return is an invaluable decision-making aid for a new entrepreneur. I started my business with $32,000. For every cent I spent, I did a mental calculation of return on my original investment. I asked myself: Will this expenditure increase my ROI or not? That constant analysis really helped me.

How to Calculate ROI

Here's how to calculate your return on investment:

1. Start with the amount of money you possess at the close of a business period. Call this your end-of-period wealth (A).
2. Subtract the amount of your original investment in the business. Call this investment your beginning-of-period wealth (B).
3. Divide the resulting number by your beginning-of-period wealth.
4. Multiply by 100 to express your return as a percentage.

$$\text{Formula:} \quad \frac{A - B}{B} \times 100 = \text{ROI}$$

Let's say you find out that your church is planning an arts-and-crafts event for local children. Fifty silkscreened shirts are needed for the children. You go down to the wholesale district and spend $200 for fifty shirts at $4 each:

$$50 \text{ shirts} \times \$4 \text{ per shirt} = \$200$$

You then sell the shirts to the church for $400. Using the four steps above, what is your return on investment?

$$\frac{\$400 - \$200}{\$200} = \frac{\$200}{\$200} = 1 \times 100 = 100\%$$

The return on your investment is 100 percent.

Here's an easy way to remember this formula:[1]

> **ROI = What you made over what you paid, times a hundred.**

$$\frac{\textbf{What you made}}{\textbf{What you paid}} \times \textbf{100} = \textbf{ROI}$$

PRACTICE SESSION

Take a few minutes here to practice ROI calculations. The return you'll realize in your own business will be critical to its success.

Return on Investment (ROI)

$$\frac{\text{End-of-period wealth} - \text{Beginning-of-period wealth}}{\text{Beginning-of-period wealth}} \times 100 = \text{ROI}$$

Assume a one-year investment period and calculate the ROI for the dollar amounts below. (Leave off the two decimal places (for cents) to make the math easier.)

End-of-Period Wealth	Beginning-of-Period Wealth	Rate of Return
$ 2	$ 1	100%*
40	10	_____
15	5	_____
20	5	_____
6	3	_____
350	175	_____
80	60	_____
1,500	1,000	_____
9	3	_____
75	25	_____

$*\dfrac{2-1}{1} = \dfrac{1}{1} = 1 \times 100 - 100\%.$

ANSWERS: RETURN ON INVESTMENT (ROI)

$$\frac{\text{End-of-period wealth} - \text{Beginning-of-period wealth}}{\text{Beginning-of-period wealth}} \times 100 = \text{ROI}$$

Assume a one-year investment period and calculate the ROI for the figures below. (Leave off the two decimal places (for cents) to make the math easier.)

End-of-Period Wealth	Beginning-of-Period Wealth	Rate of Return
$ 2	$ 1	100%
40	10	300
15	5	200
20	5	300
6	3	100
350	175	100
80	60	33
1,500	1,000	50
9	3	200
75	25	200

ROI is a decision-making tool I use every day. You can apply this concept not only to business but also to personal decisions that you make. Remember, whenever you spend your time, money, or effort on something, you are making an investment. If you can't decide whether to do something, look at the ROI.

In business formulas, "return" means "profit" and "on" means "divided by." Return on Investment means Return (A – B) divided by Investment (B).

ROI IS AFFECTED BY RISK

The return demanded by an investor depends on how risky he or she thinks an investment is. If the investment is very risky, the investor will want a high rate of return.

Risk factors include time and liquidity. The more **time** an investment is tied up, the greater the rate of return should be. The longer someone has your money, the greater the chance that it could be lost in some unforeseen way. You, as an investor, will want to be compensated for that risk.

As an investor, you also have to consider **liquidity.** Liquidity refers to the ease of getting cash in and out of an investment. How "liquid" is the investment? Can you call the business in which you have invested and get your money back if you suddenly have need for it? If so, the investment is "liquid," or easily converted into cash.

In general, the longer you have to wait for the payback on your investment, the greater the return should be. The easier your money is to retrieve, the lower your return will probably be.

SMALL BUSINESS RISK AND RETURN ARE HIGH

The rate of return on a small business can be very high. The risk of failure for most types of small businesses is also very high. The Small Business Administration has estimated that only one in seven small businesses survives. On the other hand, many entrepreneurs have survived business failures and gone on to become millionaires or billionaires with new ventures. As long as your basic reserves are not depleted by a business failure, it can be a great learning experience.

Always have a plan for failure. Sit down and imagine what could happen if you are not able to provide your product or service at a cost that is attractive to consumers. Will you go back to work for someone, or start another business? Do you have enough money put aside to cover your basic living expenses until you can start generating income again?

The higher the risk of the investment, the higher the demanded rate of return.

ENTREPRENEUR STORY
RUPERT MURDOCH,
FOX TV AND THE NEWS CORPORATION

Some entrepreneurs really thrive on risk. One risk-loving entrepreneur is Rupert Murdoch. He even started his own television channel—Fox TV—when most industry observers said it couldn't be done. But Fox's outlandish—some say, tasteless—programming, including such popular shows as "Married With Children" and "The Simpsons," has been a huge hit.

The Fox TV channel is just one piece of Murdoch's media empire. Murdoch is the owner of News Corporation, a deceptively simple name for one of the largest publishing companies in the world. Its rapid growth is the result of Murdoch's impulsive buying and willingness to take risks.

Murdoch's company owned a dozen newspapers in Australia before he moved to England in 1969 and bought the Sunday publication, *News of the World*. Most of his papers had been bought cheaply, with borrowed money. He made them profitable by turning them into scandal-loving tabloids and by running bingo contests and girlie pictures in the papers.

Getting a Kick—and Millions—Out of Risk

Murdoch was thirty-eight and relatively unknown when he made the riskiest purchase of his life (up to that time). He bought the *Sun* of London for the British equivalent of a million dollars. In 1970, the *Sun* was a dull socialist paper. After buying it, Murdoch quickly applied his tried-and-true formula. Then he swung its editorials to the political right. The *Sun* became the most profitable of Murdoch's holdings, earning him over $50 million.

Murdoch Crosses the Atlantic:
The U.S. Expansion

In 1973, Murdoch quietly came to the United States and bought two papers in San Antonio, Texas, for $18 million. He then launched the *Star*, a sensational national weekly modeled after the well-known *National Enquirer*. After that, he bought some very well-known American publications. Among them were the *New York Post*, the *Village Voice*, *New York Magazine*, and the *Boston Herald*. In 1984, Murdoch bought the Chicago *Sun-Times* for $96.5 million and applied his "brighteners," as he calls his tabloid formula.

Overseas, Murdoch acquired the London *Times,* perhaps the most historically prestigious newspaper in the world, and took a half-interest in Ansett Transport Industries, an Australian airline. Many of Murdoch's purchases look reckless when he makes them. But, in most cases, he turns a profit.

Murdoch operates with a phenomenal amount of debt, because he refuses to dilute his 46 percent stake in his company. He keeps a tight lid on expenses; after every acquisition, the first change he makes is to slash costs significantly by dismissing all nonessential employees and installing cost-cutting equipment.

Murdoch's latest foray is into satellite broadcasting. He plans a nationwide pay-TV network beamed directly into American households via satellite. This venture has so far cost $20 million and has been unsuccessful. But Rupert Murdoch is not one to give up on a risky venture.

INTERGALACTIC VENDING: A SMALL BUSINESS WITH A BIG RETURN

Most businesses that young people start face a lower risk of failure than the small businesses started by adults. The young entrepreneur usually has fewer fixed costs, such as rent or insurance. For this reason, businesses started by young people can have a high rate of return despite the lower risk.

Landon, a graduate of NFTE's Twin Cities program, bought a vending machine for $500 and installed it at his school in Minneapolis. He knew that if he could sell soda for a lower price than the stores and vending machines in and around the school, students would buy from his machine. Landon searched for the best wholesale dealer for soda. Because he found a low wholesale price, he was able to resell his soda for ten cents less than the average vendor at his school.

Soon, Landon was making a 300 percent return *per day* on his investment. He used his profit to buy a car and purchase more inventory. He named his business Intergalactic Vending.

After reading about Landon in the paper, Midwest Vending Company donated a candy vending machine and a change machine to his enterprise. Midwest was switching to computerized machines and didn't need the older machines anymore. Midwest also gave Landon a year of free machine servicing. Landon has hired someone to run his vending machine business while he looks for new business opportunities.

LOWER RISK = LOWER RATE OF RETURN

The lower the risk of the investment, the lower the demanded rate of return. Savings banks typically offer a low return of, say, 4 percent over a year because the risk of losing your money is very low. Compare the rates of return for a typical savings account and a young person's after-school business:

	A (End of Period*)	B (Beginning of Period)	Rate of Return
Savings account	$104	$100	4%
After-school business	$500	$100	400%

* Period = one year

INVESTING IN STOCK

Financial investments such as stocks and bonds also offer a return on investment. When Andrew Carnegie was persuaded by Tom Scott to buy ten shares in Adams Express for $600, he received a $10 dividend within a short time. Carnegie said, "I shall remember that check as long as I live; it gave the first penny of revenue from capital—Eureka!"

Another entrepreneur who became very excited about the prospects of using money to make more money was John D. Rockefeller. As a teen, he loaned a neighboring farmer $50. When the farmer paid him back, he added $3.50 as interest. At the time, Rockefeller had just earned only $1.12 for a full thirty hours of back-breaking work hoeing potatoes for another neighbor. As Rockefeller said in his autobiography, *Random Reminiscences*, "From that time on, I was determined to make money work for me."

One very popular investment is stock. A share of stock represents a share of ownership of a corporation. The stockholder literally owns a piece of the company.

Once a corporation sells shares, it has no control over them. The shares are bought and sold on the stock market by investors looking for return on their investment. Before we discuss this further, however, you'll need to learn to read stock tables.

READING STOCK TABLES

Reading stock tables is a great lesson in cause and effect. There's always a reason behind every stock price move. Stock prices are influenced by economic and political news, trends, and many other factors.

At first glance, stock tables appear to be written in a foreign language, but they are not hard to interpret. To prove it, study this part of a typical stock table and then answer the questions below.

| 52 WKS | | STOCK | SYM | DIV | YLD | P/E | VOL 100S | HI | LO | CLOSE | NET CHG |
HI	LO										
$8^3/_8$	5	ChockFull	CHF	1.00	—	28	132	$6^3/_8$	$6^1/_8$	$6^1/_4$	—
$58^7/_8$	$38^3/_8$	Chrysler	C	1.60	4.1	4	28650	$39^5/_8$	$38^1/_4$	$38^7/_8$	$+^1/_4$
$82^5/_8$	$68^5/_8$	Chubb	CB	1.96	2.5	13	1268	$79^7/_8$	$79^1/_4$	$79^3/_4$	$-^1/_8$
$36^1/_8$	$28^3/_4$	Citicorp Inc.	CER	2.46	6.9	14	38	$36^1/_8$	$35^7/_8$	$35^7/_8$	$+^1/_8$

1. Which stock is the most expensive? _____
2. Which stock has the highest dividend? _____
3. Which stock has the highest yield? _____
4. Which stock has the lowest P/E ratio? _____
*5. Which stock was traded the most? _____

Chart 6 gives you some experience in looking up actual stocks. Here are definitions of some of the terms you'll see:

- **52-Week High/Low (52 wks Hi/Lo):** The first figure in the column is the highest price the stock traded for in the previous 52 weeks. The second figure is the lowest. All prices are listed in dollars and fractions of dollars. The fractions are traditionally given in eighths.

---

* The answers are: 1. Chubb; 2. Citicorp; 3. Citicorp; 4. Chrysler; 5. Chrysler.

	52 WKS		STOCK	SYM	DIV	YLD	P/E	VOL 100S	HI	LO	CLOSE	NET CHG
	HI	LO										
Chemical Bank												
Colgate-Palmolive												
Disney												
Ford Motor Co.												
Reebok												

Chart 6 Reading a Stock Table. Research the Listings for These Well-Known Companies

- **Stock:** The name of the company. *The Wall Street Journal* lists both the company name and its symbol. Every stock has a symbol **(Sym),** usually consisting of from one to four letters.

- **Dividend (Div):** Corporations can pay each stockholder a dividend—a sum of money for every share each stockholder owns. A dividend is a return on investment for the stockholder. Corporations pay dividends out of their profits.

  A figure of 1.00 in this column means a dividend of $1 per share of stock was paid out to the company's stockholders over the course of the year. A stockholder who owned 100 shares was, therefore, paid $100 ($1 dividend × 100 shares) in dividends.

- **Yield (Yld):** The rate of return on the stock, expressed as a percentage:

$$\text{Dividend/Closing Price} \times 100 = \text{ROI}$$

  The yield on a stock is low compared to the ROI on some other investments. Stocks are usually purchased with the expectation that the price will go up. Reselling the stock at a higher price is how an investor's ROI is usually made in the stock market.

- **Price/Earnings Ratio (P/E):** The P/E is the price of one share of stock divided by the earnings per share. If the price of the stock is $28, and the company earned $7 for each share of stock outstanding, the P/E ratio would be: $28 \div 7 = 4$

  A P/E of 4 is considered low. A low P/E can indicate a stable company. A high P/E is about 20 and above. A P/E of 12 is more or less average. A zero P/E means that a company has no earnings.

In general, the higher a P/E, the greater the risk investors are willing to take. A new company in a new field like genetic engineering will often have a high P/E because the future earnings are as yet unknown. If the company makes a scientific breakthrough, investors could earn lots of money.

- **Volume of Shares Traded (Vol 100s):** The number of shares traded (bought and sold) during the previous day's trading period. (The New York Stock Exchange trades Monday through Friday from 9:30 A.M. to 4 P.M.)

  Volume is given in hundreds of shares. Add two zeros to a number in the Vol 100s column to get the correct figure. When a very high volume of stock is being traded, it means investors are taking an interest in that stock. Volume does not indicate whether the price will go up or down.

- **Hi Lo Close:** The highest, lowest, and last prices the stock was traded for during the previous day's trading period. Again, the figures are given in dollars and fractions of dollars.

- **Net Change (Net Chg):** The change in price—an increase (+) or decrease (−)—from the close of the previous day's trading period.*

How Would You Invest in the Stock Market?[2]

Imagine you have been given $10,000 to invest in the stock market. Which of the following stocks would you choose?

American Express

American Telephone & Telegraph (AT&T)

Bethlehem Steel

Coca-Cola Company

Eastman Kodak

General Electric

IBM

McDonald's Corp.

Procter & Gamble

---

* Additional special symbols are explained at the bottom of the published stock tables.

Sears, Roebuck
Texaco
United Technologies
Woolworth

The actual rate of return on these stocks over a ten-year period is shown in the next section.

HOW DID YOUR INVESTMENT PERFORM?

If you had invested $10,000 in any of these stocks on January 1, 1980, the value of your investment ten years later would have been:

$10,000 Stock Investment on Jan. 1, 1980	Value of Stock on Dec. 31, 1989	Percentage ROI
American Express	$46,693	+366.9%
American Telephone & Telegraph (AT&T)	36,010	+260.1
Bethlehem Steel	8,757	−12.4
Coca-Cola Company	67,174	+571.7
Eastman Kodak	19,226	+92.3
General Electric	50,964	+409.6
IBM	14,621	+46.2
McDonald's Corp.	80,532	+705.3
Procter & Gamble	37,580	+278.5
Sears, Roebuck	21,181	+111.8
Texaco	66,625	+84.4
United Technologies	25,233	+152.3
Woolworth	50,856	+408.6

CASE STUDY: CONSIGNMENT SHOP

Do you ever throw out clothes because you're tired of them? Maybe someone else would buy clothes you don't want anymore. Maybe you would like to buy clothes one of your friends doesn't want anymore.

This is the idea behind a clothing resale or "consignment" shop. A consignment shop sells used clothing. People bring in clothes they don't want anymore, and the shop sells the clothes for them. In return, the clothing donor receives a percentage of the sale, usually 30 to 50 percent.

Consignment shops are becoming more popular as people search for ways to stretch their clothing dollars. You could run a consignment shop from your house (in your garage or basement) after school or work, or on weekends. Before starting any business in your home, however, you must check on local zoning and licensing laws. Call your local city hall or Chamber of Commerce.

Janet McKinstry Cort, a close friend who helped me get NFTE started, sells vintage and antique clothing in a very popular consignment shop called Cinderella's Closet, near Boston College. Her customers receive store credit for every item they bring in. This ensures a constant flow of items. Janet is a fashion designer who can repair clothes, thereby increasing their resale value. She also makes and sells her own designs in the store.

Janet says she knew the minute she saw her storefront that her business would be successful because it's located within walking distance of a college campus. She maxed out her credit cards fixing up the store, but is currently pulling in substantial sales. Her success has enabled her to replicate Cinderella's Closet on Brown University's campus in Providence, Rhode Island.

How to Buy and Sell Clothes on Consignment

- Decide how much commission you will pay on each sale.
- Have each person who brings you clothing fill out a tag with his or her name, address, and phone number. Tell every customer how much commission you are paying.
- When you sell a piece of clothing, take off the tag and write on it the amount for which you sold the garment.
- At the end of the day, make a list of whose clothes you sold and for how much.
- Call the sellers and tell them how much money you owe them. Let's say Daphne brought you a dress that you sold for $15.00. If you have agreed to pay a commission of 30 percent, you owe Daphne $4.50 ($15.00 × .30). You make $10.50 ($15.00 − $4.50).

Tips

- Take on consignment only articles of clothing that you really think you can sell. Don't take clothes that aren't in good condition or in fashion.

- Wash, or have drycleaned, all clothing before selling it, or make a rule that you'll only take cleaned clothing.

- Create a fun atmosphere when your shop is open. Play your friends' favorite music. You can even sell refreshments.

RESOURCES

Books

Jeffrey Little explores the heart of American investment in *Understanding Wall Street* (Philadelphia: Liberty Hall Press, 1991).

Available on the stock market is *The Stock Market (7th Edition)* by Edward S. Bradley and Richard J. Teweles (New York, NY: John Wiley & Sons, 1998).

In *Common Sense: A Simple Plan for Financial Independence* by Art Williams, the author explains the basics of investment, including compound interest and return on investment, with lively examples (Minneapolis: Park Lane Publishers, Inc., 1991).

A very helpful book on decision making for entrepreneurs is *How to Make 1000 Mistakes in Business and Still Succeed: The Small Business Owner's Guide to Crucial Decisions* by Harold L. Wright (Oak Park, IL: The Wright Track, 1990).

Another resource that should be on every entrepreneur's desk is *Mancuso's Small Business Resource Guide, Revised and Updated* by Joseph Mancuso (New York: Prentice Hall Press, 1996). It's packed with valuable contacts.

Chapter 11

THE DAILY BIBLE OF AMERICAN BUSINESS

HOW TO READ (AND USE!) THE WALL STREET JOURNAL

Always do business with a man who reads.
—Andrew Carnegie (1835–1918)
American industrialist and philanthropist

A NEWSPAPER THAT PRACTICES WHAT IT PREACHES

The Wall Street Journal is the daily bible of American business; it's read by over two million people! If you are interested in business, you should read the *Journal.* It will help you think in business terms and use business vocabulary.

ENTREPRENEUR STORY
CHARLES DOW AND EDWARD JONES, DOW JONES

The Wall Street Journal began as a tiny entrepreneurial venture. In 1882, Charles Dow and Edward Jones started a service for people working in New York City's financial district. Their service provided handwritten, up-to-the-minute financial news to subscribers. Dow and Jones's first office was in a room behind a soda fountain, in a building next to the New York Stock Exchange on Wall Street. By 1889, *The Wall Street Journal*, was being sold as a newspaper for two cents.

Since then, the *Journal* has developed its worldwide circulation of over two million readers. It has become the largest daily newspaper in the United States.

ENTREPRENEUR STORY
JOHN H. JOHNSON,
EBONY MAGAZINE

Many entrepreneurs have succeeded, as Dow and Jones did, by tailoring a publication to the market they know best. John H. Johnson, the son of a mill worker, became one of the richest men in the United States by starting the first magazine written by African Americans for African Americans.

In 1918, when Johnson was born in Arkansas City, Arkansas, the local high school was open to "whites only." His mother believed strongly in the value of education, however. She moved north to Chicago so her son could attend high school there. Johnson edited the high school newspaper and yearbook and was an honor student.

As Johnson became more and more interested in journalism, he saw that very few publications reported stories that were of particular interest to the black community. Many newspapers and magazines, in fact, ignored it. Johnson decided to start a publication by African American journalists for African American readers. He approached friends and businesspeople for loans to start a magazine, but got nowhere. Finally, his mother pawned her household furniture to raise $500.00 for him. In 1942, he and his mother began publishing *Negro Digest*. After just one year, the magazine was selling 50,000 copies a month.

In 1945, Johnson started *Ebony* magazine. Most of the advertisers in *Ebony* were selling hair and skin-conditioning products to African American consumers. They were eager to advertise in a magazine that targeted their market. Today, *Ebony*'s circulation exceeds 1.5 million readers.

Johnson turned his early love of books and journalism into a multimillion-dollar empire that includes *Jet* and *Ebony* magazines, a book publishing company, a nationally syndicated TV program, real estate, and a line of cosmetics. He also owns two radio stations, one of which was Chicago's first and only black-owned station.

How to Read The Wall Street Journal[1]

In Johnson's day, it would have been hard to find a story about an African American in *The Wall Street Journal*. Today, however, the *Journal* is much bigger and more diverse. Reading the *Journal* may seem challenging at first, because each issue contains so much. Breaking it down into its three main sections—Front Page, The Marketplace, and Money & Investing—will make the paper much easier to handle.

Front Page

The front page of the *Journal* that is reproduced on page 151 has been keyed to the list below so that you can easily find the important features the *Journal* offers as openers.

1. Look first at **What's News** to get brief descriptions of the major stories of the day. Each description lists the page where the story can be found.

2. At the bottom of the front page is **Today's Contents.** This will help you find the page numbers of other features and departments.

3. Columns 1 (far left) and 6 (far right) are the spots for in-depth articles on a wide range of business topics and for profiles of business and political leaders.

4. At the top of column 4, there is usually a **performance graph** of a single aspect of the nation's economy.

5. Below the performance graph is a story about business, approached from an unusual or entertaining perspective.

6. Column 5 is reserved for what the *Journal* calls its **"Newsletter."** On Monday, it deals with the economic climate in general; on Tuesday, with issues concerning labor; on Wednesday, with taxes; on Thursday, with business developments; and on Friday, with government matters affecting business, in a feature called "Washington Wire." (The *Journal* is not published on weekends.)

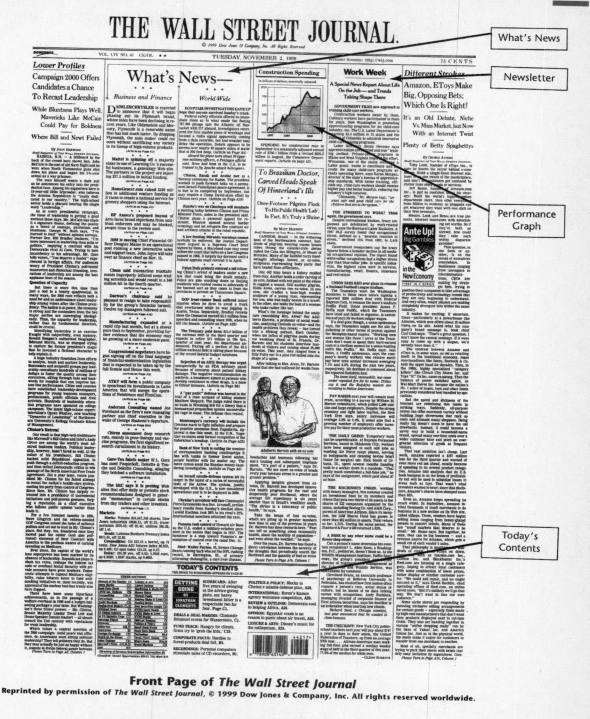

What's News

Newsletter

Performance Graph

Today's Contents

Front Page of *The Wall Street Journal*

The front page is the first page of Section A. Here is what you'll find in the rest of Section A.

1. On page A2 is the latest economic news.
2. The middle part of Section A is generally composed of the stories listed in **What's News.**
3. The daily **Industry Focus** spotlights one company or one industry.
4. Near the back of Section A are two pages devoted to **International Reports**—business and political news from overseas.
5. In its **Leisure & Arts** section, the *Journal* reviews books and music, and covers sports news.
6. The two facing pages at the end of Section A are the **editorial pages,** where the *Journal*'s editors and publisher, as well as guest columnists, present their opinions.
7. On the back page of Section A, you'll find **Politics & Policy**—news from Washington and how it affects not only business but the country as a whole.

The Marketplace

A typical front page of Section B, the *Journal*'s second section, is shown on page 153. This section contains the important business stories of the day, which are reported in depth "with a focus on the marketplace." On the first page of the section, look for:

1. The **lead story,** given the most prominent spot at the top of the page.
2. **"The orphan"**—a short, amusing, true story on a variety of topics.

Here is what you will find in the rest of Section B:

1. **Index to Business** (page B2). This is a list, by page number, of the businesses written about in that day's issue.
2. The **Enterprise** feature is about smaller, entrepreneurial companies. (This is required reading for anyone interested in small business!)

THE WALL STREET JOURNAL.

TUESDAY, NOVEMBER 2, 1999 **B1**

MARKETPLACE

Enterprise: *Investors take a gamble on 'Ben-Hur: The Musical'* **Page B2.**

Telecommunications: *AT&T to create company for Latin American push* **Page B8.**

Advertising: *Doner emerges as next shop to watch in consolidation wave* **Page B10.**

Your Career Matters: *Fannie Mae's search for a No. 2 gets complicated* **Page B20.**

Lead Story

MANAGING YOUR CAREER
By Hal Lancaster

A Founder's Lesson: Market Reality Matters More Than a Mission

UMANG GUPTA PAID the price for hubris. In the 1980s, he turned his vision of software to manage databases for vast personal-computer networks into a hot company that bore his name. Gupta Corp.'s market value eventually peaked at $400 million, giving Mr. Gupta net worth of nearly $100 million "for a few days," he says.

But when powerful new competitors piled into the market, the company suffered through seven consecutive quarters of losses and the stock price plummeted. In 1996, Mr. Gupta, as CEO, and the company changed its name to Centura Software.

Mr. Gupta now says he ignored signs of market change, partly because he listened only to his own voice. That voice was chanting a familiar Silicon Valley mantra. "The company wasn't a company, it was a cause," he explains. "We were going to change the world."

That attitude drives much of Silicon Valley, but it's a double-edged sword. While it can motivate idealistic young technologists to great heights, it can also blind them to market realities, a principal cause of the career stumbles you don't often hear about in this land of instant riches. For every new technology tycoon, there's someone who overestimated the value of his technology or underestimated the money needed to capture the market.

Umang Gupta

Now, Mr. Gupta is trying to apply the lessons he learned from his setback to his new role as chairman and CEO of Keynote Systems. His company recently had a successful initial public offering, so it has now entered the hubris danger zone.

TRAINED AS A CHEMICAL ENGINEER in India, Mr. Gupta came to the U.S. in 1971 to earn an M.B.A. at Kent State University. After working for IBM for four years, he returned to India to start a computer company but realized that the proper place for that was Silicon Valley. He relocated there with IBM in 1980 and joined Oracle a year later as its 17th employee, writing its first business plan.

But the entrepreneurial dream lingered, and in 1984, he launched a sparsely financed Gupta Corp. Instead of shopping it to venture capitalists, he financed growth with fees from early customers like Lotus and Computer Associates.

Such a strategy is risky because it requires a lengthy technological leash to withstand challenges from later, better-financed rivals. Still, the company had grown to $56 million in annual sales and 400 employees by the time it went public in 1993. A short time later, Microsoft and Oracle, among others, challenged Gupta, and the company's performance began to decline. Oracle offered to buy Gupta, but its founder couldn't sell his mission, a decision he now regrets.

Mr. Gupta went through a period of dark reflection. Why didn't he see the market change coming? "I started to think of all the things I should have done to make the company outlast me," he says.

In today's Silicon Valley, he concluded, companies that are built around the vision of a single founder will falter unless he surrounds himself with a savvy team. "No individual is smart enough to figure out all the technological moves," he says. "Bill Gates and Larry Ellison know that it, but they also built organizations that can react to change."

Companies need a lot of people who have great antennae that can sense changes in the market, he says. He didn't have those people at Gupta, or he wasn't listening to them. "Decisions can't be based just on what the founder knows or his gut feels," he says.

By 1995, he had decided the company needed to be restructured and that he didn't have the appetite for it. "The revolution was over," he says.

MR. GUPTA ALSO BLAMES his inattentiveness for not realizing the importance of the Internet. "I had people leaving Gupta to go to a little company named Netscape in 1994," he says. "Why didn't I pay attention?"

After he resigned, Mr. Gupta traveled and read a book a day for several months. He was besieged with offers to join boards or start companies. Finally, in 1997, he joined the board of Keynote Systems, which measures the performance of commercial Web sites. But when the board asked him to take over as CEO four months later, he hesitated. The company was having difficulty attracting venture capital. Its business plan wasn't fully fleshed out. Did he want to sacrifice the cheerleader and family balance he had just achieved?

The lure of running a company again was too strong. This time, though, he vowed things would be different. The business isn't constructed around a single technological revolution but a variety of technology services. "If all the Web pages got blindingly fast tomorrow," he says, "there would still be a need for us to measure other aspects of quality."

And this time, he says, "we have a lot more people reacting to market situations without my being involved." That means the company can react faster to changes, he says. "You don't hire people to do what you say. You hire people to worry for you," he adds. "I tell them I judge them by how little I have to worry about what they're doing."

Another major change: no more cramming as many meetings as possible into each day. Now, he leaves large swatches of time open so deliberation can wander in and brainstorm and he can learn what's going on. He also leaves more time to visit younger companies and attend venture capital conferences. And he believes he has recently hired executive assistant that her job is to help him, not protect him.

"I'm making sure my peripheral vision remains intact so I'm not blindsided again," he says.

E-mail comments on this or other career issues to Hal.Lancaster@wsj.com.

Adam Epstein, formerly of Brobeck, Phleger & Harrison, became general counsel at Tickets.com Inc. and hired his old employer

Becoming a Client Is the Best Revenge

Law Firm Meets the New Boss: The Junior Associate Who Quit and Joined a Dot-Com

By Richard B. Schmitt
Staff Reporter of The Wall Street Journal

ADAM EPSTEIN knows how to have a satisfying experience with a major law firm. First, you quit.

Then, you get a job with an Internet start-up, become a valued client of your old firm and get the chance to boss around your former bosses, in whose eyes your stock has suddenly soared.

"I'd be lying if I said I didn't get a charge out of it," says the 32-year-old Mr. Epstein.

For growing numbers of workers, the Internet isn't just a way to pass the time; it's a hot new exit strategy. People in all sorts of professions—from banking to journalism to pornography—are seizing the power of the Net to seize control of their careers, build new ones and upend relationships.

Now, lawyers are catching on. And it's particularly sweet revenge, given the rigid hierarchy at most big firms, where young associates have functioned mainly as well-paid worker bees.

Today, three-fourths of all associates leave firms before their seventh year, according to the National Association for Law Placement, which tracks recent law grads' comings and goings. Many of their new jobs involve technology.

"It never gets boring," says Rick Klau, who traded a legal background for a marketing job at iManage Inc., a San Mateo, Calif., software company, which teaches law firms and other businesses how to manage paper work. He's got stock options, to boot. One friend, he says, bolted law to help run an Internet site on genealogy.

In the case of Mr. Epstein, the reality check set in while clerking at a top New York firm, Willkie Farr & Gallagher, one summer during law school at Boston University. The brass tried

to impress the students with chauffeured junkets to Mets games, and other perks. But back in the office, he couldn't help but notice formerly idealistic young lawyers complaining about not having a weekend off in months or time with their growing families.

With his eyes wide open, Mr. Epstein headed West after law school, as a junior associate at one of San Francisco's largest and most prestigious firms, Brobeck, Phleger & Harrison, starting in 1993.

His plan was to learn as much as possible, without making any long-term commitments. He had a few choice assignments, but came to loathe the unrelenting contentiousness of litigation and

> *'I am very aware of how the big-firm game works', Mr. Epstein told his old pals*

the firm's emphasis on chalking up long billable hours. He really knew he was in trouble when he got a chance to work on a big antitrust case for Nintendo Co.'s U.S. unit, a firm client, and ended up alphabetizing video-game files.

He was "bringing to bear all the skills you learn by fourth grade," recalls Neil Shapiro, a former Brobeck partner who had taken Mr. Epstein under his wing for a time and was sensitive to his plight. Mr. Epstein's father's death at about the same time led him to further examine his priorities.

After three years at Brobeck, he quit, initially to open an in-line skate store with an equally disgruntled real-estate manager who had been a client of the firm. Mr. Epstein worked on his skiing, and a series of how-to lectures for lawyers looking to pursue alternative careers. He contributed columns to the local legal press, exploring what he called the "Stallionesque realities" of law-firm life.

Lawyers who read the column didn't necessarily like the message—"Get a haircut and mind your own business," one advised in an e-mail—but Mr. Epstein started catching the eye of entrepreneurial types, who considered his irregular career path and risk-taking a major plus. That led to a pair of Internet-related jobs.

Suddenly, he was applying his big-firm experience again, but from the perspective of a client, laying down the law on billing and staffing issues. In May 1999, he joined Tickets.com Inc., a fledgling online ticket vendor, as vice president and general counsel, where his duties included riding herd on outside law firms doing the company's legal work, some of whom, he determined, had developed some bad habits.

He discovered that one firm had customarily billed without itemizing expenses—a question able tactic he was wise to from his New York days. Another appeared to be billing the company for work that had been done internally. The problems were all eventually smoothed out, but James Cavato, Tickets.com's chief executive, ended up taking a phone call or two from lawyers wondering about the new regime. "It got a little contentious," he says.

Then, Mr. Epstein decided to turn to his old pals at Brobeck. He arranged a beauty contest of sorts to see what kind of team Brobeck could put together to defend his company against a major suit filed by ticket giant Ticketmaster, a unit of USA Networks Inc. The team Brobeck offered included a number of lawyers Mr. Epstein had worked with directly, some of whom played an important role in his career.

Old friends or not, Mr. Epstein laid down some ground rules only an insider would know. "We know it is not going to come cheap," he recalls saying, "but we aren't going to pay for things that aren't necessary," including long-winded memos on general subjects "where you guys are basically training young associates." Lest they all need reminding, he pointed out, "I am very aware of the way the big-firm game works." While they were meeting, he recalls, former associates walked by, and did "a double take," seeing him calling the
Please Turn to Page B39, Column 1

The New Alchemy: Turning Garbage Into Fuel

Stalks, Straw and Other Refuse Are in Demand for Making Substitutes for Gasoline

By John J. Fialka
Staff Reporter of The Wall Street Journal

Does it pay to turn garbage into a substitute for gasoline?

The U.S. government has spent almost 50 years and hundreds of millions of dollars trying to prove that it does. The research has produced many rosy policy statements about how the various sorts of organic refuse known as "biomass"—corn stalks, rice straw, even household food scraps—could be the source of an alcohol-based "fuel of tomorrow." But tomorrow never quite seemed to get here.

Now, at least four commercial ventures are gearing up to make gasoline substitutes out of stuff that people throw away or pay others to get rid of. The appearance of economically viable companies outside the government research umbrella is a radical change, says James Hettenhaus, a Charlotte, N.C., consultant who works with the Department of Energy and private companies to promote the technology.

Environmental laws, the threat of future restrictions and the nation's growing mountains of garbage are creating the new marketplace for biomass. For example, research spurred by climate change has begun to convince farmers that they can make more money and make their soil more fertile with new "no till" planting methods, which make plowing unnecessary. That will leave the upper Midwest strewn with some 250 million tons of corn stalks and other agricultural wastes, much of

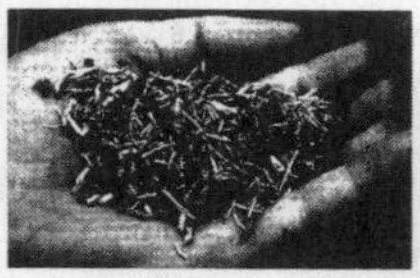

Bagasse, waste fibers from sugar cane (left), is used to make ethanol in Louisiana; rice straw is used in California

which farmers used to plow under.

"It could be a new cash crop," says Mr. Hettenhaus, who has begun to organize farm groups to collect the stuff, bale it and sell it.

One buyer he is working with is Iogen Corp., of Ottawa. Iogen is building a refinery there to turn corn stalks into ethanol, which then will be blended with gasoline and sold in the area by the Calgary oil-refiner Petro-Canada. According to Patrick Foody, Iogen's 49-year-old founder, the plant will begin producing fuel this spring.

In Louisiana, bagasse—the waste fibers left after the juice is squeezed out of sugar cane—has always posed a disposal problem. But a Dedham, Mass., company, BC International Corp., has a solution. It has bought a Louisiana refinery that was making ethanol out of corn and is modifying it to break down sugar-cane wastes with a special

process that uses genetically altered bacteria and enzymes.

"Bagasse is a no-cost feedstock," says Stephen Gatto, the company's president and chief executive. The company will extract and ferment the sugar from bagasse into ethanol and burn another chemical derived from the process—lignin—as a fuel to run the refinery. Lignin's "profligacy will sell its ethanol to companies that will process it into mouthwash, hairspray and solvents. Blended gasoline, he says, is a likely future product because it's a federal excise-tax exemption for manufacturers of ethanol-blended fuel in effect "until 2007.

"Beyond that there needs to be a change in economics to support this industry," Mr. Gatto says. Biotechnology is producing so many breakthroughs making ethanol out of corn and is modifying it to
Please Turn to Page B4, Column 2

New Therapy For Chiron: Fiscal Austerity

By Ralph King
Staff Reporter of The Wall Street Journal

EMERYVILLE, Calif.—For years, Chiron Corp. was known for having some of the sharpest minds in biotechnology. Now, it's getting a reputation for sharp pencils, too.

With pioneering feats like the discovery of the hepatitis C virus, Chiron became one of the nation's largest biotech companies. Then some of its academic-style research and pursuits on technology didn't pan out commercially, and growth stalled. Some 18 months ago, the proud scientists running Chiron reluctantly turned it over to a no-nonsense manager from the pharmaceutical industry.

Chiron now is seeing a comeback by taking fewer research risks and squeezing more profit from its assets—acting, that is, more like a traditional pharmaceutical company.

Yesterday, chairman and chief executive Sean Lance, a former Wellcome PLC veteran, unveiled the first significant research cuts ever at Chiron. The retrenchment, announced only to employees, is part of a plan to cap its bulging R&D budget by $75 million, and could result in layoffs of as many as 50 scientists, or 20% of its research staff. (R&D spending had risen to $294 million last year from $249 million in 1996.)

The cuts, mainly in gene-therapy and vaccine programs, are designed to help sustain earnings growth, a priority for Mr. Lance. In the first nine months, earnings from continuing operations, at $102.5 million, leapt 66% over the year-earlier period.

"It used to be University Chiron. We've said, 'Come on, it's Business Chiron,'" said Mr. Lance in an interview. "I've got shareholders' money, not academic grants."

The cuts set the stage for a delicate challenge at Chiron, as Mr. Lance tries to balance commerce and creativity. The danger: Big-company methods could stifle the kind of discoveries that make free-wheeling biotech firms hot. "People have been trying to figure this out for ages," says Michael King, a biotech analyst with Bancboston Robertson Stephens. "There is no cookbook approach."

Coming from Glaxo, which had $13 billion in revenue last year, Mr. Lance says he figured Chiron little Chiron, with $727 million in revenue, would be relatively easy. But after quickly arranging the sale of Chiron's lackluster diagnostics division to Bayer AG for $1.1 billion in September 1998, he hit a brick wall.

The company's sprawling research apparatus, which included dozens of projects, was divided into five separate fiefs. They communicated little and lacked accountability, Mr. Lance says. "No one in certain areas could tell me what they were going to spend. That was unacceptable to me," he says. "And they were enemies of each
Please Turn to Page B4, Column 4

CD Recorders Finally Click For Consumers

By Evan Ramstad
Staff Reporter of The Wall Street Journal

The sleepy-stereo business, which hasn't had a hit product in more than a decade, is waking up to the sound of compact-disk recorders—with most of the noise coming from personal computers.

PC makers about three years ago began offering CD-recording drives—popularly called "burners"—as add-ons, initially at prices that exceeded $1,000. Since 1996, seven million drives have been sold, with prices as low as $99. This fall, they are a standard feature in many consumer PCs that sell in the neighborhood of $1,200.

Meanwhile, compact-disk burners for home stereos recently passed one million units. Aiwa Co. and Philips Electronics NV just began selling executive-style, shelf-top stereos with built-in compact-disk recorders for around $600. Other companies are scrambling to get products to store shelves.

The scramble has been a long time coming. Recordable compact-disk technology has been around since 1988 but was stalled for years as record companies fired lawsuit after lawsuit at electronics makers.

The record companies saw digital home recording, noted for clarity of sound and durability, as a greater threat to royalties than simple cassette-tape recording. However, CD recording devices for consumers at the time were used to record data and thus were ignored in the legal crossfire.

"At the time, the threat for market in data recorders was 50,000 units, a million," says Richard Doherty, president of Envisioneering, a consulting firm in Seaford, N.Y.

The entire CD-recorder market began in 1992 when Congress approved a compromise between the recording and electronics industries. The agreement required audio CD recorders and blank CDs to carry a matching electronic code; the recorder won't record unless it finds the blank CD's code.

Artists and record labels receive a 3% royalty on the sale of each blank audio CD and a 2% royalty from sales of audio CD burners. Artists must annually file a claim with the U.S. Copyright Office, which administers the disbursement of royalties. One-third of the royalties pool goes to songwriters and composers, and two-thirds to record companies and artists.

There is a loophole: Royalties aren't required on recorders or CDs that work with PCs because no one anticipated they would be used for music. Who could anticipate that music would be flying
Please Turn to Page B4, Column 3

Orphan

---

3. **Technology** reports on "high-tech" businesses, such as computers or lasers.

4. **Marketing & Media** covers advertising and the media (television and radio, newspapers and other publications).

5. **The Law** reports on legal issues affecting business.

6. **The Mart** appears in Business Opportunities, at the end of Section B, and consists of classified pages that list employment opportunities and businesses for sale. (At the end of this chapter, you'll learn how to use The Mart to check out interesting business opportunities.)

Money & Investing

The coverage of the financial markets—in Section C, the paper's third section—is what *The Wall Street Journal* does more thoroughly than other newspapers. A typical front page of Section C is shown on page 155. It shows you why the *Journal* is so valuable to businesspeople.

1. The first two columns of the front page are titled **Markets Diary.** Activity on the five major financial markets during the previous eighteen months and the previous week is represented in **graphs.** The markets are:
   - Stocks
   - Bonds
   - Interest (rates)
   - U.S. Dollar (compared to five foreign currencies)
   - Commodities

2. Below the graphs is a **tabular summary** of the previous day's activity on the **financial markets.**

3. Depending on the day of the week, the front page of Section C will include features like "Deals & Deal Makers," or "Abreast of the Market," as well as a market roundup for the day.

4. An index to the contents of the rest of Section C is given at the top of the front page. The remainder of the front page is devoted to expert opinions on the previous day's financial developments and the financial world in general.

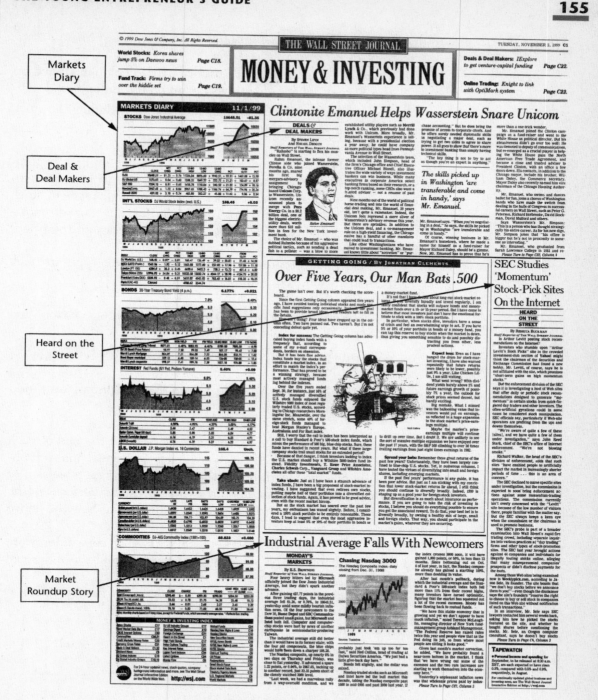

Front Page of Section C of *The Wall Street Journal*
Reprinted by permission of *The Wall Street Journal,* © 1999 Dow Jones & Company, Inc. All rights reserved worldwide.

In the rest of Section C, you will find:

1. On page C2, an important financial market column, **Heard on the Street,** which sometimes begins on C1, is continued.
2. Reports on how various financial markets, including the stock market, are performing.

You will learn about stock and corporations in Chapter 17. Corporations sell stock (shares of ownership in a company) to investors. Investors buy and sell stocks on the stock market. A single piece of stock is called a share. Back in 1889, *The Wall Street Journal* started reporting the Dow Jones Industrial Average (DJIA), an average of the prices of eleven major stocks.

Today, Dow Jones reports price averages for three types of stock and includes many more companies:

1. 30 **Industrial** stocks (such as General Motors, Exxon, and IBM).
2. 20 **Transportation** stocks (such as USAir and the Union Pacific Railroad).
3. 15 **Utilities** stocks (such as Consolidated Edison [New York] and Detroit Edison).

The price movements of these stocks are averaged at the end of each day. These averages are called the "Dow Jones Averages." You've probably heard them announced during the business news on television or on the radio. The DJIA is watched by casual investors. Changes in the leading industrial stocks are an important indication of how the entire stock market is performing.

Chart 7 compares the DJIA in 1896 (twelve companies were listed then) with the thirty companies that now yield the industrial average.

Other financial markets covered in Section C of the *Journal* are:

- Mutual Funds
- International Stocks
- Foreign Currencies
- Credit Markets
- Futures & Options

The 1896 DJIA
American Cotton Oil
American Sugar
American Tobacco
Chicago Gas
Distilling & Cattle Feeding
General Electric
Laclede Gas
National Lead
North American Co.
Tennessee Coal & Iron
U.S. Leather Preferred
U.S. Rubber

The Current DJIA		
Allied-Signal	Exxon	Procter & Gamble
Alcoa	General Electric	Sears Roebuck
American Express	General Motors	Union Carbide
AT&T	Goodyear Tire	United Technologies
Boeing	IBM	Walt Disney
Caterpillar	International Paper	Wal Mart
Chevron	McDonald's	
Citigroup	Merck & Company	
Coca-Cola	3M	
Dow	Johnson and Johnson	
Du Pont	J.P. Morgan	
Eastman Kodak	Philip Morris	

Chart 7 The Dow Jones Industrials in 1896 and in 1999

THE MART

Look in The Mart section of *The Wall Street Journal* for a business for sale that interests you. Call the person selling the business and ask some questions that would help you decide whether the business is worth buying. Some good questions to ask are:

- What is the product (or service) that you sell?
- How do you define one unit of your product or service?
- Do you have audited financial statements (statements that have been reviewed by an independent accountant)?
- What is your revenue? Your gross profit? Your profit before tax? Your net profit?
- How have your sales been over the past five years?
- What are your sales and profit forecasts?
- Do you have a business plan that you can send me?

Sample Ad

Look at this Mart advertisement from the *Journal*. The wording is simple and direct:

THE MART
INTERNATIONAL/NATIONAL/REGIONAL

Small Family Business

in Central Virginia with annual sales of $200,000. Owner interested in selling or in finding someone interested in investing in the business as a partner.

Call Frank V. at (804) 352-7191

If you were to call the owner/seller, your dialogue might go like this:

YOU: What is the product (or service) that you sell?

SELLER: This is a commercial printing company. We make printed stationery, envelopes, and other items. We define one unit of printing service as one hour. Our price per job is based on how long we think it will take, plus the cost of the paper and ink we will need.

YOU: Do you have audited financial statements?

SELLER: Yes, we do.

YOU: What is your revenue?

SELLER: Our revenue is approximately $200,000 per year.

YOU: Your gross profit?

SELLER: It's approximately $95,000 per year.

YOU: Your net profit?

SELLER: Our net profit was $72,000 this year.

YOU: How have your sales been over the past five years? What are your sales and profit forecasts?

SELLER: Our sales have been steadily increasing over the past five years. We expect our sales and profits to increase by about 10 percent per year over the next five years.

YOU: Are these numbers audited? Who's your accountant?

SELLER: Yes, our financials were prepared by Ernst & Young.

YOU: Do you have a business plan that you can send me?

SELLER: Yes, I do.

CASE STUDY: YARD WORK

John has about thirty-five customers who depend on him to keep their yards clean. He gets out of bed before dawn to mow lawns in the summer, rake leaves and resoil in the fall, and shovel snow in the winter.

John started his company, John's Four Season Care, at age fourteen, while participating in the Young Entrepreneurs of Minnesota program. "People give me business because they really like to see kids working hard—not just hanging out doing drugs, ripping off," John says. "Too many kids want to make money illegally," he adds. "This way you can do it legally and be proud."

John says the most important thing a young entrepreneur can be is reliable. "People won't ask you back if you show up late or don't do a good job," John says. "They won't recommend you to their neighbors, either," he adds. Much of John's business comes from repeat customers and referrals.

Yard work is available year-round. If, like John, you live in a four-season region, each season offers different business opportunities:

Summer	Fall	Winter	Spring
Cut grass	Rake leaves	Shovel snow	Clean up winter debris
Weed flower beds	Mulch	Salt sidewalks	Plant flowers

How many more yard work chores can you imagine?

Each season, John makes flyers announcing his services. He puts one flyer in each mailbox in his neighborhood. A week later, he visits each home that received a flyer and tries to sign up customers.

Tips

- Work quickly, but be thorough. Never leave a job until you've completely finished what the customer asked you to do.
- Always clean up after yourself. Don't leave mud or plant clippings on the sidewalk, for example!

- Don't forget to put away tools. Younger children can hurt themselves if shovels, rakes, or hedge clippers are left lying around. If it rains when they're left outdoors, they'll rust and have to be replaced.

RESOURCES

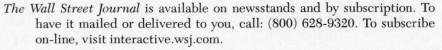

The Wall Street Journal is available on newsstands and by subscription. To have it mailed or delivered to you, call: (800) 628-9320. To subscribe on-line, visit interactive.wsj.com.

For a more detailed look at *The Wall Street Journal,* see *The Dow Jones-Irwin Guide to Using the Wall Street Journal* by Michael B. Lehmann (Homewood, IL: Dow Jones-Irwin, 1987).

12

THE ESSENCE OF SELLING IS TEACHING

LEARN TO SELL AND YOU'LL NEVER BE BROKE

When there's nothing to lose and much to gain by trying, try.
—W. Clement Stone (b. 1902)
American sales expert and author

BUSINESS IS BASED ON SELLING

All business is based on selling products or services for money. Direct selling occurs when you are face-to-face with a potential buyer, trying to persuade him or her to make a purchase.

Salespeople often become successful entrepreneurs because they hear, on a daily basis, what the consumer needs and wants. If the customer is dissatisfied, it is the salesperson who hears the complaint.

FROM SALESPERSON TO ENTREPRENEUR

Many of America's great entrepreneurs started out in sales:

• Ray Kroc, founder of McDonald's, was selling milkshake machines when he was inspired to turn the McDonald brothers' hamburger restaurant into a national operation.

161

- King C. Gillette was a traveling salesman when he invented the safety razor that millions of people now use.
- William C. Durant, the founder of General Motors, began his career as a buggy salesman. He said, "The secret of success is to have a self-seller, and if you don't have one, get one."

Durant was from my hometown, Flint, Michigan; I should have remembered his advice when I started selling. One of the first products I tried to sell was a bicycle lock from Taiwan. I was representing the lock exporter. After many phone calls, I finally secured a meeting with an importer who might order thousands of the locks. My commission on the sale would have been $5,000 a month. The importer picked up one of the locks and yanked it as hard as he could. It broke. I learned the importance of finding a self-seller—a product in which I really believed.

LISTENING BUILDS TRUST

Brian Tracy is a top sales consultant who believes that the most important thing a salesperson/entrepreneur can do is listen. Conventional sales wisdom has taught that a salesperson should spend most of his or her time on closing the sale, but Tracy believes most of the selling time should be spent on the front end of the sales call—on getting to know the customers and building their trust by listening to what they have to say after you make your pitch.

Tracy describes the sales process in three steps, which, he notes, are similar to those followed by physicians:

1. Establish rapport (the doctor's exam)
2. Identify a problem (diagnosis)
3. Present a solution (prescription)

"The prospect," Tracy writes, in *Advanced Selling Strategies* (Fireside, 1995), "cannot even seriously consider your offer until he or she is convinced that you are his friend and acting in his best interests. Therefore, you must take sufficient time to build a bridge of personal warmth and rapport between yourself and the prospect. . . ." Tracy adds that, with this approach, price should not be discussed until the "Solution" phase of the sales process.

KNOW YOUR COMPETITION

Before you venture out to visit your prospects, Tracy and other sales experts advise that you get to know your competition. Buy their products or try their services. Compare them to your own.

Here's a great tip: Try to experience a sales call from one of your competitor's salespeople. Let the person sell to you. You'll get a gold mine of information. Study the attributes and weaknesses of your competitor's product or service, because your prospects will probably bring them up during your sales calls.

If, during this stage of preparation, you begin to feel that your product or service doesn't measure up, don't try to sell it. Your business will fail if it's not built on a product or service that you believe is the best available in the marketplace for the price. Remember William C. Durant's advice about having a self-seller, "and if you don't have one, get one." Always be on the lookout for ways to improve your product or to get a better one.

PERFECT YOUR MARKETING MATERIAL <u>BEFORE</u> YOU MAKE A CALL

Before going on a single sales call, you will need to create and perfect your marketing material: brochures, order forms, samples, and so on. Take the time to get these right. They should be clear and easy to read. Test all your marketing material on friends and mentors, and listen carefully to any criticisms or reactions. All promotional items for your business should reflect and reinforce your core competence. They should include the name of your business, your logo, and any slogan. So should your marketing materials.

Good marketing materials accomplish three things:

1. Preparing them forces you to organize your thoughts.
2. They can be used to teach employees about your business quickly.
3. They help you during a sales call.

All marketing materials must be visually appealing. Compare a brochure for a furniture company that's not in color and is poorly done to a full-color brochure by Ethan Allen. Which company would you be more likely to patronize? A large part of marketing involves developing a perception of your company in your customer's mind. Good marketing material helps develop a good perception. Commit a portion of your startup budget to hiring a professional designer and writer to create your marketing materials.

ENTREPRENEUR STORY
WILLIAM C. DURANT,
GENERAL MOTORS

From 1878 to 1886, Durant started a variety of entrepreneurial ventures, primarily in the fields of insurance, real estate, and construction. None of them really took off. He had yet to find his "self-seller." When he was twenty-five, however, Durant hitched a ride to work with a friend. He noticed that his friend's new buggy rode smoother than any he had been in. His friend explained that the smooth ride was due to a new design in the buggy's springs. Durant was so impressed that he decided he wanted to own the company that made this new kind of carriage.

Durant learned that the Coldwater Road Cart Company made the buggies with the improved springs. The very next day, Durant went to Coldwater, Michigan. The owner of the cart company was willing to sell it for $1,500. Durant insisted that the deal include the patent for the springs. In two days, the deal was closed. This transaction demonstrated Durant's business philosophy: "Decide quickly, make your pitch, nail down the details, and don't worry about the money."

Making Buggies

When Durant made the deal, he didn't even have $1,500, but he didn't let that deter him from his vision. Durant borrowed $2,000 from the Citizens National Bank of Flint and made two sample buggy carts. He transported one of them to a county fair in Madison, Wisconsin. His entrepreneurial hunch was correct. The cart sold itself; within a week he had orders for 600 buggy carts.

The business was a great success. By 1893, the original $2,000 had grown to $150,000. By 1901, his company was the biggest buggy manufacturer in the country.

The Buick Partnership: Durant Finds His Second "Self-Seller"

David Dunbar Buick, a Scottish immigrant who ran a plumbing supply business in Detroit, formed the Buick Manufacturing Company in 1902. He was not having much success, however, and constantly needed capital. In 1904, the Buick Company turned to Durant, both as a fresh source of capital and for his famed selling abilities.

Durant took a ride in the still experimental "Buick." He became immediately enthusiastic about the car, which he believed was one of those natural "self-sellers" he was always on the lookout for. He agreed to come in only if he could have absolute managerial control. Durant took over the Buick Company on November 1, 1904.

Once in, Durant infused the operation with his own energy. At the 1905 auto show in New York, he "sold" 1,108 cars when the company had actually manufactured only 37. By 1906, the Buick Company was worth $3 million.

FEATURES BECOME BENEFITS

The essence of selling is teaching *how* and *why* the outstanding features of your product or service will benefit your customers. When Durant took his buggy cart to the county fair, he was able to teach potential customers how the cart's unique feature—its extra-springy seat—could benefit them by making them more comfortable during a buggy ride.

Let's say you sell hats that last long, are washable, fold without wrinkling, and come in many great colors. These features create the product's benefits: a durable hat will not have to be replaced soon; an easy-to-clean hat will save money; a hat that fits into a pocket or bag will be used often. The benefits sell the hat, not the features.

The features of a product are facts about the product. The creative art of selling is teaching customers how the features will benefit them.

PRINCIPLES OF SELLING

Like Durant, every entrepreneur has to be able to sell his or her product or service and make an effective sales call. The following principles of selling were used by Durant throughout his life. Durant was one of the great direct salespeople of this century. These principles apply to any product or service:

1. *Make a good personal impression* when selling your product or service. Prepare yourself physically. Be neat and clean.

2. *View selling as teaching*—it's your chance to teach the customer about the product or service. Explain the benefits of your product or service to your customer.

3. *Believe in your product or service.* Good salespeople believe in what they are selling.

4. *Know your product or service.* Understand how its features can benefit the consumer.

5. *Know your field.* Read the trade literature. Learn about your competitors.

6. *Know your customers.* What are their needs? How does your product or service address these needs?

7. *Prepare your sales presentation.* Know ahead of time how you want to present your product or service.

8. *Think positively.* This frame of mind will help you deal with the rejections you may experience before you sell your product or service.

9. *Keep good records.* Have your record-keeping system, including invoices and receipts, set up before you go on your first sales call.

10. *Make an appointment.* People are more likely to listen when they have set aside time to hear your sales pitch. They will be less patient if you interrupt their day unannounced.

11. *Stay in touch with your customers and potential customers.* Cultivate your customers for repeat sales. Build relationships.

The essence of selling is teaching.

THE SALES CALL

A sales call is an appointment with a potential customer to explain or demonstrate your product or service. During the sales call, you will want to:

- Make the customer aware of your product or service.
- Make the customer *want* to buy that product or service.
- Make the customer want to buy it from *you*.

PREQUALIFY YOUR SALES CALL

Before calling to make an appointment for any sales call, ask yourself these questions:

- Is this person in my market?
- Does this person need my product?
- Can this person afford it?

If the answer to any of these questions is No, making a sales call on that person may be a waste of time. Asking yourself these questions is called "prequalifying" a sales call.

THE SEVEN-STEP SALES CALL

Many people don't realize how strong you have to be mentally to conduct sales calls. I went on over 1,100 sales calls while running my import–export business. I went on 400 calls before I closed my first sale of more than $1,000. This experience allowed me to hone my ability to make a sales call. I still make frequent sales calls today, only now I'm selling the NFTE mission to potential donors. I use the same seven steps when talking to billionaire donors that I used when I was trying to sell wooden carvings.

1. *Preparation.* Prepare yourself mentally. Think about how your product or service will benefit this customer. Have the price, discounts, all technical information, and any other details "on the tip of your tongue." Be willing to obtain further information should your customer request it.

2. *Greeting.* Greet the customer graciously. Do not plunge immediately into business talk. The first few words you say can be the most important. Keep a two-way conversation going. Maintain eye contact and keep the customer's attention.

3. *Showing the product or service.* Try to "personalize" it. Point out the benefits for this particular customer. Use props and models (or the real thing) where appropriate.

4. *Dealing with objections.* Always acknowledge objections and deal with them. Don't pretend you didn't hear. Don't overreact to objections, and don't be afraid to listen. A famous real-estate entrepreneur, William Zeckendorf, said, "I never lost money on a sales pitch when I listened to the customer."

5. *Closing the sale.* Review the benefits of your product or service. Narrow the choices the customer has to make. Close the sale. Don't overstay your welcome. There is a rule of thumb that if a customer says No three times, you still have a chance. If he or she says it the fourth time, it's really No. If the answer is No, take it gracefully. You may make a sale to this customer in the future.

6. *Follow-up.* Make regular follow-up calls to find out how your customer likes the product or service. Ask if you can be of any further help. If the customer has a complaint, don't ignore it. Remember, *the most successful business is built on repeat customers.*

7. *Ask for references.* If you did a good job for customers who needed your product or service, ask them to refer you to other potential customers.

USE TECHNOLOGY TO SELL

Where appropriate and applicable, use the latest advances in technology to sell your product by (1) helping customers understand and use the product and (2) staying in touch with them. You can, for example:

- Videotape a demonstration or presentation of your product.
- Create a Web site customers can visit for updates or product facts.
- Use e-mail and faxes to stay in touch with customers.

- Use digital planners to keep prospect lists organized and log sales calls.

All the technological concepts used in marketing to identify customers and do market research can be used to sell to your market, too.

THE ONE-MINUTE SALES CALL

Another good suggestion is to keep your sales calls under one minute. Believe it or not, it's a challenge for most people to pay attention to someone for more than a minute. Write down your sales pitch and practice delivering it to a friend or relative. Have your listener time you. You'll be shocked at how fast a minute can go by!

Here's an example to get you started. Let's say you make baby food from organic fruits and vegetables. You are trying to convince the owner of Johnson's General Store to buy some of your baby food to sell in his store.

YOU: Hello, Mr. Johnson. Thank you for agreeing to see me today. I'm excited about this product and think you and your customers will be, too.

I brought you a jar of our baby applesauce. It's nicely packaged, don't you think? We hand-decorate each jar. They make nice gifts for new or expecting parents. The eye-catching ribbons will be sure to attract your customers.

We use only organic fruits and vegetables, no sugar, and very little salt. Our label explains that some babies are sensitive to the additives and dyes found in some commercial baby foods. These may give sensitive babies headaches or upset stomachs. Our food is very gentle on the baby—and that makes the parents' life much easier!

I understand your concern that our baby food costs twenty-five cents per jar more than the brand you presently stock. I think your customers will pay more for our high quality and for knowing that their babies are protected from harmful additives or high levels of sugar and salt. Because we add very little water to our product, we actually offer more food for the money than some cheaper brands.

I really think you could start a trend by stocking our baby food here, Mr. Johnson. There's been a shift in the food market toward healthy food for adults—and those adults are looking for healthy baby food. Our products combine an eye-catching look with healthy ingredients that new parents and their friends and relatives won't be able to resist. How many jars would you like to order?

Entrepreneur Story
Sandra Kurtzig, ASK Computer Systems

In the late 1960s, Sandra Kurtzig made hundreds of sales calls. She was selling computer time for General Electric. In those days, there were no personal computers. Computers were enormous machines called mainframes that many people shared by buying computer time. As a result, using a computer was a complicated and time-consuming process. If you wanted to solve a problem using a computer, you had to hire a computer programmer to write a program that would solve your problem.

Kurtzig's customers complained frequently that they wanted a more efficient way to use computers. She realized that what her customers wanted was programs that were already written to meet their needs. In 1971, Kurtzig started her own company, ASK Computer Systems, Inc., to develop software programs that would meet this consumer need.

Kurtzig started ASK (in a spare bedroom in her house) with $2,000.00 when she was age twenty-four. By 1973, ASK had developed a simple, universal program that could be used by thousands of manufacturers to keep track of their inventory. No one had done this before. Business software that people everywhere use today had not yet been invented.

By the end of the decade, ASK was worth $400 million. ASK became the first high-tech company owned by a woman to sell stock, and the largest company founded and run by a woman.

Kurtzig has said that almost every ASK product evolved from customer requests or suggestions. One important ASK invention was financial software (developed when a customer asked for help managing his financial accounts). You can never go wrong by listening to the customer, Kurtzig recommends.

Turning Objections into Advantages

Initially, Kurtzig's customers were worried that paying ASK to design software for them would be too expensive. Kurtzig did not respond by arguing with the customer's perception of the software as expensive. Rather, she explained that the expense reflected the product's high quality and ASK's commitment to making sure that it worked when installed and that it would satisfy the customer's needs.

The key to selling is to show the customer that his or her objection to buying a product is really an advantage. Remember this acronym[1] during your sales call:

Smile, **A**gree, **D**eflect **O**bjection, **N**ext **O**ffer
"SAD - O - NO"

Sales Commission

Many salespeople are paid sales commissions—percentages of each sale made. A car salesperson who makes a 10 percent sales commission, for example, would earn $1,000 after selling a car for $10,000.

$$.10 \times \$10,000 = \$1,000$$

I earned a 5 percent sales commission on any products I sold for my friends from Africa and Bangladesh.

Direct Sales

The Direct Selling Association (DSA) is the national trade association of companies that manufacture and distribute products and services sold directly to consumers. Its membership includes Avon Products, Mary Kay Cosmetics, Artistic Impressions, Amway, Tupperware Worldwide, and many other popular direct sellers.

Direct selling companies tap into the entrepreneurial dream by training people who want to build their own businesses. A Mary Kay salesperson, for example, purchases skin-care products and makeup from Mary Kay Cosmetics at a 40 to 50 percent discount. The salesperson gives facials and skin-care classes in her home or at a customer's home to attract customers, and sells the products directly to them.

A Mary Kay salesperson can also recruit people to sell Mary Kay products. The recruiter receives a percentage of the sales of her recruits. In this way, direct selling has enabled thousands of people to build very profitable businesses with very little capital investment.

Some disreputable companies focus almost exclusively on the recruiting aspect of direct sales, luring salespeople with promises of instant riches. The DSA has been instrumental in educating the public about the dangers of these so-called pyramid schemes. The primary purpose of a direct selling company should be to sell products that meet consumer needs. Before getting involved with any direct sales company, call or write the Direct Selling Association for an evaluation or advice.

THE SALES RECEIPT

When you make a sale, don't forget to fill out a receipt for the customer. A sample receipt is shown in Chart 8.

The receipt must include the date of the sale, the amount of the sale, and the item. The receipt is the customer's proof that the item

---

GINA'S T-SHIRT CO.

Date *June 13* 1999

Sold to: *George Braxton*

Address: *123 E. Orange St.*

Reg. No.	Clerk		
1	*1 red T-shirt (#28)*	*$10.99*	*$10.99*
2			
3		*8% Sales Tax*	*.88*
4			
5		*Total*	*$11.87*
6			
7			
8			
9			
10			

Style 1200   **495-1**

Chart 8 A Typical Sales Receipt

or service was purchased. The carbon copy is a record of income for you.

CASE STUDY: TURNING RECIPES INTO CASH

What do Paul Newman, Debbi Fields, and a group of high school students from Los Angeles have in common? They've all turned their favorite recipes into profitable businesses. Newman's Own popcorn, pasta sauces, and salad dressings raise funds for his favorite charities. Debbi Fields has turned her teenage chocolate-chip cookie recipe into Mrs. Fields Cookies, a multimillion-dollar international enterprise. And, in the early 1990s, thirty students from Crenshaw High School formed a company called Food From The 'Hood that marketed one of the hottest selling items in southern California—Straight Out The Garden salad dressing. They were mentored by their teacher, Tammy Bird, who is now a NFTE teacher, and a publicist named Melinda McMillan, who actually took a leave of absence from her job to help get Food From The 'Hood off the ground.

The students had already been selling produce from their school garden when they decided to concoct a dressing. They wanted the dressing to be low in fat and salt because diseases linked to high sodium diets, such as high-blood pressure, are prevalent in their urban community.

Next, the students met with Rebuild L.A., a nonprofit organization formed to help L.A. businesses recover from the 1994 riots. Rebuild L.A. introduced them to the owners of a minority investment firm, who helped the students write a business plan. The plan landed the budding entrepreneurs a partnership with Sweet Adelaide Enterprises, a large salad dressing packer.

In 1994, the students were awarded a grant from Rebuild L.A. to help them to get their product into local grocery stores. Today, Straight Out The Garden is sold by over 2,000 grocery stores in southern California. All profits go toward college scholarships for the student owners.

Tips

- To place your product in grocery chain stores requires some clout. Crenshaw students consulted Bromar, a professional food broker, for advice on how to get their product accepted by grocery chains.
- Believe in your product. The other thing Newman, Fields, and the Crenshaw students have in common is a tremendous belief in the quality of their products.

RESOURCES

Books

Some of the best books published about selling are:

The Joy of Selling by J. T. Auer (Holbrook, MA: Adams, Inc., 1991).

Swim with the Sharks Without Being Eaten Alive by Harvey Mackay (New York: William Morrow & Co., 1988).

How to Sell Yourself by Joe Girard (New York: Warner Books, 1988).

Face-to-Face Selling by Bart Breighner (Indianapolis, IN: Jist Works, Inc., 1995).

If you think a career in sales might interest you, or you just want to read the latest theories on selling, check out *Sales and Marketing Magazine* at your library or call (800) 253-6708 to subscribe.

Associations

The Direct Selling Association has a wealth of information on the craft of direct selling and on how to contact direct sales firms.

Direct Selling Association
1666 K Street, NW, Suite 1010
Washington, DC 20006-2808
(202) 293-5760
Fax (202) 463-4569

Chapter **13**

MARKETING—THE ART OF GETTING THE CUSTOMER TO COME TO YOU

A PLAN FOR ESTABLISHING YOUR BRAND

In my factory we make cosmetics, but in my stores we sell hope.
—Charles Revson (1906–1975)
American founder of Revlon Cosmetics, Inc.

When you go on a sales call, you are bringing the product to the customer. **Marketing** is the art of getting the customer to come to the product. It is the plan an entrepreneur develops for introducing a product or service to the market.

Nike, for example, sells sneakers. It distributes sneakers to stores where customers can buy them. But Nike also **markets** sneakers. Its marketing department creates advertisements and promotions designed to persuade customers that Nike sneakers will inspire them to "Just Do It."

To market a product successfully, ask yourself: What does the customer need this product to do? Answering that question will help you identify a benefit. Show your customer that your product produces that benefit.

Why does a customer go to a hardware store to buy a drill? Because he or she needs to make a hole. The *hole* is what the customer needs, not the drill. If the hole could be bought at the hardware store, the customer wouldn't bother to buy the drill. If you are marketing a drill, therefore, you should explain to the customer what good holes your drill makes![1]

ENTREPRENEUR STORY
RAY KROC, MCDONALD'S

Many great fortunes have been based on a single marketing insight. Ray Kroc, the president of McDonald's, did not invent or even improve the hamburger. He invented a new way of *marketing* hamburgers. He realized that customers cared more about fast service, consistent product, and a low price than they did about the ultimate hamburger. These were the benefits that brought them to the product. By marketing those benefits, Kroc made McDonald's the huge success it is today.

Turning a Marketing Insight into a Fortune

The original McDonald's restaurant was a small hamburger stand in San Bernardino, California. Two brothers, Maurice and Richard McDonald, ran the stand. Kroc was a fifty-two-year-old salesman of Multimixers, the mixers the McDonald brothers used to make their shakes. When Kroc received an order for eight Multimixers—enough to make forty milkshakes at once—from this hamburger stand on the edge of the desert, he flew out to see the business for himself.

With sales of over $350,000 a year, McDonald's was one of the most successful little restaurants in America. Customers loved the simple, cheap food and the fast service. The McDonald brothers knew they had a hot business that they could expand around the country, but there was just one problem—both brothers hated to fly. When Kroc flew in and offered to form a partnership with them and take care of franchising their business, they signed on the dotted line.

In 1961, Kroc bought out the brothers for $2.7 million, but he followed rigidly their original recipes for their hamburgers, fries, and shakes. Kroc wanted every McDonald's customer, from Anchorage to Miami, to get an identical product. According to Bill Bryson's fascinating book *Made in America*, Kroc "dictated that McDonald's burgers must be exactly 3.875 inches across, weigh 1.6 ounces, and contain precisely 19 percent fat. Big Mac buns should have an average of 178 sesame seeds."

CORE COMPETENCE:
YOUR MARKETING FOUNDATION

What product or service can you deliver better than anyone else? If you can answer that question with confidence, you can develop your

core competence—your advantage over your competitors because you offer customers greater value, through either lower prices or more benefits. If you are clear about your core competence, your marketing decisions will start to fall into place. Every ad, every promotion should be designed to get customers excited about your core competence.

ESTABLISHING A BRAND IN THE CUSTOMER'S MIND

More valuable to McDonald's than all the Big Macs it sells every year is the perception, in the minds of McDonald's customers, that every time they patronize a McDonald's they will receive food that tastes exactly the same as it does at every other McDonald's franchise around the world, and fast, friendly service. That's how a business establishes its **brand.** A brand is a name that represents, in the customer's mind, an image associated with the business's product. By keeping its food and service so consistent, McDonald's has established a brand. Whenever you see the golden arches, you know what kind of food, service, and price to expect.

What example does this set for you, as a small business owner?

1. Determine your core competence.
2. Explore how your core competence can be turned into a competitive advantage that customers will associate with your brand name.

You don't have to be first to be successful; you just have to discover a competitive advantage and attack by creating a new category in the customer's mind. Domino's Pizza, for example, decided its competitive advantage was going to be delivering pizzas in under thirty minutes. That marketing insight created a hugely successful company.

MARKETING DICTATES YOUR BUSINESS MOVES

Remember Russell Simmons and Def Jam described in Chapter 2? Simmons, like Kroc, built his entire career on marketing. Kroc decided that consumers cared more about fast service and a low price than about the ultimate hamburger. He identified that as the core competence of his business, and he made it the focus of every marketing decision. Every decision Kroc made about McDonald's was a direct result of that marketing vision. McDonald's will never branch into gourmet food, for example.

Simmons's marketing decision was to sell black urban culture to the entire world. Every decision he has made about his parent company, Rush Communications, has stemmed from that marketing vision.

All your decisions about your business should reinforce your marketing vision, too. To discover your marketing vision, identify the most important benefit the customers in your market will receive from your product or service. All your advertisements and other promotions should tell your customers about this benefit. Next, choose the four essential elements of your marketing plan—The Four "Ps."

THE FOUR "PS" OF MARKETING

1. **Product**—the product (or service) should meet or create a consumer need.
2. **Price**—the product (or service) has to be priced low enough for the public to buy it and high enough for the business to make a profit.
3. **Place**—the product (or service) should be sold where there will be a demand for it and where customers can easily find it. (Don't try to sell bathing suits in Alaska in February!) Location is extremely important. Ideally, you'll want your store or business to be in a place where *your* market is.
4. **Promotion**—the advertising and publicity for your product (or service) should constantly remind potential customers of its unique ability to satisfy their needs.

PREPARING A MARKETING PLAN

Once you've chosen the Four Ps of your business, you will be ready to complete a marketing plan for your business. Using Y for Yes and N for No, fill out the marketing plan shown in Chart 9. (To suit your own market, you may want to use different selling methods and locations; for example, you may be using e-mail on the Internet.)

MARKETING PLAN LOCATIONS (WHERE TO SELL)

S E L L I N G M E T H O D S	Door to Door	Flea Markets	School/ Church Functions	Street (Street Vendors)	Through Local Stores	Your Own Home	Internet
Business Cards	N	N	Y	Y	Y	N	N
Posters	N	N	N	N	N	N	N
Flyers	Y	Y	Y	N	Y	N	N
Phone	N	N	N	N	N	N	N
Sales Calls	N	N	N	N	N	N	N
Brochure	Y	N	Y	Y	N	N	N
Mailings							
Other							

Chart 9 Sample Marketing Plan

PROMOTION = PUBLICITY + ADVERTISING

Your marketing plan indicates how you plan to promote your business. Entrepreneurs use **promotion** to attract customers and increase sales. Promotion is the use of **publicity** and **advertising.** Publicity is free; advertising is purchased. If your business is providing an unusual service, for instance, you might be able to get a local newspaper to do an article on your business. That article would give your business publicity. If you buy an ad in that newspaper, you're using advertising to promote your business. Publicity is sometimes referred to as public relations or "PR."

Valuable promotions include:

- **Business cards.** Your business card bears the name, address, and phone number of your business, as well as your name and title. Carry some cards with you wherever you go.

- **Discount coupons.** Give a discount, or price break, to first-time customers or to all customers for a limited time. This will encourage potential customers to try your product or service.
- **Flyers.** Flyers are one-page ads you can create by hand or on a typewriter or computer. Photoprint your flyer and distribute it at school, at church functions, at sporting events, or on the street. Chart 10 shows a simple but explicit flyer.
- **Promotional items.** T-shirts or caps bearing the name of your business can turn you and your friends into walking advertisements

Chart 10 Advertising via a Flyer

for your business. You can even put the name of your business on your shopping bags.

VISUALIZE THE CUSTOMERS

There is one more step to take before you begin following your marketing plan: Visualize your customers. How old are they? What kind of income do they earn? What benefit of your product or service would attract your ideal customer? Make that benefit the center of your promotion plans.

If you are advertising a rap concert, for example, it would be a waste of money to take out an ad in a magazine for senior citizens. By visualizing your customer, you avoid wasting money on advertising to customers who aren't interested in your product or service.

Turning a Knack for Marketing into a Successful Business

If you have a knack for marketing, that in itself can be your business. When Doug Mellinger was in college, he knew some computer programmers and engineers whose ability to sell themselves was not nearly as developed as their technical skills were. He decided to start a business that would market them to companies that needed their services.

Doug's PRT Corp. of America acts as a go-between for corporations that need to hire people who are skilled in advanced computer technology for various projects. PRT secures the job, puts the technical team together, and makes sure everything runs smoothly between the client and the technicians.

Since its inception in 1989, PRT has successfully completed projects in artificial intelligence, data security, imaging, and other high-tech areas for over forty Fortune 200 companies in the United States, Japan, and Europe. Today, Doug is widely acknowledged as one of the most successful young entrepreneurs in America.

One of the reasons Doug is so successful with PRT is that he had already run a number of small businesses while in college. He visited a NFTE class in the South Bronx and gave a very inspirational talk about how his experiences as a young entrepreneur had prepared him to handle PRT's incredible growth (the company grew from 1 to 100 employees in four years, and its revenue increased over 100 percent during each of those years). Today, he is one of NFTE's strongest supporters.

He serves on a number of advisory boards to government agencies and to public and private universities that are committed to improving educational and career opportunities for economically disadvantaged youth.

Effective Advertising

An effective ad for a small business typically concentrates on the aspect of the product or service that is most important to the customer. That aspect is usually one of these three:

1. Price
2. Product/Service
3. Location

The Media

There are many places to advertise your business. These are referred to collectively as the **media.** The main types of media are print, television, radio, and the Internet.

- **Print.** Newspapers, magazines, and newsletters are examples of print media. A good spot for a print ad is the Yellow Pages. Consider running a coupon in your neighborhood or school newspaper.
- **Television.** Even though commercial TV rates are very expensive, a young entrepreneur can sometimes get low rates or even a free mention (publicity) of his or her business on local cable stations.
- **Radio.** University and local stations are usually willing to mention a young person's business venture.
- **The Internet.** Some Web sites may let you post a "banner" ad (a small ad at the top or bottom of a Web site) in exchange for allowing them to put a similar ad for their own product on your Web page. (See Chapter 15, "Technology Is Your Generation's Competitive Advantage" for more information about using the Internet in your business.)

To generate publicity, consider mailing to the local media a **press release**—a few paragraphs that give information about your business. Chart 11 gives you a model to imitate.

For Immediate Release
January 24, 2000

For More Information Contact:
John Davies—(718) 555-7839

SOUTH BRONX HIGH SCHOOL
STUDENT OPENS TIE-SELLING BUSINESS

Sixteen-year-old John Davies of 34 Fordham Road, in the South Bronx, announced today the creation of "John's Tie Service." A junior at Longfellow High School, John purchases his ties from the wholesale market and orders them through catalogs. He will be selling ties on weekends at the Mott Haven Flea Market.

John is starting his own enterprise as a way to learn about business and supplement his income. His short-term goal is to raise enough capital to help pay for his college education. John's long-term plan is to own a string of soul-food restaurants in urban communities.

John believes that creating a successful business is a great way to help not only himself but his community.

For interviews with this young entrepreneur, please call (718) 555-7839.

Chart 11 Format for a Press Release to the Media

How Print Ads Work

There are many ways to create a print ad for a newspaper or magazine, but most successful ads include five basic parts:

1. **Headline.** This is the "title" of the ad. It's usually the first thing people see, so it should be short and clear, to grab their attention.
2. **Deck.** Also called a subhead, it amplifies the headline and explains the subject or purpose of the ad a little more.
3. **Copy.** This is where you can really explain your core competence in detail.
4. **Graphics.** Photos or drawings attract attention *and* illustrate your product's features. Like headlines, they are often among the first things people notice.
5. **Logo.** A symbol or distinctive design feature is an important part of branding.

You can find all five parts in the ad pictured in Chart 12.

Logos and Trademarks

A **logo** (short for logotype) is an identifying symbol for a product or business. The logo is printed on the business's stationery, business cards, and flyers. Some logos appear on the products as well. When a logo has been registered with the United States Patent Office to protect it from being used by others, it is called a **trademark.**

A company uses a trademark so that people will recognize its product instantly, without having to read the company name or even having to think about it. The Nutrasweet™ red swirl is an example of a trademark most people recognize. Rights to a trademark are reserved exclusively for its owner. To infringe on a trademark is illegal.

To file for a trademark, request an application from the **Patent and Trademark Office.** Call **(703) 308-4357.** After you receive the application, gather these items into one packet:

1. The completed application form
2. A drawing of the trademark

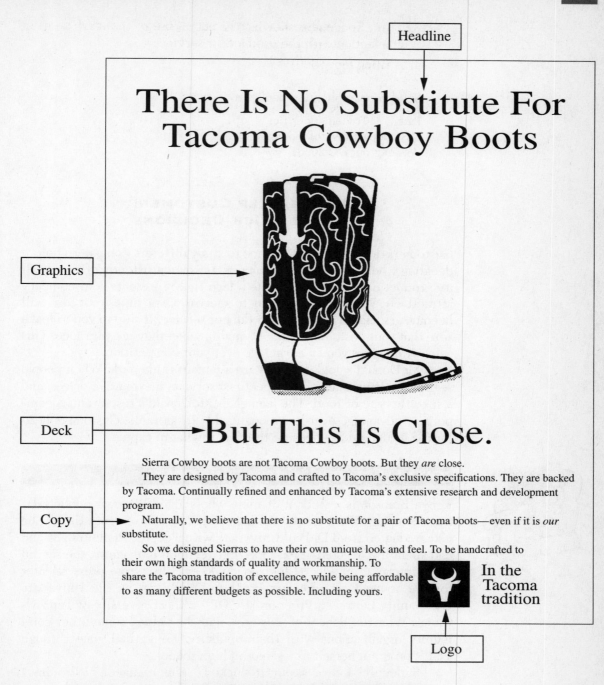

Headline

There Is No Substitute For Tacoma Cowboy Boots

Graphics

But This Is Close.

Deck

Sierra Cowboy boots are not Tacoma Cowboy boots. But they *are* close.

They are designed by Tacoma and crafted to Tacoma's exclusive specifications. They are backed by Tacoma. Continually refined and enhanced by Tacoma's extensive research and development program.

Copy

Naturally, we believe that there is no substitute for a pair of Tacoma boots—even if it is *our* substitute.

So we designed Sierras to have their own unique look and feel. To be handcrafted to their own high standards of quality and workmanship. To share the Tacoma tradition of excellence, while being affordable to as many different budgets as possible. Including yours.

In the Tacoma tradition

Logo

Chart 12 A Classic Five-Part Print Ad

3. Three specimens showing the actual use of the mark on or in connection with the products or services

4. A filing fee ($320)

Send your application packet to:

Patent & Trademark Office
U.S. Department of Commerce
Washington, DC 20231

LOGOS HELP CUSTOMERS
MAKE QUICK DECISIONS

Customers don't have a lot of time to study different companies before deciding where to spend their money. If you consistently offer a quality product or service and create a logo that represents your company attractively, you are on your way to success. Over time, your logo will become associated with your product or service. It's up to you to make sure that your customers think of quality when they see your logo. This association gives you an advantage over your competition.

McDonald's golden arches are a famous trademark. When people see the golden arches, they expect fast service, inexpensive prices, and a specific type of food. The logo gives McDonald's restaurants a competitive advantage over less recognizable restaurants. Customers head for the golden arches because they know what to expect.

CASE STUDY: PUBLIC RELATIONS FIRM

Keeya Branson is a student of mine who started her own public relations company, Wide Awake Publicity, when she was twenty-three. She had graduated from DePaul University with a degree in philosophy and had spent a year looking for a job. Between job interviews, she served as an intern at an advertising agency. Keeya also wrote press releases for the Young Entrepreneurs Program (YEP) run by the University Community Outreach Program (UCOP) at the University of Pennsylvania's Wharton School of Business, and she helped some other community organizations with their publicity. Keeya had gone through YEP's program herself as a senior in high school.

Suddenly, Keeya says, "It clicked." She realized, "Why am I spending this energy looking for a job? I have a job." YEP became

Wide Awake Publicity's first client. Today, Keeya is generating publicity for several other nonprofit groups and various individuals.

Wide Awake Publicity's most important tool is the media kit, Keeya says. The media kit is a folder that holds a black-and-white photograph that represents the client, a press release, a biography of the business or its owner(s), and copies of any press coverage the client has already received. Keeya sends the media kit to newspapers and to radio and television stations she thinks might be interested in spotlighting the client's business. She always follows up with several phone calls. The most important aspect of her business, in fact, is her relationship with "the press."

Keeya says entrepreneurship is a viable alternative to the unemployment so many recent college grads face. "You can't always live and die in a company anymore. The only person you can count on is yourself," Keeya says. She adds, "Entrepreneurship is not an impossibility; in fact, it's a definite possibility."

Tips

- Consider serving an internship in the field of your choice. Although interns are not usually paid (some receive stipends), the experience and networking opportunities are invaluable. Many companies hire from their pool of interns before looking to outside applicants to fill a position.

- Most small publicity firms specialize in certain types of clients. Some may represent only rock bands, for example. Others, like Wide Awake, focus on meeting the needs of nonprofit organizations. Specialization will make it easier for your firm to build strong media ties.

RESOURCES

Books

A small business is, by definition, a "do-it-yourself" project. Learn how from *Do-It-Yourself Advertising: How to Produce Great Ads, Brochures, Catalogs, Direct Mail, and Much More* by Fred Hahn (John Wiley & Sons, Inc., 1993).

Bill Bryson's often hilarious book, *Made in America: An Informal History of the English Language in the United States* (New York: William Morrow, and Co., 1995), tells the stories of many American entrepreneurs as it explores American linguistics.

Another valuable source is *The Handbook of Small Business Advertising* by Michael Anthony (Addison-Wesley Publishing Co., 1981).

Other Resources

The bible of Madison Avenue is *Advertising Age* magazine. It's available on newsstands and in libraries. For a subscription, contact:

Advertising Age
Crain Communications
740 N. Rush Street
Chicago, IL 60611
(800) 678-9595
www.adage.com

Chapter

14

MARKET RESEARCH FOR ENTREPRENEURS

HOW TO FIND OUT WHO YOUR CUSTOMERS ARE AND WHAT THEY <u>WANT</u>

If you give the consumer a snapshot where he could see himself as he really is and the way he wants to be portrayed, people really respond to it. That emotionalism translates into behavior in the marketplace.

—Thomas Burrell (b. 1939)
Founder of the largest African American-owned
advertising agency, Burrell Communications Group

MARKET RESEARCH HELPS YOU GET TO KNOW YOUR CUSTOMERS

We've talked about the importance of knowing your customers and marketing your product or service to them. But we haven't talked about *how* to get to know your customers.

Market research is the process and technique of finding out *who* your potential customers are and what they want.

Through market research, business owners ask consumers questions and listen to their answers.

You can—and should—conduct some market research for your business. Market research can vary from a simple survey of friends and neighbors, which can be completed in one day, to detailed statistical studies of a large population over a long period of time.

Let's say, for example, that you've invented a new type of frisbee and you want to sell it on the campus of your college, which has 20,000 students. One way to research your market would be to survey a random sample of 200 students, showing them the product and asking these questions:

- Do you play frisbee? How often?
- Would you be interested in purchasing this frisbee, if it were available?
- Where do you currently purchase your frisbees? What do you like or dislike about the current seller?

If 50 of the 200 students surveyed seem interested in your frisbee, you can expect that roughly 5,000 of the 20,000 students on your campus represent your market.

TYPES OF MARKET RESEARCH

The three main types of market research are:

1. **Surveys.** People are asked directly, in interviews or through questionnaires, what they would think about a product or service if it were available. At NFTE, for example, we often form focus groups with young people or with teachers. A focus group is comprised of people who do use or might use a product. The focus group is typically led by a facilitator trained in market research, who questions the group about a product or service. We've used feedback from our focus groups to help us make many decisions—from what color the BizBag™ should be to how to improve our textbooks.

2. **General research.** Businesspeople check libraries, city agencies, or other resources for information. If you want to start a sporting goods shop in a neighborhood, for instance, you will need to know how many sporting goods shops are already in that area.

3. **Statistical research. Statistics** are facts collected and presented in a numerical fashion so we can find useful patterns. Market research companies keep records of the typical

consumers in a given area. They can then provide statistics based on age, occupation, geographic location, income, and ethnic or religious background. Market researchers also delve into consumers' hobbies and interests and find out whether they own or rent their homes. Consumer statistics that deal with the behavior of groups of people are called **demographics.**

Large corporations with nationally distributed products will spend a great deal of time and money on market research in order to get a product "just right."

Ford and Chrysler each spent millions on market research *before* producing, respectively, the Mustang and the minivan. It was worth millions of dollars to these companies to determine whether the public wanted these vehicles, because producing them was going to cost *tens* of millions.

Both the Mustang and the minivan were successful. One of the best-known examples of market research failure, however, was Ford's 1956 Edsel. The car was introduced with great fanfare, but was so poorly made and clumsily designed that very few were purchased. When the Edsel made its national debut on a live television special, in fact, it wouldn't start. Two years and $450 million later, Ford pulled the plug on the Edsel assembly line.

ENTREPRENEUR STORY
THOMAS BURRELL, BURRELL ADVERTISING

To market a product or service to a particular group of people, you have to know exactly what those people want. In the late 1960s, major corporations became more conscious of the potential clout of black consumers but were unsure how to reach them.

Marketing to African Americans

In 1971, Thomas Burrell opened one of the first black-owned advertising agencies in the United States. By 1972, Burrell had convinced McDonald's that Burrell Advertising Inc. could help the huge company expand its inroads into the African American market. Today, Burrell Advertising is the fastest growing and largest black-owned advertising agency in the United States, with annual billings over $60 million.

Burrell Advertising has created over one hundred commercials for McDonald's. The list of Burrell's corporate clients includes Coca-Cola, Ford Motor Company, Johnson Products, Joseph Schlitz Brewing, Blockbuster Entertainment, Procter & Gamble, Jack Daniel Distillery, Polaroid, Stroh Brewing, and First National Bank of Chicago.

Burrell Advertising specializes in advertising for special market segments, such as African American consumers. The company is always first or second on the short list of companies seeking to target the African American market. Burrell himself could probably quote the demographics of the African American market off the top of his head. By combining his company's detailed market research with his own experiences as a black man, he has created powerful appeals to that market.

Burrell describes his marketing philosophy as "positive realism." He adds, "We wanted to make sure the consumer understood the advertiser was inviting that consumer—that black consumer—to participate as a consumer of the product. Black consumers have not felt they were being extended an invitation."

Researching Market Segments

Burrell also caters to nonminority consumers. Within this large category are groups that require "target advertising"—that is, advertising tailor-made to their particular needs, values, and lifestyles. Among these groups are the youth market, the "mature" (or older) market, and the urban market.

In 1988, Burrell founded two related companies: Burrell Public Relations Inc. and Burrell Consumer Promotions Inc. Together with Burrell Advertising, the three companies provide clients with a total marketing package. The three companies' revenues total over $70 million annually, ensuring Burrell's reputation as a world-class player in the field of marketing communications.

The public relations company helps clients communicate more effectively with their target markets. In 1989, for example, Burrell Public Relations created a Hispanic Marketing Division in order to respond more effectively to the needs of Hispanic consumers.

Burrell's second entrepreneurial extension was Burrell Consumer Promotions Inc. This arm designs promotional packs, in-store sampling, direct mail, sweepstakes and contests, and other promotions for clients.

Breaking Through the Race Barrier

Burrell still considers himself, first and foremost, an entrepreneur. A fit and imposing man at 6'4", Burrell speaks candidly of the two influences that originally triggered his entrepreneurial energy. One was his mother, who, from the time he was a child, encouraged him to be self-reliant. The other was the fact that he is African American. It is not surprising that a powerful five-foot-tall statue of Martin Luther King, Jr. stands in the waiting room of his office.

Burrell himself best describes why being African American encouraged him to try entrepreneurship: "I felt that no matter how successful I might have been at that time [the late 1960s], there was a ceiling that would certainly prevent me from going all the way in someone else's company. And even if I could go all the way it would still not be my company. I felt I had something special to say. I had a special approach to running an advertising business that I could do best in my own establishment. And, I figured I had nothing to lose."

Despite the original orientation of his firm toward the African American market, Burrell feels his agency has proven by now that it can handle advertising to any market. "It's an unfortunate thing," he says, "that being a black-owned company means, for some people, that you should be limited to addressing blacks only. I've got to believe that who owns an ad agency will at some point become irrelevant. What will matter will be the kind of advertising the agency does, how capable the agency is."

Smiling, he adds, "I've been a black person all my life and I will be for the rest of my life. The only thing I know how to do is stay positive. You stay positive and something good will happen."

Collecting Data

No matter what market a Burrell Advertising campaign is targeting, market research is the first step. Market research identifies the Four Ps discussed in the previous chapter: (1) Product, (2) Price, (3) Place, and (4) Promotion.

You can collect market research data by interviewing your friends, neighbors, and relatives. Here are a few questions you can adapt to your own product or service:

1. Would you buy this product/service?
2. How much would you be willing to pay for it?
3. Where would you buy it?
4. How would you improve on it?

Say you created a design and silkscreened it on five dozen plain white T-shirts. After six weeks, you have sold only six. Friends tell you they would have bought your product if:

- The shirt came in red or blue.
- The shirt was available in a different size.
- The shirt came in a different style.
- The shirt was silkscreened with a different design.

With a little market research, you could have determined your customers' needs and wishes *before* you made the shirts. You would have sold many more.

KNOW THE COMPETITION

Researching the competition is another important part of market research. Have you found out who else offers your product/service in your area? Visit your competitors' stores and Web sites. Talk to their customers. Buy something from your competitors, and make sure you get on their mailing lists. In that way, you'll always hear about their sales and other promotions.

Your market research should include collecting specific data about your competition. List the names of your competitors and the prices they charge. Compare your quality to theirs.

Name of Competitor	Product/Service	Price	Quality
1. _____	_____	_____	_____
2. _____	_____	_____	_____
3. _____	_____	_____	_____
4. _____	_____	_____	_____

Why is your product going to beat the competition? Remember, to develop a brand, you simply have to decide what you want your company's name to stand for in the customer's mind. What is your company's competitive advantage? How does it distinguish itself from the competition?

> **Buy something from a competitor and get on its mailing list.**

ANALYZE THE BUYING PROCESS

How do you identify the potential customers for *your* business? First, ask yourself what need your product serves. Arm & Hammer has turned this marketing question into a gold mine by developing baking soda tooth paste, air and carpet fresheners, and deodorant products.

Next, think about who might actually buy your product. Remember that the people who use it are not always the buyers. Mothers buy children's clothes, for example, so if you are making kids' playsuits, they have to be easy to clean.

Analyze the "buying process" that will lead consumers to your product. This is taught in MBA programs as follows (while you read, think about how you could reach the consumer with marketing at each step):

1. **Awareness.** The consumer realizes a need for something. Advertising is designed to make consumers aware of potential needs for everything from dandruff shampoo to a new car.

2. **Information search.** The consumer seeks information about what product could fulfill the need. A consumer looking for a multivitamin might take a brochure from a stack on the counter of the local health food store.

3. **Evaluation of alternatives.** The consumer looking for a multivitamin might check out the vitamins available in the local health food store and compare them, for price and content, with the more commercial brands sold in the supermarket.

4. **Decision to purchase.** The first purchase is really a test; the consumer is trying the product to see how well it performs.

5. **Evaluation of purchase.** If the product performs well, the consumer may begin to develop loyalty to that brand.

How do you keep this consumer for life? After you have figured out *what* need the product/service fulfills, *who* will buy it, and *how* they will buy it, you will have a much better idea of how to market it.

CASE STUDY: ON-LINE COMMUNITY

In 1991, while just a freshman at Williams College, Bo Peabody founded Tripod, a Web site that marketed to college students in their early to mid-20s. At first, Tripod hired freelance writers to create stories that Peabody thought would be of interest to that market segment. But Peabody soon realized that most visitors to the site were ignoring the content. They were much more interested in reading, and responding to, what other visitors to the site were writing and posting. To build the site's brand, Peabody went with what the consumers in his market obviously wanted—an opportunity to express themselves.

"The biggest mistake most Web sites have made is not embracing the idea that the Web is fundamentally an interactive medium," Peabody told *Success* magazine (January 1999, page 47). "People want to participate and create the media experience for themselves."

So, instead of offering more or different content, Tripod began to offer free personal home pages, e-mail, message boards, and chat rooms. "One of the hardest things to do is take something you have been working on for months and drop it one day to pursue something else," Peabody admitted. But that's what successful marketing is all about—responding to what your market research is telling you.

The new marketing strategy paid off—big time. Tripod's on-line community boomed until it became one of the largest ever, with over 2.3 million members. At age twenty-seven, Peabody sold his one-time small venture to Lycos for $58 million. That's the power of building a brand on-line.

Tips

- Consider starting a business in your home or a relative's home. If the business takes off, you can always move to an office. Starting a business with very low overhead is a good way to protect it from insolvency during the lean times any new business will face.

- Don't limit yourself to one service if your equipment can handle more than one. If you silkscreen T-shirts, for example, you have the equipment to silkscreen posters, invitations, shorts, and so on. Concentrate on your main business, but don't overlook other money-making opportunities. And always listen to the customer!

RESOURCES

Book

For the full story of Ford's Edsel fiasco, see *Made in America: An Informed History of the English Language in the United States* by Bill Bryson (New York: William Morrow and Co., 1995). This book offers a wealth of fascinating anecdotes about American businesses.

Other Resources

If you need help analyzing your market, or you want to expand your business into a market with which you are not familiar, a demographic consultant can be useful. Demographic information is usually not cheap, so check prices carefully before you order any. American Demographics, Inc. is one of several market research organizations that sells demographic information. Contact:

American Demographics, Inc.
P.O. Box 68
Ithaca, NY 14851
(800) 828-1133

Another resource is Business Demographics, an on-line service that offers market reports tailored to geographical regions.

Business Demographics can be contacted at *CompuServe::go BUSDEM*.

If you're thinking about a career in marketing and would like some brochures or other instructive materials, contact:

The American Marketing Association
25 S. Wacker Drive, Suite 200
Chicago, IL 60606
(312) 648-0536

Chapter

TECHNOLOGY IS YOUR GENERATION'S COMPETITIVE ADVANTAGE

USE THE WEB, AND MORE, TO BETTER SERVE YOUR CUSTOMERS

Business is going to change more in the next ten years than it has in the last fifty.

—Bill Gates
Founder of Microsoft, Inc.

You may already know more about business technology than entrepreneurs twice your age, because so many innovations in computing and other technologies have occurred during your lifetime. Fifteen years ago, hardly anyone used a fax or a cell phone. Many entrepreneurs kept their records in handwritten accounting journals.

We tend to be most comfortable with the **technology** we grow up with. Technology is science that has been applied to industry or commerce. You can turn your generation's familiarity with the Internet, laptop computers, beepers, and the like, into a competitive advantage for your business.

A video rental store that does its ordering and record keeping by hand, for example, is likely to lose customers to a video rental store that uses scanners and computer lists. Why? Because customers know they won't have to wait in line as long in the technology-savvy store.

WHAT TECHNOLOGY DO YOU ALREADY OWN?

You can turn technology that you already own into a business. Do you own a good quality camera? Start a photography business. How about a VCR and a video camera? You could tape weddings, parties, and other events. A sewing machine can be used to start all kinds of businesses, from clothing alterations to making dolls or pillows.

A van or pickup truck can become the centerpiece of a trucking or delivery business. A washing machine can be turned into a laundry service. Use your kitchen to start a catering service or a cooking school. Or sell your homemade baked goods. Your personal computer, of course, can be used in many types of businesses, from word processing to graphic design.

Think about any technological knowledge you have. Can you teach someone else how to use a computer? A camera? Put what you *know* to work.

ENTREPRENEUR STORY
MICHAEL DELL, DELL COMPUTER

Michael Dell did just that at age nineteen, when he was still in college. Dell borrowed $1,000 from his parents and used it to buy computer parts, which he assembled into customized computers that he sold to other students at the University of Texas. Today, Dell Computer is basically in the same business: It buys parts wholesale, builds computers to customers' specifications, and sells them direct. By eliminating "the middleman" (the computer stores), Dell can offer customers exactly what they want, at lower prices. In addition, Dell doesn't have to pay to store a lot of inventory. It only builds computers after they are ordered by customers.

TOOL NUMBER ONE: THE PHONE

Your phone is a powerful business tool. Turn your phone into an answering service for your business by buying an answering machine. If you can't afford a machine, check out the answering services that charge only a few dollars a month. Your telephone company may also offer an inexpensive voice mail account as part of its service package.

Whether you use an answering machine or a phone company service, make sure the message callers hear gives the full name of your business and sounds clear and professional. Change your message often, to advertise specials and sales and to keep customers listening. Use beepers and cell phones to stay in touch with customers, employees, and suppliers.

If you can afford it, consider a separate telephone line for your business. You can then have it listed by your business name in the phone book, and you'll know to always answer with your business name when that phone rings. For a small charge, many phone companies offer a way to have two or more phone numbers go to the same line. Each number has a unique way of ringing so you know whether someone is calling from one number or the other.

ADD A FAX

Make your phone even more useful by attaching a fax machine to it. Fax machines enable you to send and receive letters, flyers, contracts— anything printed on a page. You can also use your computer to send faxes through a **modem.** A modem translates signals from your computer into a digital stream that can be sent over telephone lines.

Instead of mailing coupons to prospective customers, why not fax them? If you have a modem hooked up to your computer and fax machine, program your computer to fax your coupon to a list of fax numbers. The computer will automatically send your fax to the numbers on the list, leaving you free to do something else.

POCKET ORGANIZERS

A pocket organizer is a good investment for any entrepreneur. It includes a calculator and an electronic calendar for keeping track of appointments, and it stores memos, notes, and important addresses and phone numbers. The latest pocket organizers let you transfer information from the organizer to your computer, which is useful for turning the addresses in your organizer into, say, mailing labels for flyers.

When you're in the middle of a negotiation, the last thing you want to do is fumble for figures. If you can't afford a pocket organizer, carry a super-cheap pocket calculator to keep you from getting flustered by math. Some digital watches have built-in calculators, so you can always have one on your wrist.

Gotta Have It: A Computer

One of the best investments you can make for your business is to buy or borrow a computer. Even the most bare-bones model can help you:

- Create stationery for your business.
- Type professional-looking letters and check your spelling.
- Keep financial records.
- Make flyers and posters.
- Send e-mail and faxes to customers.
- Keep a list of customers' addresses, and print labels for mailing.

Most important, a computer will allow you to access the Internet, an amazingly useful source of information and marketing opportunities.

Remember, you don't need the latest model computer to surf the Web or make flyers, and older models cost much, much less. If you can't afford even an older computer, try to borrow one or use one part-time. You can buy computer time at Internet cafés or office stores, and many public libraries and community colleges now offer free Internet access.

Protect Your Data

The information you store on your computer is called **data.** Important business data on your computer might include mailing lists, invoices, letters, and financial records. Because your computer is an electronic device, you'll need to protect it from four data destroyers:

1. **Power outages.** A power blackout can destroy data that you haven't saved yet. Office supply stores carry an uninterrupt-ible power supply (UPS) that will keep your computer running when the lights go out.

2. **Power surges.** A power surge can send *too much* electricity through your computer and fry the circuits. Plug all your

computer equipment into a power strip with a surge protector (available at office supply stores or hardware stores).

3. **Computer viruses.** A **virus** is a small piece of computer software that can attach itself to other software (like your word processing files) and ruin it. Protect your computer with virus protection software like *Norton Antivirus* or *SAM*.

4. **Disk failures.** Your computer's **hard drive** (the place where it stores all of your files) can crash, destroying valuable data. To prevent this, save everything you do by copying it onto a back-up floppy disk. With file sizes getting larger and larger, an even better method is to attach a removable hard drive to your computer and periodically back up your entire drive. You can also use many other removable storage media, such as a Zip or SyQuest drive.

How to Buy Software

New software for small business owners is being created every day. Mail-order companies offer some of the best deals on computer software, and they'll mail you catalogs that keep you up to date on the latest developments. Some of the best are:

- **Micro Warehouse.** Call (800) 367-7080 to order a catalog, or visit www.warehouse.com.
- **Mac Warehouse.** Call (800) 255-6227 to order a catalog, or visit www.warehouse.com/macwarehouse.
- **The PC Zone.** Call (800) 258-2088 to order a catalog, or visit www.zones.com.

Shareware and Freeware

Surprisingly, a lot of software is available for free or at low cost on the Internet. Free software is called **freeware.** This is software that has been developed by (1) an individual who is simply eager to share it with the computer world, or (2) a company that wants you to use the free program so that, later, you will buy other programs that are associated with it. Many large companies—such as Apple, with its Quicktime multimedia software, and Microsoft, with its Explorer Web browser—use this strategy very effectively to increase interest in their other products.

Shareware is also distributed for free, but only as a demonstration—it usually has an expiration date, after which it will no longer be usable. To unlock the expired shareware, or to upgrade it to include more features, you must pay a fee (usually quite low). The supplier of a shareware program gambles that people who use it will like it so much that they will decide to pay for the full program, including upgrades and technical support.

If you are using a proprietary service, such as America Online or CompuServe, the service can direct you to shareware. If you are using a direct connection to the Internet, visit **www.download.com** for an archive of the most popular programs.

Be sure to run all software through your virus detection program before installing it on your hard drive.

Exploring the Internet

When you have a computer and a modem, you can access the Internet. But what exactly is the Internet? It began in the late 1960s as a new kind of technology for the Department of Defense; it allowed the hundreds of different kinds of computers at the Pentagon to talk to each other. The network was very flexible—any computer, running just about any kind of software, could communicate with any other computer on the system. The network became popular among university researchers, who used it to share files and send e-mail to each other, and its size doubled every year for nearly two decades. Now, the Internet is the world's largest computer network. It connects almost 300 million users, and it is no longer controlled by one government or organization.

In 1989, an Englishman named Tim Berners-Lee invented a way to use the Internet that allowed users to create, on their computers, pages with **links** in them. The links were words that, if clicked on with a mouse, could connect to any other page, on any computer, anywhere on the Internet. And so the World Wide Web was born.

Web pages are called **hypertext** documents because the text (and now pictures, and even video) on each page links to another page. Every Web page has its own address, called a **URL,** which stands for Uniform Resource Locator. (The URL for NFTE, for example, is www.nfte.com.) You can surf from one URL to the next with a click of the mouse.

The Web makes using the Internet much easier. As a result, it has become a powerful tool for marketing to the millions of people on-line. And where there are customers, entrepreneurs must follow!

Getting Connected

At one time, you needed an account at a university or government agency and a working knowledge of sophisticated computer terminology to ride the information highway. Now, all you need is a computer, a modem, and an account with an **Internet service provider** (ISP). You have three options:

1. **Proprietary service.** On-line services such as America On-line, CompuServe, Prodigy, and Delphi are called proprietary services. When they started, subscribers could only access **proprietary** data on one big set of computers at the service's headquarters. The data were proprietary because they were owned by the service and were available only to people who paid a subscription fee. Proprietary services also offered some access to the Internet—at least e-mail—but they were successful mostly because they offered information that was unavailable elsewhere. With the advent of the Web, the companies saw a new market and began to offer direct access to the Internet (and therefore the Web), in addition to their proprietary services. Now, they are the most common way for people to get on-line. They are easy for beginning surfers to use, and many of them continue to offer special services that set them apart from the competition.

2. **Basic ISP.** Once you get your feet wet, you may find that the access to the Internet provided by the proprietary services is somewhat limited, or that the special services they offer don't appeal to you. (Many advanced users, for example, don't like the special software that many proprietary services require them to use.) Smaller local ISPs, as well as national ISPs such as NetCom and EarthLink, can provide a connection to the Internet without the bells and whistles. Such basic ISPs are becoming more and more competitive with proprietary services in convenience and ease of use, and they are often cheaper. You can find a list of them in the Yellow Pages under Internet service providers.

3. **Bulletin board service (BBS).** If what you really want out of the Net is a sense of community, try a local or subject-specific BBS. Like proprietary services, BBSs began as a way for people to get proprietary information from a single

computer. Now, most BBSs offer regular Internet access in addition to a host of local interest message boards and specialized services.

A Web Site Is a Storefront to the World

An **electronic storefront** is a place on-line, usually a Web site, that customers can visit to view a company's catalog, price list, and other information. Some electronic storefronts even allow customers to make purchases on-line with a credit card.

The most powerful aspect of the World Wide Web is that it is, as the name says, worldwide. Opening an electronic storefront on the Web can put a small businessperson on a level playing field with more established, larger businesses by allowing contact with more customers at a lower cost than ever before. Any business can use a Web site as part of its marketing strategy. Some businesses, like the bookseller Amazon.com, exist *only* as Web sites.

There are three approaches to operating a business over the Internet:

1. Charging a subscription fee to people who want to visit your site.
2. Selling goods, services, and information.
3. Selling advertising space, particularly if you're getting many "hits" (visits to your Web site) on a daily basis.

Some Web sites use more than one approach. *The Wall Street Journal Interactive Edition,* for example, uses all three. It charges an annual fee for access to its Web site; it sells individual stories from its archives for a few dollars each; and, because so many people visit the site every day, it sells advertisements.

Building Your Web Site

It's getting increasingly easy to design your own Web site. Many ISPs help by offering home pages as part of their deal, and Web sites such as Yahoo!/GeoCities allow you to set up a personal Web page on their server for free. (They make money by putting advertisements on your site.)

Your ISP probably will be able to provide you with step-by-step instructions for creating a simple home page. If not, you will have to learn to use HTML (HyperText Markup Language), the computer programming language that is used to create Web pages. That sounds scary, but HTML is easy to learn. Try *HTML For Dummies* (IDG Books) for a good introduction. With just a few hours of studying, you'll be able to make a good-looking page.

A Web site can allow you to reach customers far beyond your immediate geographical area. In addition, advertisers are sometimes willing to pay big bucks to place ads on Web sites that attract a lot of viewers. Yahoo! and I-Village, for example, are two Web sites that many people visit every day. They earn almost all of their revenues from advertising.

Make sure your Web page is easy to find. Most people find Web sites by going to a **search engine** such as Yahoo or Lycos. A search engine helps people sift through the millions of pages on the Web to find the one that is of interest to them.

Search engines find Web sites by searching the Web for new pages and then storing those URLs, along with some key words, in a database. When people type in key words, the engine spits out a list of URLs that match them. The search engines sometimes miss new Web sites, so when you launch your Web page, make sure you **register** it with at least two or three of the major search engines. When you register your page, you let the search engine know that your URL exists, and, just as important, you choose key words to associate with it. For example, Yahoo! will let you register on-line at docs.yahoo.com/info/suggest/.

And, of course, don't forget to put the URL on your stationery and business cards.

E-mail and Newsgroups

E-mail is short for "electronic mail"—mail sent via the Internet. **Newsgroups** are groups of people with common interests who send e-mail to a server, called Usenet, where everyone else in the group can read it and respond. There are thousands of different newsgroups on Usenet; they specialize in discussions on nearly every imaginable topic. Almost every ISP offers e-mail and Usenet server access as part of its Internet package.

Sending e-mail or posting messages on newsgroups can help get your message out to very focused groups of sales prospects and keep you in touch with customers you already have, but you must use these methods carefully. In the physical world, you can fish for sales prospects by distributing flyers or cold-calling people on a list. Using e-mail or newsgroups in a similar fashion can result in your e-mail box being jammed with **flames,** or hate mail. Most newsgroups do not appreciate blitzes of advertisements (called "spam"), and members will respond angrily.

Becoming involved in a newsgroup can lead to sales prospects, however, if done correctly. Let's say you sell photography supplies and you hear about an interesting newsgroup for photographers (for example, rec.photo.marketplace). Don't blitz it with ads for your business! Instead, before posting any messages, "lurk" for a while. Just read messages for a week and get a feel for the discussions taking place. Once you feel comfortable, try posting a message like this:

> The discussion this week on the advantages of the new Nikon mini-camera was very interesting. I'm in the photography supply business and am looking for interesting items to add to my Web site. I already post articles from *Advanced Photography* magazine and tips from some of my clients. Does anyone have any ideas for other useful information I could post? Thanks!
>
> Sandra Bowling
> PhotoSupply Online
> www.photosupply.com
> photosupply@AOL.com
> The Photographer's Source for Supplies and Advice

Because this is not a sales pitch, no one in the newsgroup will take offense, and your message may attract some potential sales prospects to your Web site.

Mailing Lists

The best people to market to are those who have already bought or shown interest in your product or service. When a customer makes a purchase or a potential customer asks about your business, ask for his or her e-mail address. Use this information to set up a simple **database** for your computer. A database is a collection of information stored and organized for easy searching. Some databases are very complicated and require special software, but you can create a simple (and very useful!) database by creating a table using any good word-processing program.

Your customer database should include the person's name and e-mail address, the date of your last contact, and a note that indicates what the person asked about or bought. As your database grows, you can organize it by region or customer interest and use it as a mailing list to send out targeted e-mail. If you sell gourmet sauces, for example, your notes could tell you whether a customer is interested in hot sauces or dessert sauces. When you add a new hot sauce to your line, you will know whom to target with e-mail introducing the sauce, possibly with a special offer.

Make sure that your subject line is effective and interesting. If it isn't, your prospect may not even bother to read your message. Remember, most people resent getting e-mail that doesn't interest them and may even retaliate by flaming you. It's a good idea, in fact, to always include an offer to drop people from your mailing list at the end of each message. This shows that you are respectful of their "cyberspace."

A Final Word

As a young entrepreneur, you are especially well-positioned to take advantage of the Internet's rapid growth and the technology developing along with it. You will probably find the Internet a more comfortable business environment than the office of a millionaire businessman twice your age, for example. This could be your generation's competitive advantage. Go for it!

CASE STUDY: ON-LINE JOB LISTINGS SERVICE

When starting an on-line business, it's vital to remember that the Internet is not unlike the Wild West in the mid-1800s—the laws ain't been made yet!

Laurel Touby found that out when a competitor challenged her claim to the **domain name** of her Web site, www.hireminds.com, a job listing service for New York City writers and editors. (The domain name is the first part of a URL and usually ends in something like ".com" or ".org" or ".net.")

Touby is a freelance journalist who began hosting cocktail parties in downtown bars for her journalist friends. Pretty soon, her parties were mobbed with journalists looking for writing jobs, and editors looking for journalists. In 1997, Touby created her Web site, where she posted job listings for free. In July 1998, for $70, she purchased the domain name www.hireminds.com—but she didn't trademark it (trademarking costs $200).

By April 1999, Touby's business was cranking. She began charging publishers looking for writers and editors $100 an ad; her clients included *Cosmopolitan, Ms., The Nation, SmartMoney,* and many other national publications. But a phone call from a recruiter for computer companies in Boston threatened to bring down her whole operation.

"I got a phone call from this fellow who says, 'I've bought up all the domain names around yours. I've applied for the trademark.' I felt like he was saying, 'You've got nothing,'" Touby told *The Village Voice* ("Hiring Squad," June 8, 1999).

Touby's problem was that her registered domain name protected only the specific domain, "www.hireminds.com." However, very similar names such as "higherminds.com" or "www.hireminds.org" were still up for grabs. With a trademark, however, she would have protection against competitors using even similar names, so she quickly applied for a trademark, too.

According to the U.S. Patent and Trade Office, the trademark would be awarded to whoever did business first under that name. Touby had to scramble to prove that she was using the name before her competitor. She sent out a mass e-mail to over 2,000 of the journalists who had used her service. If they had gotten work via her site before August 3, 1999, when her competitor began using the name, she requested that they send her proof. According to the *Voice* article, Touby encourages anyone starting an on-line business to check with the U.S. Patent and Trade Office first, to make sure no one else is using the same domain name.

RESOURCES

Books

If you decide to program your own Web site, look no further than *HTML for Dummies* by Ed Tittel, et al. (IDG Books, 1998) for help.

101 Businesses You Can Start on the Internet by Daniel S. Janal (Van Nostrand Rheinhold, 1996) gives an exciting glimpse of the future of on-line business.

Other Resources

Find free software for both Macs and PCs at:
shareware.com
www.download.com

Free space for Web sites at:
    angelfire.com
    geocities.yahoo.com/home

Business Owner's Toolkit, www.toolkit.cch.com, is loaded with tax, legal, and business info for entrepreneurs.

To research or apply for a domain name, visit InterNIC at:
    www.networksolutions.com.

To research or apply for a trademark, visit the U.S. Patent and Trade Office at:
    uspto.gov.

Chapter 16

PRACTICAL DAYDREAMING

DEVELOPING AND PROTECTING INVENTIONS

Don't ask whether something can be done; find a way to do it.
—An Wang (b. 1920)
Chinese American inventor and founder of Wang Laboratories

ENTREPRENEUR STORY
STEVE PERLMAN, WEBTV

While you're out there conducting market research, you might find yourself daydreaming about new products and services that the customers you are meeting might want to buy. Everyone daydreams, but entrepreneurs daydream with a market in mind. Some entrepreneurial daydreams have become inventions that have changed the world—and made the inventors rich beyond their wildest . . . well, daydreams!

Steve Perlman, the inventor of WebTV, built his first home computer when he was only fifteen years old. A gifted child, he had earned straight As until he discovered computers. Pretty soon, he was neglecting his homework in favor of taking apart the family TV set so he could play video games on it. (The details given here come from a story by Janice Maloney, in the July 1999 issue of *Wired* magazine.)

Perlman still managed to get into Columbia University, where he hacked into the school's mainframe computer and used it to run his word-processing programs. Upon graduation in 1983, he was recruited by Apple and joined its Advanced Technology Group in Cupertino, California. By 1990, though, Perlman had quit. He was frustrated that nothing he had invented while at Apple had been brought to market. He came back when Apple agreed that he could retain the rights to his inventions if Apple didn't use them.

Perlman daydreamed into existence a new way to surf the Web. Instead of using an expensive, complicated personal computer to access the Internet, he would create a simple, relatively cheap box that would sit on top of a TV. When Apple killed the idea, Perlman left again—but this time he took his invention with him. By 1995, he'd created a working prototype of the WebTV box. He and a friend, Bruce Leak, started a company with another friend, Phil Goldman, and began to sell WebTV out of the guest bedroom in Perlman's house.

Perlman, being something of a mad scientist, buried himself in development and let his partners worry about the money. He made some exciting breakthroughs—for example, he built WebTV service on top of what's called a "managed appliance" platform. This means that each WebTV box is equipped to automatically dial a local server to update its software as needed. The consumer didn't have to do anything—just plug the box into a phone jack and a TV, and start surfing the Web.

By 1997, Perlman had raised and burned through $46 million developing WebTV. Luckily, that's when Microsoft came calling. Microsoft was excited about the prospect not only of WebTV, but also of using Perlman's "managed appliance" invention to enable owners of Windows PCs to automatically upgrade their computers while they were sleeping.

Joining Microsoft's team netted Perlman and his two partners around $70 million apiece. But money has never been Perlman's primary motivation. He's a visionary who sees money as merely the means to continue inventing. Now that WebTV is in 21,000 stores nationwide, Perlman is already immersed in his next obsession—digital movies. He's building a digital production studio to start creating programs for what he calls "smart TV." "The line between what we today think of as a video game and what we today think of as a TV show will blur," Perlman told Maloney.

DEVELOP YOUR OWN
PRACTICAL DAYDREAMING

Successful businesses have been built on much humbler inventions than Perlman's futuristic fancies. The Sandbagger, a machine that fills sandbags, was invented in 1993 by Stacey Kanzler after she was surprised to see news footage of soldiers hand-filling sandbags during the heavy flooding in the Midwest that year. Within two weeks, Kanzler's prototype was being tested by the National Guard. Today, her company is worth over $2 million, but Kanzler is even happier that her invention helps save lives and property.

My friend Sylvia Stein has invented several products, including The Nose™, an eyeglass holder. When I asked her how she jump-starts her imagination, she said she tries to complete this sentence:[1]

I wish someone would make a _____ that _____.

Another way to start thinking like an inventor is to imagine solutions to problems in your neighborhood or community, or in the world. Write or sketch your solutions, pretending that anything is possible.

TURNING AN IDEA INTO A REAL PRODUCT

When you've come up with an idea for a product, make a model of it. This model can be rough. Use cheap materials such as paper, wood, paint, cloth, or plaster of Paris. You may go through many models.

Conduct some market research by showing the model to friends, acquaintances, and storekeepers. Collect ideas and suggestions, and use any suggestions that will improve your design. Don't be afraid to experiment.

Once you've perfected your model, the next step is to have a **prototype** made. A prototype is an exact model of the product, made by the manufacturing process that would be used in actual production of your invention. This can be an expensive step: prototypes cost many times the final production cost per item. If you are serious about turning your invention into a business, however, you will need a prototype to show investors or buyers.

To find a manufacturer for your prototype, check your library for the *Thomas Register of American Manufacturers*. This reference lists all U.S. manufacturers.

USING THE THOMAS REGISTER OF AMERICAN MANUFACTURERS

The *Thomas Register* is published every year and contains twenty-six volumes. It is an excellent source for names of manufacturers you can contact about having a prototype of your invention made. You should be able to find the *Thomas Register* in the reference room at a public library. If you can't find it, don't hesitate to ask the reference librarian. (Budding entrepreneurs should always be nice to their local reference librarians! I've relied on them greatly for help on many occasions.)

The twenty-six volumes are divided into three groups:

- Group One—Volumes 1–16 contain a list of categories of products and services arranged alphabetically. Within each product or service category, you can look up companies alphabetically by state and city. Use Group One to locate manufacturers in your area that make products similar to your invention.
- Group Two—Volumes 17 and 18 give profiles of different companies, listed alphabetically by company name. After you find a manufacturer (in Group One) that looks interesting, look up its profile in Group Two. The profile will include the manufacturer's address, telephone numbers, and office locations, and the names of company officials.
- Group Three—Volumes 19–26 offer catalogs arranged alphabetically by company name. These catalogs include product information such as drawings, photos, and statistics.

REALITY CHECK

- Does your invention solve a big enough problem—that is, a problem faced by many people?
- Can you locate these people easily?
- Is the manufacturing cost too high?
- Is there competition? Is someone else selling a similar product? How is yours better? Different?
- Try **test marketing.** Put a display, along with the product, in a store and see how it sells.

PATENTS

If you develop a good invention, you can either go into business for yourself or sell the idea to a manufacturer. Before taking either step, however, you must patent the invention to protect your rights as the inventor.

A **patent** grants to the inventor the exclusive privilege of making, using, selling, and authorizing others to make, use, and sell his or her invention. A patent can be obtained for any original, non-obvious, and useful device or process and is valid for twenty years. After that time, anyone may sell the invention, without paying the inventor.

Thomas Jefferson wrote: "The issue of patents for new discoveries has given a spring to invention beyond my conception." Later, Abraham Lincoln said, "The Patent System added the fuel of interest to the fire of genius." The first patent and copyright law was passed in 1790. The United States Patent Office was established in 1836.

When Filing a Patent Is Necessary

A patent cannot be obtained on a mere idea or suggestion. Your invention must be fully developed and working consistently before you can seek patent protection. You will have to prepare detailed drawings showing exactly how it works.

You don't need to obtain a patent unless you:

- Invent a product that you intend to market yourself or sell (or license) to a manufacturer *and*
- Believe that someone else could successfully sell the product by copying your invention.

On average, a patent takes about two years to obtain. A patent search has to be undertaken to make certain that the idea is not **infringing** on, or violating, someone else's patent. Obtaining a patent is a complex legal process. Before starting it, see a registered patent attorney.

A patent application must include the following:

1. An in-depth description of the invention.
2. A drawing of the invention, where necessary.
3. A completed "Declaration for Patent Application."
4. A notarized statement from the inventor to the effect that he or she is the original inventor of the subject of the application.
5. The filing fee ($380 or more).

The completed packet containing these five items should be sent, via registered mail, to:

Patent & Trademark Office
U.S. Department of Commerce
Washington, DC 20231
(703) 557-4636
www.uspto.gov

You can look at patents filed by other inventors at www.uspto.gov.

A Patent Can Build a
Fortune: Fred C. Koch

In the 1920s, when Fred C. Koch patented a process for making gasoline out of heavy crude oil, it transformed the oil industry and made Koch a very wealthy man—but not without a fight.

The major oil companies, which used competing technologies, immediately sued Koch for patent infringement. Some forty lawsuits were filed, and Koch eventually won them all.

While his legal battle was ongoing in the United States, Koch took his process to the Soviet Union, where he helped upgrade fifteen oil refineries. This provided him with the capital he needed, in 1940, to build his first refinery when he could finally use his technology in the United States. Under the leadership of Fred's son, Charles Koch, who has pioneered many management techniques, Koch Industries grew from a company with annual revenues of $177 million in 1966 to about $30 billion in 1998.

PUBLIC DOMAIN

Failure to obtain a patent can prevent an inventor from profiting from his or her invention. If an invention is put into use by the inventor for more than one year without obtaining a patent, the invention is considered **public domain** and a patent will no longer be granted.

An unfortunate example of public domain involved Louis Temple, an African American who lived in New Bedford, Massachusetts, and invented the toggle harpoon in the early 1800s. This invention greatly increased the efficiency of whaling at a time when whale oil was extremely valuable for lighting lamps and making candles.

To test the harpoon, Temple gave prototypes to several New Bedford ship captains. In those days, whaling voyages took about two years. By the time the ships returned and reported the harpoon's great success, Temple's invention had become public domain. Temple was never able to profit from his invention and died in poverty.

> **Don't go to the trouble and expense of applying for a patent unless your invention is unique and you intend to sell it.**

COPYRIGHTS

Literary, artistic, and musical works also need protection from copy-cats, but they cannot be patented. A **copyright** is the form of legal protection offered to literary, musical, and artistic works. The owner of a copyright has the sole right to print, reprint, sell and distribute, revise, record, and perform the work under copyright. The copyright protects a work for the life of the author/artist plus seventy years thereafter.

To file for a copyright, request forms from the Copyright Office. The forms are easy to fill out. To secure a copyright, send a completed form and two examples of the work, with a registration fee of $30, to:

Copyright Office
Information and Publications Section, LM-455
Library of Congress
101 Independence Avenue, S.E.
Washington, DC 20559-6000

These are the phone numbers you'll need:

Public information: (202) 707-3000
To order forms: (202) 707-9100

AFRICAN AMERICANS BEGIN PATENTING THEIR INVENTIONS

Like Temple, many African American inventors made important contributions to American business, yet failed to profit from them. Nobody knows how many inventions were thought up by slaves before the Civil War, for example, because credit for them was taken by their masters. There were probably quite a few, because ideas for making a job easier or completing it faster often come to those who have to do the actual work.

In 1895, an African American Congressman, George Washington Murray, read into the *Congressional Record* a list of ninety-two patents that had been issued to Americans of color. Murray wanted the general public to know that African Americans had made important contributions to the industrial revolution. Murray himself received eight patents for farm machinery improvements.

EARLY AFRICAN AMERICAN INVENTORS

After the Civil War, many African Americans went to work for the railroads. Some received patents for inventions to make the trains run more smoothly. In 1872, for example, Elijah McCoy invented a device for the self-oiling of railroad locomotives. This invention saved a great deal of time and money. Before it was available, the train's foreman had to get out of the cab and oil the parts by hand so they would not wear out prematurely.

McCoy was inspired to invent this device because he had often been assigned to do this tiresome job. The railroad was the only reliable form of long-distance transportation at the time, so McCoy's invention was very important. When Elijah McCoy died in 1929, he was both financially secure and respected by the engineering community.

Another African American's invention revolutionized the shoe industry. Jan E. Matzeliger invented an automatic shoe-stitching machine, called a "lasting" machine, in 1883. It could stitch 700 pairs of shoes a day, instead of the few pairs a day that could be sewn by hand. This invention greatly reduced the average price of a pair of shoes.

INVENTOR OF THE LIGHT BULB

Few people know that an African American named Lewis H. Latimer invented the light bulb that made the practical application of Edison's electric light system possible. Latimer worked closely with Edison and installed the first city electric light systems in New York, Philadelphia, London, and Montreal.

Dr. George Washington Carver is one black inventor who was internationally known during his lifetime. Born at the end of the Civil War, Carver completely transformed farming in the South by developing ways to use the peanut (peanut butter being only the most famous), the sweet potato, and the soybean. Because of his efforts, the South's dependency on cotton as the only exportable cash crop ended. Although Dr. Carver did not become rich from his work, he did receive honor and fame.

MORE RECENT SUCCESS STORIES

In this century, African American inventors have been better positioned to profit directly from their inventions. When Garret A. Morgan invented a gas mask in 1914, he already had a very profitable business based on a hair-straightening cream he had accidentally discovered and successfully marketed. Although his gas mask was originally meant for use in mines and tunnels, the U.S. Army used it extensively in World War I. In 1923, Morgan invented the first three-way traffic signal, the forerunner of today's traffic light. For the rights to his signal, General Electric paid him $40,000—a considerable sum at the time.

In the 1960s, Dr. Meredith Gourdine developed a million-dollar company based on inventions in the field of "electrogas dynamics"—converting gas into electricity. Even though Dr. Gourdine became blind in 1973, he is still very active in the company he founded.

WOMEN INVENTORS

Like the stories of early African American inventors, the stories of women inventors are finally coming to light as interest in women's history has increased. Nuclear fission, solar heating, bras, drip coffee, the ice cream cone, the Barbie™ doll, dishwashers, rolling pins, windshield wipers, medical syringes—these are just some products invented by women.

Many early women inventors created new products to help them where they spent most of their time—in the home—cooking, cleaning, and sewing. Mary Kies became the first woman patentee in 1809. She invented a process for weaving straw with silk or cotton thread. Her idea was instrumental in boosting New England's hat-making industry. When the War of 1812 cut off supplies of hats from Europe, New England hat makers used the Kies process to take over the hat market.

As women began to work outside the home, they invented helpful office products. Bette Graham invented "Liquid Paper," or whiteout, which saves secretaries the trouble of typing over an entire page when they make a typing error.

Women Inventors Today

As women have moved into traditionally male fields, such as medicine and science, their inventions in these areas have been increasing. In 1988, for example, Gertrude Elion became the first woman inducted into the Inventors' Hall of Fame. During the thirty-nine years she worked for Burroughs-Wellcome, a drug company, Elion patented forty-five medical compounds. She shared the 1988 Nobel Prize for medicine with George H. Hitchings. They invented a compound that prevents recipient patients' immune systems from rejecting transplanted organs.

Ann Moore's invention of the child-carrying Snugli™ led to a valuable medical application. The Snugli can be seen on almost every American street, but Moore got the idea for it during her service with the Peace Corps in Africa in the 1960s. In Togo, West Africa, mothers carry their babies around with them all day in a fabric harness. Moore developed this concept into a pouchlike child carrier that is comfortable and washable. Moore began selling the Snugli in 1979. By 1984, annual sales were $6 million—and rising. Moore has used her Snugli technology to develop the Airlift™—a padded, portable oxygen tank carrier for patients who need a steady supply of oxygen.

IMMIGRANT INVENTORS

As they establish themselves in this country, Asian, Hispanic, and other new Americans are inventing important new products and processes.

Dr. Eloy Rodrìguez, for example, has developed some important drugs from tropical and desert plants. His formulas are being tested against viruses and cancer. He was drawn to these discoveries by noting that monkeys and other primates eat certain plants when they are sick. Dr. Rodrìguez has established a new biology field called "Zoopharmacognosy"—the study of self-medication by primates.

Another recent medical breakthrough by a Hispanic American is the invention, by Dr. Lydia Villa-Komaroff and her team of researchers, of the process of harvesting insulin from bacterial cells.

SOME POPULAR INVENTIONS

Listed below are some popular products and their inventors. The interesting stories behind many of these inventions can be found in the NFTE book *Inventions In Profile*.

Product	Inventors
Post-It notes	Silver/Fry/Nichols
Frisbee	Walter Morrison
Silly Putty	James Wright
Slinky	Richard James
Band-Aids	Earle Dickson
Vaseline	Robert Chesebrough
The Nose	Sylvia Stein
Yo-Yo	Donald Duncan
Toothpick	Charles Forster
Safety razor	King Gillette
Motorcycle	Sylvester Roper
Safety pin	Walter Hunt
Drive-in theater	Richard Hollingshead
Bathtub	Michael Kohler
Levi jeans	Levi Strauss
Shopping cart	Sylvan Goldman

CASE STUDY: SELLING COLLECTIBLES ON THE WEB

Although many great businesses have been built on inventions, you don't need to be a brilliant inventor to be a brilliant entrepreneur. Sometimes, using an existing invention to sell a product in a fresh way or in a new place can generate big bucks.

Steve Milo was always crazy about entertainment-linked collectibles—toys, mugs, T-shirts, and other items decorated with images from comic books, TV shows, and movies. He dreamed about turning his obsession into a business. In 1984, even though he was a busy student at the University of Virginia at Charlottesville, Milo found time to create a direct-mail catalog to sell entertainment collectibles. He called his mail-order business American Entertainment.

When he heard about the World Wide Web, Milo saw an opportunity to use the new technology to reach a much larger market. He started by putting his catalog on-line. When he realized that customers wanted to actually purchase his stuff on-line, too, he incorporated then-new technology that allowed Web sites to take credit card orders securely. Next, he added daily articles and weekly updates on movies, TV shows, and other popular entertainments to keep customers informed of the latest merchandise (or "swag," as entertainment-linked collectibles are known in the biz). With each improvement, his business increased.

Today, at age 34, Milo is running a $20 million company, now called AnotherUniverse.com to reflect its Internet presence. He expects to continue to take advantage of every new development in Web technology. In an interview in the November 1998 issue of *Entrepreneur* magazine, he said, "There are some tremendous opportunities on the Internet, and we've only begun to scratch the surface."

RESOURCES

Books

The U.S. Patent and Trademark Office offers a booklet called *General Information on Patents*. It can be ordered by calling the U.S. Government Printing Office at (202) 512-1800.

Here are three books that cover the basics of obtaining patents, copyrights, and trademarks:

The Copyright Handbook: How To Protect and Use Written Works by Stephan Fishman (Berkeley, CA: NoLo Press, 1991).

Inventing and Patenting Sourcebook by Richard Levy (Detroit, MI: Gale Research, Inc., 1992).

Trademark: How to Name Your Business & Product by Kate McGrath and Stephan Elias (Berkeley, CA: NoLo Press, 1992).

Feminine Ingenuity: How Women Inventors Changed America by Anne L. Macdonald (New York: Ballantine Books, 1992) is a very entertaining and informative look at American female inventors.

Other Resources

Many public libraries provide trademark searches for a small fee. Or, you can contact:

United States Trademark Association
6 East 45th Street
New York, NY 10017-1487
(212) 986-5880

Chapter  17

How to Make Your Business Legal

Choosing the Right Legal Structure Is Crucial

> When two men in a business always agree,
> one of them is unnecessary.
>
> —**William Wrigley, Jr. (1861–1932)**
> **American businessman**

... **L INTO**
... **ORIES**

... during your lifetime,
... ories:[1]

... ngible product.
... om manufactur-

... ectly to the final consumer.

... intangibles such as time or

... will see when you start working on your business plan, each type of business has different accounting, marketing, and promotional needs. That's why it's important to be able to categorize your business.

As I've mentioned previously, my first small business was an import–export business. This was a service business. I represented manufacturers from West Africa, Pakistan, and Bangladesh. I was providing a service to them by taking their products around to dealers in New York City and trying to sell them. I was selling the manufacturers my time and my familiarity with New York.

Today, I am the president of NFTE, which is also a service business. We provide expertise in the teaching of entrepreneurship.

Manufacturing

A **manufacturing** business is one that makes a tangible product. A manufacturer rarely sells its products directly to consumers. It typically sells large quantities of its product to wholesalers, or it may hire a manufacturer's representative to sell its products directly to retailers. Some examples of manufacturing businesses are:

- Kohler, Inc., which manufactures plumbing fixtures. You've probably seen faucets imprinted with the Kohler name.
- Sony Corporation. Sony manufactures the Sony Walkman™, the Trinitron™ television, and other consumer electronic products.

Wholesale

A **wholesale** business rarely sells directly to the public, and it doesn't manufacture anything. It buys products from manufacturers in bulk and sells smaller quantities to retailers from warehouses. Some wholesalers also have store outlets, but they will not sell to consumers. If you see a store with a sign that reads "To the Trade Only," it is a wholesaler. A wholesaler is sometimes called a **middleman.** Wholesalers perform the business activity between manufacturers and retailers. Here are some examples of wholesale businesses:

- Dial-A-Floor buys carpets from manufacturers and sells them to carpet retailers.
- Hudson Wholesale buys clothing from manufacturers and sells it to boutiques.
- Butler Lumber, Inc. sells lumber to hardware stores and lumber companies.

RETAIL

Retail businesses sell directly to the consumer. Retailers buy products from a wholesaler and sell them directly to the final consumer. Retailers run stores or other selling units that are open to the public. Examples of retail businesses are:

- The Body Shop, Inc. Body Shop stores sell to consumers a variety of skin care products made from natural ingredients.
- Mrs. Fields Cookies. Although Mrs. Fields Cookies bakes its own cookies, the company sells them directly to consumers from its retail stores.
- East Side Sports. In Chapter 24, you'll read about this sporting goods store started by a NFTE graduate.

SERVICE

A **service** business provides intangibles such as time, skills, or expertise in exchange for a fee. Examples of service businesses are:

- H & R Block, Inc., the largest preparer of federal income tax returns for individuals. H & R Block prepares over 10 million returns each year.
- Charles Schwab & Company, which provides stock trading service.
- Wide Awake Publicity. Keeya Branson's firm helps clients secure publicity.

The above examples are *retail* service businesses because they sell directly to the end consumer. There are also service businesses that serve wholesale or manufacturing customers.

THE FOUR PARTS OF A BUSINESS

Each business is composed basically of four parts. Large businesses (or corporations) employ many experts who oversee different aspects of these four parts. An entrepreneur, though, might have to handle all four parts alone. These parts are:

1. **Production**—making or obtaining the product.

2. **Financing**—securing and efficiently using money to develop the business.

3. **Marketing**—developing strategies for getting the consumer interested in the product or service.

4. **Customer service**—maintaining and servicing a product or service once it has been sold; the art of keeping customers happy and loyal to the business. Don't confuse customer service with a service business. Every kind of business should pay attention to customer service. If your business offers good customer service, your customers will become repeat purchasers. They will return to your business again and again. Repeat customers make a business successful.

In their book *Fast Cash for Kids* (Hawthorne, NJ: Career Press, 1995), Bonnie and Noel Drew suggest that young entrepreneurs take these three steps to excellent customer service:

1. **Get a written agreement.** Discuss the price of your product or service with the customer before agreeing to a transaction. Write down on an order form:
   - The work you are going to do or the product you are going to deliver.
   - The amount you will be paid.
   - The date the job is to be completed or the product is to be delivered.

   Have the customer sign the order form.

2. **Underpromise and overdeliver.** Always "expect the unexpected." For instance, if you think you can do a job in three days, tell the customer you'll have it done in five days. In that way, you're covered if you run into a problem. If you can finish "early," the customer will be pleasantly surprised.

3. **Make your customers your number-one priority.**
   - Do something extra without being asked.
   - Offer a money-back guarantee on your product or service.
   - Thank the customer for the business.
   - Keep appointments; if you can't keep an appointment, call and explain why.

- Follow up on every sale. Check with the customer to make sure he or she is satisfied with your product or service. A follow-up call or visit can often lead to another sale.

PICKING THE BEST LEGAL BUSINESS STRUCTURE

After you pick the kind of business you want to be in, you will have to choose a legal structure. There are five basic legal business structures:

1. Sole proprietorship
2. Partnership
3. Corporation
4. Subchapter S corporation
5. Limited Liability Company (LLC)
6. Nonprofit corporation

Sole Proprietorship

A **sole proprietorship** is owned by one person, who may also be the only employee. The owner receives all the business profits and must bear all the losses. Most student businesses are sole proprietorships.

The sole proprietor is personally **liable,** or responsible, for any lawsuits that arise from accidents, faulty merchandise, unpaid bills, or other business problems. This means the winner of a lawsuit against a sole proprietor can not only collect money from the business but also ask a court to force the owner to sell private possessions. The owner could lose his house or car, for example. The entrepreneur can always protect him- or herself, however, by buying insurance.

To avoid lawsuits, a young person starting a business should sell only products or services that are highly unlikely to hurt anyone. Avoid selling skateboards, for example, or offering rock-climbing lessons!

Partnership

A **general partnership** consists of two or more owners who make decisions for the business together and share profits, losses, and liability. Partners can bring different strengths, skills, and resources to the business. You may need a partner to make your business idea a reality. Herbert, for example, had a business plan for a T-shirt screening business, but he had no place to set up a business. He formed a partnership with Koung because Koung had a garage.

Sometimes, partnership disagreements can destroy a business. Also, one partner can make decisions that obligate the entire business. We recommend that partners always see a lawyer and draw up a **partnership agreement** that carefully defines the responsibilities of each partner and how profits and investments will be shared. Before Herbert and Koung went into business together, I warned them that their partnership could ruin their friendship. I counseled them to write down all their agreements. They did, and their business (and friendship) has lasted seven years so far.

Corporation

The word "corporation" is derived from *corpus,* Latin for "body." A **corporation** is a legal body composed of one or more stockholders united under a common name. Corporations issue stock and elect a board of directors, who manage the company. The board of directors differs from a board of advisers in that a board of directors has the power to hire and fire and to spend or not spend the company's money. Some entrepreneurs, in fact, have lost control of their companies to their boards of directors.

The corporate legal structure offers two key advantages:

1. A corporation may issue stock to raise money. Essentially, the company sells pieces of itself to stockholders, who then become co-owners of the company. This is called selling **equity** (ownership) to raise money.

2. A corporation has limited liability. Unlike sole proprietorships and partnerships, the owners of a corporation cannot have their personal assets used to pay business lawsuit settlements or debts. Only the assets of the corporation can be used to pay corporate debts.

The main disadvantage of corporations is that corporate income is taxed twice. First, the corporation must pay corporate income tax on its earnings. Later, when the corporation distributes its earnings as dividends to stockholders, the stockholders must include the dividends as personal income on their tax returns.

A business needs to incorporate when the owner wants to raise money by selling equity or when the owner needs protection from being liable for lawsuit settlements or debts that could be incurred by the business.

When Harold started his DJ business at age sixteen, he was spinning records for local parties. Today, his Nu X-Perience Sound and Lighting Company provides sound and lights for parties and parades. Now that he's dealing with sound and lighting equipment that could conceivably hurt someone in an accident, Harold has incorporated to protect his personal assets.

Subchapter S Corporation

This type of corporation limits the number of stockholders to seventy-five. It offers most of the limited liability protection of the corporation, but Subchapter S corporate income is taxed only once—as the personal income of the owners. Many small companies are Subchapter S corporations because it's a good way for a small company to avoid the double taxation of corporations.

Limited Liability Company

A new business structure, called a limited liability company (LLC), has finally been approved in all fifty states and the District of Columbia. Because it combines the best features of partnerships and corporations, it is an excellent choice for many small businesses. The LLC offers a more flexible structure and more flexible cost- and profit-sharing arrangements.

With an LLC, income is taxed only once, as the personal income of the partners. The partners receive the same protection of their personal assets from creditors and lawsuits that they would receive within a corporate business structure.

In addition, many of the restrictions—for example, regarding number and type of shareholders—that apply to the Subchapter S corporation do not apply to an LLC, making it even more attractive.

Nonprofit Corporation

A nonprofit corporation is set up with a specific mission to improve society. Churches, museums, charitable foundations, and trade associations are examples of nonprofit corporations.

Nonprofit corporations are **tax-exempt.** They do not pay taxes on their income because the income is being used to help society. On the other hand, nonprofits may not sell stock or pay dividends. No one owns a nonprofit corporation.

Why NFTE Is a Nonprofit Corporation

Initially, I funded my entrepreneurship program with personal savings. When I saw how well young people were responding to learning about business through hands-on experience, I decided to build a national movement so that every child born into poverty could have the opportunity to start his or her own business.

In 1987, I registered NFTE as a nonprofit corporation. As a "nonprofit," I could ask for donations. I wrote to everyone on the list of the 400 wealthiest people in America, published by *Forbes* magazine, and told them about my mission. Raymond Chambers, a wonderful entrepreneur from Newark, New Jersey, responded to that letter. After I met with him and his adviser, Barbara Bell, he agreed to finance NFTE for its first year at the Boys and Girls Clubs of Newark.

Management

As a small business grows, it will reach a point where the entrepreneur and a few employees cannot handle the business efficiently. At that stage, the business needs **management.** Management is the art of planning and organizing a business so it can meet its goals.

Many successful entrepreneurs are creative people who tend to get bored with the everyday details of running a large business. I'm that way, myself. Successful entrepreneurs realize this and hire managers to actually run the business. Once NFTE outgrew my home office and moved into our headquarters in downtown Manhattan, I hired Mike Caslin to help me with fund-raising and strategy. Mike has been my partner and NFTE's CEO since 1988 and is responsible for much of NFTE's success. So is Chris Meenan, the first, and one of the finest, teachers I ever met. Today Chris oversees NFTE's teachers worldwide.

As a nonprofit, NFTE had to raise money from funders to hire Chris and Mike, but entrepreneurs with growing *for-profit* corporations can raise capital by selling stock. These entrepreneurs can use some of the capital they raise to hire managers who can organize their businesses. The entrepreneurs can then spend less time managing and more time thinking up new business ideas.

Some entrepreneurs have made the mistake of giving management too much power or not paying attention to what managers are doing. Steve Jobs of Apple, for example, was actually booted out of the company in a coup led by a manager who was able to convince the Apple board of directors to fire Jobs. (More on that story in Chapter 19, "Financing Strategies That Work for Young Entrepreneurs.")

EVERY ENTREPRENEUR NEEDS A BOARD OF ADVISERS

You might not be ready for a board of directors for a while, but nothing says you can't start building a board of *advisers* for yourself right now. A *board of advisers* is a group of people who agree to advise you on your business and to help you with it. If you want to start designing your own line of clothing for snowboarding, for example, your board of advisers might include:

- An uncle who has worked in the fashion industry for years and can connect you with pattern makers and suppliers.
- A friend with a degree in fashion design who's working for a major designer.
- A sibling who has his or her own business.

You get the picture—choose advisers who can help your business because they have (1) some knowledge that you don't have and (2) contacts they are willing to share with you. Advisers can make key introductions that could help your business tremendously.

Ask your advisers for a commitment to meet personally with you for a brainstorming session at least once a month.

ENTREPRENEUR STORY
DEBBI FIELDS, MRS. FIELDS COOKIES

Some entrepreneurs will fail to hire adequate management because they don't want to give up overseeing the daily details of their businesses.

Debbi Fields, the owner of Mrs. Fields Cookies, made this mistake in the late 1980s. By 1987, Fields had opened over 500 stores in six countries. The rapid growth, combined with Debbi's unwillingness to let other people take much responsibility, almost caused the business to fall apart in 1988.

Sales were falling because too many new stores had opened too close to existing ones. Fields was forced to close ninety-seven stores that year. She realized that she would have to find good managers and trust them with helping her and her husband, Randy, run the business. She hired a chief financial officer from a top accounting firm, and a head of operations who had long experience in the food business. She delegated the day-to-day details of running the business to them.

This left her free to develop new ideas. The name Mrs. Fields meant top-quality baked goods to customers all over the world, so she began thinking up ways to use the name for more than just cookies and brownies. Fields made a deal with Ambrosia Chocolate to make and market Mrs. Fields semisweet chocolate chips, and she began testing recipes for muffins, bread, sandwiches, and soups for her new Mrs. Fields Bakeries. Soon, the stock price began to recover and profits improved.

Letting go of the daily details also gave Fields more time to read every comment sent to the company by customers and to travel around visiting her stores and meeting with local managers. She learned the hard way that a successful entrepreneur should not try to do everything alone.

ENTREPRENEUR STORY
SAM WALTON, WAL-MART

No matter what legal structure you use for your business or what managers you hire, motivating yourself and your employees is very important. One of the masters of motivation was Sam Walton, who built Wal-Mart, the largest retailer in the world, from a single five-and-dime store.

Walton grew up during the Great Depression in the small, hardscrabble town of Bentonville, Arkansas. He picked up entrepreneurship from his mother, who started a small milk business to help the family make ends meet. Walton began selling magazine subscriptions when he was only eight years old, and he had paper routes from seventh grade through college. He also raised and sold rabbits and pigeons, "nothing unusual for country boys," as he noted in his autobiography, *Sam Walton: Made in America* (with John Huey, New York: Doubleday, 1992).

Although Walton passed away in 1992, his folksy style remains the key to a business that is now worth over $50 billion. Even when *Forbes* named him America's richest man in 1985, Walton preferred pickup trucks to Rolls Royces, and hunting and fishing to attending celebrity-studded events.

Walton expected his managers and executives to share his aversion to flashy spending. This wasn't just a billionaire's quirk; it was part of his motivational strategy. In his autobiography, he said, "If American management is going to say to their workers that we're all in this together, they're going to have to stop this foolishness of paying themselves $3 million and $4 million bonuses every year and riding around everywhere in limos and corporate jets like they're so much better than everybody else."

Walton Introduces Profit Sharing

Walton wasn't just paying lip service to this idea. He put money behind it. In 1970, Walton introduced profit sharing for Wal-Mart managers. By 1971, he had extended it to every "associate" (as he called his employees) in the company. Using a formula based on profit growth, Wal-Mart contributes a percentage of each associate's wages to a profit-sharing plan, which the associate can take along—in either cash or Wal-Mart stock—when he or she leaves the company. In 1991, for example, Wal-Mart contributed $125 million to the profit-sharing plan.

The profit-sharing plan has created significant wealth for many Wal-Mart employees. More importantly, it makes each employee eager to work hard and come up with innovations to improve the profitability of the company. In *Sam Walton: Made in America,* a Wal-Mart truck driver notes that he worked for one large company for thirteen years and left with $700. After working for Wal-Mart for twenty years, he has built up over $700,000 through profit sharing. "When folks ask me how I like working for Wal-Mart," he says, "I tell them about my profit sharing and ask them, 'How do you think I feel about Wal-Mart?'"

Profit sharing was just one of Walton's motivational innovations. No matter how enormous the company became, his door was open to any employee who needed to talk to him. He constantly visited stores and made people feel that they were an important part of the Wal-Mart team. He encouraged and rewarded healthy competition among his stores.

I visited the Wal-Mart museum in Bentonville recently. People there are still sad about Walton's passing. His office has been reconstructed, and a copy of the profit-sharing plan hangs on the wall. Although he didn't have a computer in his office, Walton was a great proponent of technology. An incredible inventory control system has helped Wal-Mart keep prices low. The chain also uses video technology to train people across the country.

I'm sure Walton would approve. He wrote: "Our country desperately needs a revolution in education. Without a strong educational system, the very free enterprise system that allows a Wal-Mart or an IBM or a Procter & Gamble to appear on the scene and strengthen our nation's economy simply won't work."

CASE STUDY: DIRECTORY SERVICE

By the time she was age twenty-one, Jennifer Kushell had already owned three small businesses. She had noticed that young entrepreneurs can feel more isolated than older entrepreneurs. Even if they've never started a business before, older entrepreneurs may already be "in the loop" because they've built up many business contacts over the years. Jennifer decided that her fourth business would help young entrepreneurs network.

In November 1993, Jennifer and her partner, Benjamin Kyan, began producing *The International Directory of Young Entrepreneurs* (IDYE). The print directory developed into The Young Entrepreneurs Network, an on-line community and consulting service for young entrepreneurs.

Today, the directory includes around 500 members from thirty countries. The entrepreneurs listed range in age from ten to early thirties. The directory also includes information on professional business resources such as venture capital groups.

Meanwhile, the on-line community serves many more entrepreneurs with chat rooms, on-line advisers, member discounts, a quarterly newsletter, a library, and bartering and classified ads. When she's not working on the site, Jennifer lectures about entrepreneurship around the country, and works as a consultant with other young entrepreneurs as they build their own ventures.

According to Jennifer, the most important thing young entrepreneurs should remember is: "Starting and operating your own small business should be fun. Pick something you love to do and let your imagination lead you."

The growth of Jennifer's business is a natural result of her knowledge of her market. The directory was a great way for her to research her market while providing it with an important service. Next, she was able to combine her market research with Internet technology to create her successful on-line community. Like Jennifer, as you get to know your market better, ideas for expanding your business will multiply.

RESOURCES

Books

The Partnership Book: How to Write a Partnership Agreement by Dennis Clifford and Ralph Warner (Berkeley, CA: NoLo Press, 1991).

The Small Business Incorporation Kit by Robert L. Davidson III (New York: John Wiley & Sons, Inc., 1992).

One of the most popular books on customer service is *Delivering Knock Your Socks Off Service* by Kristin Anderson and Ron Zemke (New York: American Management Association, 1991).

On the Web, a resource that is also fun for young entrepreneurs is the Young Entrepreneurs Network, at www.youngandsuccessful.com. Touch base with other entrepreneurs and ask them any questions you may have about how to structure your business.

Other Resources

Starting and Operating a Small Business in . . . . Packets under this title have been prepared for every state. Each packet includes up-to-date information regarding both federal and state laws and regulations that affect a small business. Contact:

Oasis Press/PSI Research
300 North Valley Drive
Grant's Pass, OR 97526
(800) 228-2275

The National Association for the Self-Employed (NASE) keeps track of tax issues for small business owners. It also arranges bulk discounts for small

businesses. More than 88 percent of its 300,000 members are business owners with five or fewer employees. The NASE offers a toll-free small business
advice hotline and other helpful services. Contact:

> National Association for the Self-Employed
> 1023 15th Street, N.W., Suite 1200
> Washington, DC 20005-2600
> (202) 466-2100
> Fax (202) 466-2123
> (800) 232-NASE

Women who need advice starting their own business can contact:

> American Women's Economic Development Corporation (AWED)
> 641 Lexington Avenue, 9th Floor
> New York, NY 10022
> (800) 222-AWED

Chapter 18

SELECTING YOUR BUSINESS

LET YOUR TALENTS LEAD YOU

The propensity to truck, barter, and exchange one thing for another . . . is common to all men, and to be found in no other race of animals.

—Adam Smith (1723–1790)
Scottish economist

LET YOUR TALENTS LEAD YOU

You may think of yourself as more artistic than businesslike. You may have no idea what kind of business you could start. You may wonder whether artists can ever be successful entrepreneurs. They can!

ENTREPRENEUR STORY
SPIKE LEE, SPIKE'S JOINT

Spike Lee's business success disproves the notion that a creative artist can't also be a shrewd businessperson. Lee began selling merchandise connected with his films through an informal mail-order operation after the success of his first feature film, *She's Gotta Have It*. By the time Lee's movie *Do the Right Thing* became a huge hit, he was selling $50,000 worth *a month* of T-shirts and baseball caps. To sell his merchandise, Lee opened a store called Spike's Joint, in Fort Greene, Brooklyn, a few blocks from where he was raised.

Lee's style-setting ability was confirmed by the incredible popularity of the "X" cap he designed to promote the film *Malcolm X* in 1991. So many imitation "X" caps flooded the market, however, that Lee was inspired to become more serious about properly promoting and protecting his merchandise and fashion ideas.

In June 1992, Macy's opened a Spike's Joint in its Manhattan store. This was soon followed by Spike's Joints in sixteen other Macy's stores. Lee even opened a Spike's Joint on trendy Melrose Avenue in Los Angeles. He opened negotiations for a licensing deal to bring five Spike's Joint stores to Japan, and he began developing three lines of sportswear. He also formed his own record company: 40 Acres and a Mule Musicworks.

Lee equates owning a business with freedom and power. He strongly believes that African Americans should become entrepreneurs. He has said, "For so long, we African American people have been taught to work for other people and not to build our own businesses . . . but anytime you're in business and you can unify things, it gives you that much more power."

TURNING HOBBIES, SKILLS, AND INTERESTS INTO BUSINESSES

The possibilities for young people starting businesses are almost limitless. If you still haven't settled on a business idea, list some of your hobbies and skills below. What you enjoy doing in your spare time might be turned into a profitable business. Making money through doing what you enjoy is a winning combination.

Match up business opportunities with your hobbies, interests, and skills.

Hobbies and Interests	Business Opportunities
_____	_____
_____	_____
_____	_____
_____	_____

Skills	Business Opportunities

Anita Roddick, the founder of The Body Shop, Inc., suggests that new entrepreneurs ask themselves three questions when trying to choose a business to pursue:

1. What makes me mad?
2. What am I good at?
3. What separates me from the pack?

When selecting your business, choose something you enjoy doing.

THINGS TO CONSIDER WHEN CHOOSING A BUSINESS

Imagine yourself for a moment in the business of your choice. Is it a "good fit"? Are you going to stay interested in it and enthusiastic about it for a long time?

Keep your business simple. This is going to be your very first enterprise, so don't bite off more than you can chew. Many successful entrepreneurs start more than one business over the course of their lifetime. *Start with something simple that you know you can do well.* View yourself as growing into business by starting small. Choose something you are going to enjoy selling.

For now, if you choose a simple business and follow these three rules, your business should succeed:

1. Satisfy a consumer need
2. Buy low, sell high
3. Keep good records

Successful entrepreneurs listen to what people in the community are saying. Think about the people you know. What do they like? What do they want? What do they need? Could you fill one of their needs? Consider what your friends, family, and schoolmates want and need. They are your market.

By now, you may have several ideas but can't decide which one would be best. Try writing down several possible businesses. Eliminate them one by one until you end up with the business you like best.

If you haven't yet come up with a business idea you like, this chapter's money-making ideas may help. For further guidance, check out the resources at the end of the chapter.

Throughout this book, I have included detailed examples of businesses run by young entrepreneurs. I hope these narratives will help you select a business of your own. Here is a list of some of the most common businesses run by young people. The first section suggests businesses that can be started on-line!

Internet Business Ideas

- **Astrology charts.** If you know how to create any personalized service, such as an astrology or biorhythm chart, you could reach and serve many potential customers on-line. There are even on-line Tarot card readers!

- **Collectibles.** Create a forum for people to trade collectible items, such as sports cards, coins, or stamps. Charge a commission for trades made through your Web site.

- **Fashion.** Clothing sales—from new designs to consignment sales of greatly used clothing—are doing well on-line. T-shirt vendors, for example, have reported brisk sales to college students, who tend to have free Internet accounts at school, via the World Wide Web.

- **Jewelry.** This enterprise can take advantage of the nice graphics available on the Web. Jewelry designers can post photos of their work and sell directly to on-line consumers. Even if you aren't a jewelry designer yourself, you could set up an on-line jewelry store and promote your friends' designs for a percentage of the sales.

- **Record label.** With new MP3 technology, musicians can put their albums on-line, and customers can download them directly into their computers, bypassing the record industry completely.

Very small, specialized on-line record labels may be the wave of the future.

- **Specialty foods.** The nice thing about selling specialty food items on-line is that you can customize packages for different customers and send them exactly what they want to buy. Post new recipes regularly on your home page, to draw customers back often.

- **Visual art.** Artists and photographers can show samples of their work on home pages and make sales without having to wait to show their work in galleries. Even if you aren't an artist, you could own a virtual art gallery.

- **Zine.** Just as records can be sampled and sold on-line, so can magazines. To make money with a "digizine," you can sell subscriptions and advertising.

"Off-line" Business Ideas

- **Baby-sitting Service**

  Are you reliable and responsible? Do you like children? Provide a baby-sitting service.

- **Baking**

  Do you like to bake? You can sell freshly made bread, cookies, cakes, and pastries. For this business, "word of mouth" is truly the best advertising!

- **Bicycle/Auto/Appliance Repair**

  Are you mechanically inclined? Fix bicycles, cars, appliances, or other machinery that you know well.

- **Catering**

  Are you into cooking in a big way? Start a catering business and supply whole meals or buffets for parties and other occasions.

- **Distributing Flyers**

  Do stores in your neighborhood need people to hand out flyers? These can be distributed on the street, put on car windshields, or given out at social functions. This service could be offered to shopkeepers on a regular basis.

- **Entertaining**

  Are you a natural ham who enjoys being in front of an audience? Do you know any magic tricks or have any acting experience? You might like being a magician or a clown and entertaining at birthday parties and other events. If you have musical talent, you could get a band together and play for weddings and parties.

- **Gardening/Lawn Cutting**

  Do you like working outdoors? From the street, you can often spot lawns and gardens that are not being kept up by their owners as well as they should be. You could also shovel snow in the winter (if you live in a four-season area).

- **Growing Plants**

  Is there a room in your house or apartment that gets a lot of sunlight? You can grow herbs, flowers, or other plants for sale. This can be a good "second" business because plants don't have to be watched every minute of the day.

- **Handicrafts**

  Do you like to make jewelry, leather goods, or other handicrafts? Do you have friends who make nice handicrafts but don't want to be involved in the selling process? Sell your own crafts and, for a commission, your friends' crafts, too.

- **Holiday Selling**

  Do you have spare time during the holidays? Try selling seasonal specialties, such as Christmas decorations or Valentine's Day candy, which have short but intense sales seasons. If you are willing to put in the time, you can make a lot of money in a relatively short period.

- **House/Office Cleaning**

  Do you like to see things clean and neat? Houses and offices need to be cleaned. Many people and businesses do not have time to clean.

- **Laundry Service**

  Do you have access to a good washer and dryer? Doing laundry (like dog walking and house cleaning) is another chore many people do not have time to do.

- **Messenger Service**

  Do you enjoy running around? Try a messenger/small-package delivery service. This business has low start-up costs. The service can expand rapidly as you build up a reputation for reliability.

- **Music Lessons**

  Do you play an instrument well enough to teach someone else? Even if you have only intermediate knowledge of an instrument, you could probably teach young beginners.

- **Painting/Furniture Refinishing**

  Do you like to paint? Paint rooms and apartments; repaint or refinish old furniture.

- **Pet Care**

  Do you like animals? Dog walking and taking care of pets are possibilities.

- **Photography**

  Do you have a good camera or a camcorder? More and more, people are having their weddings, birthdays, parties, and other events photographed or videotaped (or both). You'll need samples of your work to show to prospective clients.

- **Plant Care**

  Offices sometimes hire a service to come in once a week or so to water, clean, and fertilize plants. As more and more people work outside the home, there is more demand for household plant care, too.

- **Translating**

  Are you bilingual? Translate ads, flyers, signs, and other printed media for local shopkeepers who want to reach customers who speak different languages.

- **T-Shirts**

  Are you artistically inclined? Design and print your own customized T-shirts.

- **Tutoring**

  Do you know one of your school subjects well enough to teach other students? Do you know how to dance, act, sing, or draw well enough to teach it to young children? Giving lessons (tutoring) requires patience, but you will discover the rewards and satisfaction of teaching.

- **Typing Service**

  Are you a fast and accurate typist? If you can type well or use a word processor, you can offer a wide variety of services: typing papers for other students, organizing and printing out mailing lists, or making up brochures, newsletters, or flyers.

- **Wake-up Service**

Are you an early riser? Start a wake-up service for your fellow students.

Naming Your Business

Once you've selected a business, the next step is to name it. The name of a business represents the character of the enterprise to customers, investors, and advisers.

It is common for entrepreneurs to name their businesses after themselves. Using your first name to identify your business—showing the pride you take in it—can be a good idea (Joe's Pizza, for example).

Attaching your last (family) name to your business is not such a good idea. If you name your business with your last name, several risks are involved:

- If your family's name is common among other families in your area, your business won't be distinctively identified as yours and no one else's.

- If the business fails, your name becomes associated with a failed business. This can hurt you if you decide to start a new business and potential investors remember that your earlier business failed.

- If the business succeeds, you might decide to sell it for a tidy profit. But what if you hate what the new owner does with it? What if he or she engages in dishonest business practices? Your name is still on the door.

Business owners can get carried away when naming a business. Naming a photography studio "Timeless Expression," for example, is creative but doesn't give customers any information about the business. A more straightforward name, such as "The Portrait Place," might draw more customers.

The Best Name Is One That Tells Customers What the Company Does, Sells, or Makes

In his best-selling book, *Have You Got What It Takes? How To Tell If You Should Start Your Own Business* (Englewood Cliffs, NJ: Prentice-Hall,

1982), Joseph Mancuso says, "Naming the company is the first move of many in which you should keep the customer's needs first and foremost in mind." NFTE's name—The National Foundation for Teaching Entrepreneurship, Inc.—for example, explains that we teach entrepreneurship nationally and that we are a nonprofit foundation.

REGISTERING A SOLE PROPRIETORSHIP

To sell a product or service legally, you need to register your business. In most areas, it is easy and inexpensive to register a sole proprietorship. Once you do, you will have a real business! Contact the county courthouse or local Chamber of Commerce to find out which licenses and permits are necessary in your area.

Registration usually takes the following steps:

1. Choose a name for your business.
2. Fill out a "Doing Business As" (DBA) form, indicating the name of your business and your name. The certificate in Chart 13 is an example of a standard DBA. The state will then have a record of the name of the person doing business.
3. Be prepared to have an official conduct a name search to make sure the name you've chosen isn't already being used.
4. Fill out a registration form and pay the fee required in your area.
5. Find out whether a **notary public** must witness your signature on the DBA. A notary is a person authorized to witness the signing of documents and to certify them as valid. Most banks have a notary or can refer you to one. There may be one at the registration office. You will have to show the notary photo identification.

SALES TAX IDENTIFICATION NUMBER

In most towns, every business must obtain a sales tax identification number and collect sales tax. To find out what sales taxes are required in your area, call your state's sales tax office. The office can send you an application for a sales tax number. Chart 14 will familiarize you with the format of the application.

BUSINESS CERTIFICATE

I HEREBY CERTIFY *that I am conducting or transacting business under the name or designation*

of

at

City or Town of　　　　　　　　*County of*　　　　　　　　　　　　*State of New York*

　　My name is*

and I reside at

　　I FURTHER CERTIFY *that I am the successor in interest to*

the person or persons heretofore using such name or names to carry on or conduct or transact business.

IN WITNESS HEREOF, *I have this*　　　　*day of*　　　　　　　　　　　*20____, made and signed this certificate*

....

*Print or type name.
*If under 21 years of age, state "I am .... years of age."

STATE OF NEW YORK
COUNTY OF　　　　　　　　} *ss.:*

　　On this　　　*day of*　　　　　*20____, before me personally appeared*

to me known and known to me to be the individual described in and who executed the foregoing certificate, and he (she) thereupon duly acknowledged to me that he (she) executed the same.

....

Chart 13 A Standard DBA Form

DTF-17 (11/96) New York State Department of Taxation and Finance

Application for Registration as a Sales Tax Vendor

Department use only

Please print or type

1 What type of certificate are you applying for?
(You must check one box - see instructions): ☐ Regular ☐ Temporary ☐ Show ☐ Entertainment

2 Legal name

3 Trade name (if different from item 2)

4 Federal employer identification number

5 Address of principal place of business (show/entertainment or temporary vendors use home address, regular vendors use physical address of business)
Number and street   City   State   ZIP code

6 Telephone number (include area code) ( )
7 County of principal place of business
8 Country, if not U.S.
9 Date you will begin business in New York *(see instructions)* / /

10 Mailing address, if different from business address on line 5
C/O name   Number and street   City   State   ZIP code
Date you will end business in New York if you are a temporary vendor / /

11 Type of organization ☐ Individual (sole proprietor) ☐ Partnership ☐ Corporation ☐ Trust ☐ Governmental ☐ Exempt organization
☐ Other *(specify)* ☐ Limited Liability Partnership ☐ Limited Liability Company

12 Reason for applying ☐ Started new business ☐ Purchased existing business ☐ Adding a new location ☐ Change in organization ☐ Other (specify)

13 List all owners/officers. Attach a separate sheet if necessary. This section must be completed by all applicants.

Name	Title	Social security number
Home address		City, State, ZIP code	Telephone number ( )
Name	Title	Social security number
Home address		City, State, ZIP code	Telephone number ( )
Name	Title	Social security number
Home address		City, State, ZIP code	Telephone number ( )

14 Does your business currently have tax accounts with New York State for the following taxes? If yes, enter identification number.
Corporation Tax ☐ Yes ☐ No ID # _____ Withholding Tax ☐ Yes ☐ No ID # _____
Other Taxes - enter type of tax and identification number _____

15 If you have ever registered as a sales tax vendor before with New York State enter information shown on the last sales tax retun you filed:
Name   Identification number

Questions 16 and 17 apply to regular vendors only. All other vendors go to question 18.

16 Will you operate more than one place of business? ☐ Yes ☐ No If *Yes*, check the appropriate box below and follow the instructions.

A ☐ Separate return will be filed for each location. Fill out and return a **complete** application for **each** business location.
B ☐ Consolidated return will be filed to cover all places of business. List your business locations on Form DTF-17-ATT and return with this application.

17 Do you expect to collect any sales or use tax or pay any sales or use tax directly to the Department of Taxation and Finance? ☐ Yes ☐ No

18 Fill in the boxes below, describing your major business activities:

	Describe your business activity in detail *(attach a separate sheet if necessary)*	Enter letter of major division from Form DTF-17-I, page 2-3	Enter Standard Industrial Code (SIC) *(see instructions)*	Percent of time spent on activity *(total should = 100%)*
Primary Business Activity				
Secondary Business Activity *(if any)*				

19 Are you a sidewalk vendor?.. ☐ Yes ☐ No
If *Yes*, do you sell food? .... ☐ Yes ☐ No
20 Do you participate solely in flea markets, antique shows or other "shows"?.. ☐ Yes ☐ No
21 Do you intend to make retail sales of cigarettes or other tobacco products?.. ☐ Yes ☐ No
22 Are you liable for paying the New York State beverage container tax?....... ☐ Yes ☐ No
23 Do you sell merchandise from door to door or through party plans?......... ☐ Yes ☐ No

Department use only

Mail code		Certificate No
Type	Status	Sch. Ind.	Aux. sch.
SIC P		SIC S

Chart 14 One State's Application Form for a Sales Tax Identification Number

BUSINESS CARDS

After you have registered your business, you should have business cards made. A business card bears your name, title, business name, and phone/fax/Web contacts. The card should fit into the credit-card section of your wallet. Always carry business cards with you. Give them to business contacts and prospective customers.

CASE STUDY: WEB CONSULTING[1]

The most important lesson I want you to take from this book is that starting and operating your own small business should be fun. Pick something you love to do, and let your imagination lead you.

That's exactly what Omar Wasow, 24, and Peta Hoyes, 25, did when they began New York OnLine (NYO), an on-line community focused on thoughtful discussion about New York life. Omar and Peta were raised in New York and love the city's ethnic diversity and cultural offerings. The pair met at Stanford University and decided to return to New York after college. New York OnLine started operating from Omar's Brooklyn brownstone apartment in April, 1994.

Omar borrowed most of the $50,000 startup capital from his parents. Soon, three computer terminals and twenty-five phone lines were hooked up in his living room. Omar and Peta (who has a degree in mechanical engineering) taught themselves how to wire everything.

Subscribers to New York OnLine paid a base charge of $6 a month. In return, they got access to restaurant, movie, and television reviews, and trendy magazines like *Wired* and *Vibe*. Users also participated in debates on subjects dear to New Yorkers' hearts—such as why Pat Riley *really* quit coaching the Knicks. On-line services attract mostly white males, but 40 percent of New York OnLine's users were females and 50 percent were people of color. Even though the site had only around 1,200 subscribers in 1995, interest from advertisers was intense because they wanted to tap into its demographic diversity.

Peta and Omar succeeded in attracting a young, ethnically diverse crowd, which made New York Online very appealing to advertisers and to clients who hired Peta and Omar to develop Web sites for them. The first client was TimeWarner's *Vibe* magazine. By 1995, New York Online had landed its first international client, The Martinique Promotion Bureau. In December of that year, NYO began developing a targeted, Web-based, on-line community with Newhouse Newspapers

New Media. Clients and awards have followed, including *Black Enterprise* magazine's Innovator of the Year Award in 1996. Today, NYO maintains its popular on-line community while also conducting new media consulting and Web development. According to Peta and Omar, these businesses, and any future businesses NYO will develop, stem from two principles that have formed their marketing vision from the beginning: (1) Community—"the ability for people with common interests to communicate" and (2) Utility—"the ability to facilitate useful exchanges and functions of information."

RESOURCES

Books

Better Than a Lemonade Stand: Small Business Ideas for Kids by Daryl Bernstein (Hillsboro, OR: Beyond Words Publishing, Inc., 1992).

Fast Cash for Kids: 101 Money-Making Projects for Young Entrepreneurs, 2nd Edition by Bonnie and Noel Drew (Hawthorne, NJ: The Career Press, 1995).

Other Resources

Call your local Chamber of Commerce to find out whether any youth entrepreneurship clubs or programs are being run in your town. You might also check with your local Boys & Girls Club.

For a list of programs that NFTE runs nationally, contact:

The National Foundation for Teaching Entrepreneurship, Inc.
120 Wall Street, 29th Floor
New York, NY 10005
(212) 232-3333
Fax (212) 232-2244
www.nfte.com

For information on the fine entrepreneurship education programs run by the University Community Outreach Program (UCOP), contact Lisa Hoffstein at:

UCOP
Milken Institute
401 City Avenue, Suite 204
Balacynwyd, PA 19004
(610) 668-5330

Entrepreneurship programs are also run by EDTECH. The directors of EDTECH, George Walters and Aaron Bocage, befriended me in the early 1980s when I was a teacher. Contact:

EDTECH
313 Market Street
Camden, NJ 08102
(609) 342-8277

Joline Godfrey runs business summer camps for teen women. For more information, contact:

An Income of Her Own
Joline Godfrey, Director
P.O. Box 987
Santa Barbara, CA 93102
(800) 350-2978

For information about entrepreneurship programs, contact:

The Kauffman Foundation
4900 Oak
Kansas City, MO 64112-2776
(816) 932-1000

and:

The Young Entrepreneurs of Kansas
Devlin Hall
1845 Fairmount
Wichita, KS 67260-0157

for a great program in the Midwest.

Chapter 19

FINANCING STRATEGIES THAT WORK FOR YOUNG ENTREPRENEURS

SHOULD YOU BORROW OR SELL?

> We [at Polaroid] grow and grow and grow not on the basis of the bottom line but on the basis of the faith that if you do your job well, the last thing you have to worry about is money, just as if you live right, you'll be happy.
>
> —Edwin Land (b. 1909)
> Founder of Polaroid, Inc.

Anita Roddick didn't expect The Body Shop, Inc. to change the cosmetics industry, be a force for social awareness, *and* make millions of dollars—but it has done all of these. The Body Shop would have never gotten that far, though, if Roddick hadn't sold half the company to her friend, Ian McGlinn, for his £4,000 (around $7,000) investment in her company. Local banks refused to lend Roddick money because she had been in business for only a few months. In return for his investment in Roddick's business, McGlinn received a share of The Body Shop's profits.

Today, McGlinn's investment is worth over £140 million (around $240 million). Roddick says she has no regrets. Without McGlinn's financing, she would not have been able to grow her company.

FINANCING

Financing is the use and manipulation of money. Raising money for a business is one aspect of financing.

If an entrepreneur cannot personally supply the necessary amount of money, another option is **other people's money** (OPM). There are two ways to raise OPM. Each affects a business differently.

1. **Debt.** The business borrows the money and pays it back over a set period of time at a set rate of interest. Corporations sell debt in the form of bonds. You could borrow money from family and friends to finance your business. Roddick was unable to raise any debt financing for her business so she turned to equity.

2. **Equity.** The business gives up a percentage of ownership for money. Like McGlinn, the equity investor receives a percentage of future profits from the business, based on the percentage of ownership purchased. Corporations sell equity in the form of stock. You cannot sell stock unless your business is incorporated, but you *can* sell equity. You can offer ownership and a share of your future profits in exchange for financing.

DEBT

To finance through debt, the entrepreneur borrows from a person or an institution that has money. The entrepreneur signs a promise to repay the borrowed sum with interest. That promise is called a **promissory note.**

Interest is figured by multiplying the **principal** by the interest rate. The principal is the amount of the loan, not including interest payments. If $1,200 is borrowed at 10 percent, to be paid back over one year, the interest on the loan is $1,200 \times .10 = $120.

One advantage of debt is that the lender has no say in the future or direction of the business as long as the loan payments are made. Another is that the loan payments are predictable.

The disadvantage of debt is that if the loan payments are not made, the lender can force the business into bankruptcy to get the loan back, even if that loan is only a fraction of what the business is worth. The lender can even take the home and possessions of the owner of a sole proprietorship, or of a partner in a partnership, as substitutes for the money owed.

Borrowing should be carefully considered by the beginning entrepreneur. It often takes a long time for a new business to show a profit. *The risk of debt is that failure to make loan payments can destroy the business before it gets the chance to prove itself.*

Advantages of Debt Financing (Loans, Bonds)

1. The lender has no say in the future or direction of the business as long as the loan payments are made.

2. Loan payments are predictable—they do not change with the fortunes of the business.

Disadvantages of Debt Financing

1. If loan payments are not made, the lender can force the business into bankruptcy.

2. To settle a debt, the lender can take the home and possessions of the owner of a sole proprietorship or a partner in a partnership.

EQUITY—EXCHANGING OWNERSHIP FOR CAPITAL

Equity means that, in return for money, the investor receives a percentage of ownership in the company. For the $1,200 investment we discussed above, an equity investor might want 10 percent ownership of the company, which would give the investor 10 percent of the business's profits. The investor is hoping that, over time, 10 percent of the profits will provide a high rate of return on the initial investment of $1,200.

The equity investor assumes greater risk than the debt lender. If the business doesn't make profits, neither does the investor. An equity investor cannot force a business into bankruptcy to get back the original investment. If a business is forced into bankruptcy by its creditors, they get paid off first from the sale of the business's assets. Equity investors have a claim on whatever is left over after debt investors have been paid.

Although the equity investor's *risk* is higher than that of the debt lender, so is the potential for *return on equity*. The equity investor could make the investment back many times over if the business prospers. For that reason, he or she accepts a higher level of risk than the debt lender. The debt lender's risk of losing his or her investment is lower, but so is the debt lender's return.

With equity financing, the money doesn't have to be paid back unless the business is successful. However, through giving up ownership, the entrepreneur can lose control of the business to the equity holders.

Advantages of Equity Financing (Stock, Percentage of Company)

1. If the business doesn't make a profit, the investor does not get paid. The equity investor cannot force the business into bankruptcy in order to get paid.
2. The equity investor has an interest in seeing the business succeed, and may, therefore, offer helpful advice and valuable contacts.

Disadvantages of Equity Financing

1. Through giving up ownership, the entrepreneur can lose control of the business to the equity holders.
2. Equity financing is riskier for the investor, so the investor frequently wants both a say in how the company is run and a higher rate of return than a lender.

FINANCIAL RATIOS

Large companies are usually financed by both debt and equity. The mix of debt and equity is grasped quickly by dividing equity into debt to obtain a debt-to-equity ratio.

The financial strategy of a company is expressed by its **debt-to-equity ratio.** If a company has a debt-to-equity ratio of one-to-one (expressed as 1:1), the company has one dollar of assets for every dollar of its debt.

$$\frac{\text{Debt}}{\text{Equity}} = \text{Debt-to-equity ratio}$$

Another ratio that gives a picture of financial strategy is the **debt ratio**—the ratio of debt to assets. A debt ratio of .50 means that every dollar of assets is financed by 50 cents of debt and 50 cents of equity.

$$\frac{\text{Amount of debt}}{\text{Amount of assets}} = \text{Debt ratio}$$

Example:

$$\frac{0.50}{1.00} = 0.50$$

Whether a ratio is good or bad depends on the amount of debt considered acceptable in a given industry. In general, however, companies with lower debt ratios are considered more solvent because they owe fewer creditors if they go bankrupt.

STEVEN JOBS: LOSING CONTROL OF APPLE

Relying too heavily on equity can be the downfall of a business owner. Steve Jobs, co-founder of Apple Computer, made that mistake. Because Jobs and his partner, Stephen Wozniak, were young men with very little money, debt financing was out of their reach. To raise money, they sold off chunks of the company.

By the late 1980s, Apple was very successful—so successful that Jobs was able to hire a prominent Pepsico executive, John Sculley, to take over as Apple's chief executive. Unfortunately for Jobs, Sculley set out to persuade Apple's board of directors that Jobs was a disruptive influence on the company. Eventually, a vote was taken. The number of votes each shareholder had was related to the number of shares he or she owned. Jobs didn't own enough of Apple's equity to fight off Sculley's effort to fire him. He was outvoted and thrown out of the company he had started.

ENTREPRENEUR STORY
DONALD TRUMP, DANGERS OF HEAVY
DEBT FINANCING

Companies that rely heavily on debt financing are described as "highly **leveraged.**" Leveraged means financed with debt. This financial strategy works well only when business is very good. When business is slow, debt payments are more difficult to meet.

Reliance solely on debt is very dangerous for a company. Creditors can force the company into bankruptcy or take over company property.

Businesses sometimes are in this predicament because the business owner has been unwilling to give up any control of the company by issuing equity and has relied too heavily on debt financing.

Real estate tycoon Donald Trump made exactly this mistake in the 1980s. Trump invested millions of dollars in revitalization of Atlantic City's gambling strip. He also bought New York's landmark Plaza Hotel and built Trump Tower, a skyscraper of ultraluxurious apartments purchased by oil sheiks and movie stars. As you'll see when we take a closer look at Trump's financing strategy on pages 256–259, by 1988, Trump owned some very valuable properties. He was also deeply in debt, however.

Trump did not want to give up managerial control by selling stock when he needed to raise money to build a new casino or buy a hotel. Because of his reputation, banks were willing to lend him a great deal of money. The lender banks took several of Trump's important assets and properties when the economy took a downturn in the late 1980s and he couldn't make his loan payments. Trump was forced by the banks to sell off his airline, Trump Shuttle, and some of his casinos. By pruning his real estate holdings and paying off some of his debt, Trump was able to make a comeback in the 1990s.

Evaluating Donald Trump's Financing Strategy

Below is Donald Trump's balance sheet (in millions) as of December 31, 1988.[1] Calculate the debt ratios for each of his properties, then answer questions 1 through 7.

| Assets | Millions of Dollars | | | |
	Estimated Worth of Assets	Debt	Net Worth	Debt Ratio*
Taj Mahal	$834	$834	$ 0	1
West Side Yards	480	172	308	_____
Trump Plaza Casino	637	273	343	_____
Trump Casino	606	410	196	_____
Trump Shuttle	400	400	0	_____
Trump Tower	200	100	100	_____
Cash	130	157	−27	_____
Trump Condos	111	6	105	_____
Marketable securities	88	75	13	_____
Trump Palace	77	77	0	_____
Trump Plaza	70	48	22	_____
Grand Hyatt (50%)	70	30	40	_____
Trump Regency	63	85	−22	_____
Trump Plaza Co-ops	46	0	46	_____
Trump Air	41	0	41	_____
Personal transportation	37	0	37	_____
Personal housing	30	39	−9	_____
Total	$	$	$	_____

$$*\text{Debt ratio} = \frac{\text{Debt}}{\text{Estimated worth of assets}}$$

1. What was Trump's highest priced asset?

2. What was Trump's net worth for the Trump Shuttle? Why?

3. On which asset was Trump's net worth the greatest?

4. Which asset carried the most debt?

5. Which properties did Trump own free of debt?

6. On which properties did Trump owe one dollar of debt for each dollar of the asset?

7. Why do you think Trump separately incorporated each of his properties?

ANSWERS: EVALUATING DONALD TRUMP'S FINANCING STRATEGY

The debt ratios for each of Donald Trump's properties as of December 31, 1988, were:

Assets	Estimated Worth of Assets	Debt	Net Worth	Debt Ratio*
	Millions of Dollars			
Taj Mahal	$ 834	$ 834	$ 0	1.00
West Side Yards	480	172	308	.36
Trump Plaza Casino	637	273	343	.44
Trump Casino	606	410	196	.68
Trump Shuttle	400	400	0	1.00
Trump Tower	200	100	100	.50
Cash	130	157	−27	1.20
Trump Condos	111	6	105	.05
Marketable securities	88	75	13	.85
Trump Palace	77	77	0	1.00
Trump Plaza	70	48	22	.66
Grand Hyatt (50%)	70	30	40	.43
Trump Regency	63	85	−22	1.35
Trump Plaza Co-ops	46	0	46	0
Trump Air	41	0	41	0
Personal transportation	37	0	37	0
Personal housing	30	39	−9	1.30
Total	**$3,920**	**$2,706**	**$1,214**	.69

*Debt ratio = $\dfrac{\text{Debt}}{\text{Estimated worth of assets}}$

1. Highest priced asset: The Taj Mahal.
2. The net worth for the Trump Shuttle was zero because it was financed completely with debt.
3. Asset with greatest net worth: Trump Plaza Casino.
4. Asset with most debt: The Taj Mahal.
5. Properties owned free of debt: Trump Plaza Co-ops, Trump Air, personal transportation.
6. Properties with dollar-for-dollar debt: The Taj Mahal, Trump Shuttle, Trump Palace.

7. Trump separately incorporated each of his properties in order to protect them from creditors. His creditors on The Taj Mahal, for example, could not force him to sell Trump Air to pay them. They could only force him to sell The Taj Mahal.

BUSINESS INCUBATORS

OK, so you're not Donald Trump, but you want some help starting up your business. Why not see whether there are any business incubators in your area? An incubator is a place that provides entrepreneurs with everything from office space to access to equipment like xerox machines, computers, and fax machines.

The West Philadelphia Enterprise Center (WPEC) is one such incubator. To Philadelphia entrepreneurs who qualify, it provides super-cheap office space. WPEC uses a scoring system to decide which entrepreneurs to take on—applicants are extensively interviewed to determine their commitment to their business idea, for example. Norman Bond and Keith Ellison qualified for WPEC assistance after Ellison completed a business plan and feasibility study for a new magazine, *Next Step: The International Diversity Guide.* In 1997, they moved into the incubator, paying only $165 per month for their office. That year, the magazine generated total revenues of $180,000. It's presently distributed in 500 bookstores nationwide.

Another incubator, The Business Development Incubator sponsored by the Temple University Small Business Development Center, works with entrepreneurs between ages fifteen and twenty-two. Entrepreneurs who qualify pay $25 a month for a desk and file space, a computer, a phone, and a fax. They also receive counseling and can attend entrepreneurship workshops and seminars.

To look for an incubator near you, start with your local universities and colleges. This could be a great option for you!

PLAYING WITH THE BIG GUNS:
VENTURE CAPITALISTS

If incubators are one end of the entrepreneurship spectrum, venture capitalists are the other. These are investors and investment companies whose specialty is financing new, high-potential entrepreneurial companies. Because they often provide the initial equity investment to start up a business, they are called venture capitalists.

Venture capital is the money given to a new venture by an investor. Venture capitalists are looking for a high rate of return. They typically expect to earn back, over a five-year period, six times the amount they invest. That works out to about a 45 percent return on investment. Professional venture capitalists won't usually invest in a company unless its business plan shows it is likely to generate sales of at least $25 million within five years.

Venture Capitalists Want Equity

Venture capitalists want **equity,** or some share of ownership, in return for their capital. They are willing to take the higher risk of losing their capital for a chance to profit from the business's success. Henry Ford turned to venture capitalists to finance the Ford Motor Company. He gave up 75 percent of the business for $28,000 of badly needed capital.

It took Ford many years to regain control of his company. Still, many small business owners have turned to venture capital when they wanted to start or grow a business and couldn't persuade banks to lend them money.

How Venture Capitalists Get Their ROI

Venture capitalists typically reap the return on their investment (ROI) in one of two ways:

1. The venture capitalist sells his or her percentage of the business to another investor.
2. The venture capitalist waits until the company "goes public" (starts selling stock) and sells his or her stock in the business on the stock market.

A Business Plan Is Necessary to Raise Capital

No matter whom you approach to raise money for your business, you'll need a business plan. Venture capitalists and bankers will refuse to see an entrepreneur who doesn't have a business plan—and your friends and relatives will be a lot more willing to lend or invest if you have a good plan. You may have a brilliant business idea, but if it is not set forth in a well-written business plan, no potential investor will be interested.

A well-written business plan shows potential investors that the business owner has carefully thought through the business. All investors—bankers, friends, family, neighbors, or venture capitalists—crave information. The more information you offer investors about how their money will be used, the more willing they will be to invest in your business. Your plan should be so thoughtful and thorough that the only question it raises in an investor's mind is: "How much can I invest?" Chapter 25, "How to Write a Super Business Plan," provides more detailed information on how to write a business plan.

Nearly all the young entrepreneurs profiled in this book succeeded, in part, because they wrote a business plan before they made a single sale. A well-written plan not only helps you raise money, it also guides you as you develop your business.

A sample business plan drawn from a real business run by a young entrepreneur is reproduced on pages 324–334. Following the sample are worksheets that will take you, step-by-step, through writing a business plan for *your* business. As you write the plan, problems you might not have thought of before will be uncovered. Working them out on paper will save you time and money. Before you serve your first customer, you will have answered every question that you might be asked. How much are you charging for your product or service? What exactly *is* your product or service? What is one unit? What are your costs? How are you going to market your product or service? How do you plan to sell it?

Questions like these can quickly overwhelm you if you start a business without a plan. By using the worksheets on pages 335–348, you will have both the answers you need *and* a rough draft of a business plan for your own business.

CASE STUDY: HOME-BAKED GOODS

Debbi Fields, of Mrs. Fields Cookies, Inc., built a multimillion-dollar business from cookies. Do you bake anything really well? Cookies? Banana bread? You can sell your home-baked goods at flea markets, garage sales, or school events.

When Fields was nineteen, she married an older man who was a brilliant economist. Being the wife of an older man who was getting a lot of attention for his career made Fields want to accomplish something, too. Fields had baked her popular chocolate chip cookies for friends and families since she was thirteen, so she decided to start a business selling her cookies to the public.

No one—not her family, not her friends, not even her husband—thought this was a good idea. Her cookies were soft and chewy, not crisp like store brands. They needed to be eaten fresh to taste their best.

Fields refused to abandon her idea, so her husband decided to give her his full support, even though he thought it would never work. The banker who had given her and her husband the mortgage on their house arranged a loan. He, too, told her that her business would never work, but he trusted the Fields to pay back the loan.

Fields opened a small store in Palo Alto, California, in August 1977. On her first day of business, she hadn't sold a single cookie by noon. Trying not to panic, Fields loaded up a tray with cookies and walked around the shopping arcade offering them to shoppers for free.

Her strategy worked: within an hour, customers were at her store buying cookies. She sold $50.00 worth that day and $75.00 worth the next. She was in business, and she had discovered a strategy. To this day, Mrs. Fields stores give customers free samples to encourage them to buy cookies.

The business grew rapidly, but most of the profits were earmarked to pay off bank loans used to open new stores. Despite her success, Fields constantly had to fight for financing from the banks. Again and again she was told that selling cookies was not a "real" business like selling steel or cars.

In 1986, her husband quit doing economic consulting and joined her business. Although the company was now profitable, bank loans were still needed to open new stores. The Fields were very tired of dealing with bankers so they set out to try to replace their debt financing with equity financing. They decided to sell shares in the company to the public and use the cash to pay off the banks and finance further expansion.

The Fields sold stock on the London Stock Exchange's unlisted securities market first, because this approach was easier and cheaper than selling stock on the American market. The stock was offered in London in the spring of 1986. It did not do well at first because the company was not that well known in Britain, but eventually the stock price did improve.

When the stock was offered in the United States the following year, it did very well. Today, Mrs. Fields Cookies is financed with a blend of debt and equity. The Fieldses have more flexibility than when they relied exclusively on debt financing.

Tips for Starting a Business with Home-Baked Goods

- Don't get too elaborate. Stick to one or two products that you can consistently make really well.

- Figure out your cost of goods sold—the cost of making one additional unit (your unit might be one cookie or one cake, for example). Set your price high enough to cover your cost of goods sold and your labor.

- Offer a baking service to busy families. Make up a flyer that advertises your service. You could offer to supply fifty cookies a week, for example.

- Buy ingredients in bulk at warehouse or grocery club stores. Bulk purchases are cheaper.

- Make your baked goods extra-irresistible by packaging them attractively. Tie a yellow ribbon around banana bread, or sell cookies in colorful boxes. Make up batches of special items around holidays—heart-shaped cakes for St. Valentine's Day, or green cookies for St. Patrick's Day.

- Give away samples to attract customers.

These tips also apply to businesses selling homemade soups, jams and jellies, or any other food item you might make that people really like.

RESOURCES

Books

A particularly good book on creative entrepreneurship financing is *Guerrilla Financing: Alternative Techniques to Finance Any Small Business* by Bruce Brechman and Jay Conrad-Levinson (Boston: Houghton Mifflin, 1991).

Another excellent resource is *Money Sources for Small Business: How You Can Find Private, State, Federal, and Corporate Financing* by William Alarid (Santa Maria, CA: Puma Press, 1991).

If you'd like to learn more about Donald Trump's flamboyant career, look for *The Art of the Deal* (New York: Random House, 1988), and *Surviving at the Top* (New York: Random House, 1990).

Debbi Fields tells her story in *One Smart Cookie* (New York: Simon & Schuster, 1987).

Other Resources

The National Association of Small Business Investment Companies is an association of companies that give financial assistance to small businesses. A membership directory is available for $1.00.

National Association of Small Business Investment Companies
1156 15th Street, N.W., Suite 1101
Washington, DC 20005
(202) 833-8230

Chapter

20

FROM THE WHOLESALER TO THE CONSUMER

TEST DRIVE YOUR ENTREPRENEURIAL SKILLS

Commerce is the great civilizer. We exchange ideas when we exchange goods.

—R. G. Ingersoll (1833–1899)
American lawyer

Chrissie had no room for a dog or cat in the basement apartment she lived in with her little girl, so she bought a fish. This gave the NFTE student the idea for a business she calls "The Best Pet." Chrissie brought home some brandy snifters from the distribution house for which she worked. She put some colored sand in each snifter and then added water and a fish that matched the color of the sand.

Chrissie took ten of her "Best Pets" to the flea market that her class was participating in at the Mall of America, in Minnesota. To her surprise, she sold all ten and received orders for four more. Today, Chrissie sells ten to twenty Best Pets a week while she attends technical college. Between attending college and taking care of her child, Chrissie can devote only a few hours a week to her business, but she estimates that those few hours bring her about four times more income than she would earn from a part-time job. Best of all, Chrissie can make her Best Pets while she's home with her daughter.

A flea market is a great place for a budding entrepreneur to test-market a product and launch a business. This chapter outlines how to buy goods from a wholesaler and resell them for a profit at a flea market. This experience will allow you to practice many concepts you have studied so far, including salesmanship, negotiation, and the preparation of an income statement.

FINDING A WHOLESALER

Wholesalers buy goods in large quantities from manufacturers and sell those goods in smaller quantities to retailers. If you live in a city, there will be wholesale stores close enough for you to visit in person. Find them by looking through your local *Business-to-Business Directory.* This is a Yellow Pages publication in which businesses advertise the products and services they offer to other businesses.

If you live in a small town or rural area that has no wholesale suppliers nearby, pick the major city nearest you and look in its *Business-to-Business Directory.* You can call wholesalers whose products interest you, and order goods from them through the mail.

In addition, NFTE is launching a wholesale catalog and mail-order business called NFTE On Broadway. Entrepreneurs who don't live near a wholesale district can use the catalog to order products for resale. The business is run by NFTE students, overseen by Janet McKinstry Cort of NFTE. The catalog includes a variety of products from New York City's wholesale district. All products are marked up only slightly from the original wholesale price. Young entrepreneurs are able to advertise their products in the catalog.

Another way to locate wholesalers is to contact manufacturers' representatives. To do so, write to or call the Manufacturers' Agents National Association. It can direct you to wholesalers in your area that carry the products you are seeking.

Manufacturers' Agents National Association
23016 Millcreek Road
Laguna Hills, CA 92653
(714) 859-4040

Most major product lines (lingerie, candy, and so on) have trade associations located in Washington, DC. These associations are listed in the Washington phone book and will be happy to tell you about wholesalers in your area. Most public libraries have phone books from around the country in their reference sections.

SELLING AT THE FLEA MARKET

A flea market is an open-air market made up of entrepreneurs who rent space by the day or by the season. The space may be free, on a first-come, first-served basis. More often, there is a fee for renting a space.

Traditionally, prices at flea markets are low. Consumers shopping at flea markets are looking for bargains.

You can get a list of flea markets in any community by calling the local Chamber of Commerce.

FLEA MARKET SALES RULES

1. **Arrive early to get a spot where as many people as possible will see your merchandise.**

2. **Have plenty of business cards and flyers to give away, even to people who don't buy anything.**

3. **Display posters or other eye-catching advertisements.**

4. **Bring plenty of change.**

5. **Keep track of your merchandise on inventory/record sheets.**

6. **Write a sales receipt for every sale.**

7. **Put on your "sales personality"—be outgoing and friendly.**

INVENTORY SHEETS

Use an inventory sheet to keep track of the sales you make at the flea market. An inventory sheet also shows at a glance how much profit you made on each sale. This record will make it easy to prepare an income statement for your flea market day.

Inventory sheets also keep track of the markup—the difference between what you paid for an item and the amount you get when you sell it—on each unit you sell. Markup is expressed as a percentage. To calculate markup, divide the wholesale cost per unit into the gross profit per unit and multiply by 100:

$$\text{Markup} = \frac{\text{Gross profit per unit}}{\text{Wholesale cost per unit}} \times 100$$

Chart 15 shows a sample inventory sheet. Notice how easily the income statement develops from the information on the inventory sheet. Remember: This information is for your eyes alone. *Never* place your records where your customers can see them.

TRADE SHOWS

Another great opportunity to sell may come with a trade show. A trade show is, in essence, an industry-specific flea market. Trade shows are usually run by industry or artist associations. For entrepreneurs who can't afford to—or don't want to—open their own stores, a trade show is an excellent way to show products off to store buyers.

FLEA MARKET INVENTORY SHEET (SAMPLE)

Product	A Units Sold (make mark for each sale)	×	B Wholesale Cost Per Unit	=	C Total Cost of Goods Sold	D Selling Price Per Unit	E (A × D) Total Sales
Hat	‖‖‖		$9.00		$45.00	$15.00	$75.00
Lipstick	‖‖‖I		.50		3.00	2.00	12.00

MY INCOME STATEMENT

My total sales are:		$87.00	($75.00 + $12.00)
My total cost of goods sold is:		−48.00	($45.00 + $ 3.00)
My gross profit is:		$39.00	($87.00 − $48.00)
My operating costs are:			
My fixed costs are:	$4.00		
My variable costs are:	0	$ 4.00	
My net profit/(loss) is:		$35.00	($39.00 − $4.00)

Chart 15 Flea Market Inventory Sheet and Income Statement

ENTREPRENEUR STORY
SUE SCOTT, PRIMAL LITE

Sue Scott[1] is a sculptor who made her living working in galleries, but really wanted to support herself with her art. She never thought of herself as the entrepreneurial type, but she knew she was unhappy with her life. One day, she experimented with putting a light in one of her sculptures. She was so taken with the result that she decided to go into business designing lights. She used her credit cards for the capital she needed to make samples of her novelty lights.

Scott named her company Primal Lite and went to trade shows to display her samples. Ninety-five sales representatives across the country snapped up her line of dinosaur, fried egg, lizard, and other lights. Today, Primal Lite's annual sales are almost $10 million.

To find out about trade shows in your area, call your local civic center. A schedule of upcoming trade shows should be available there. To learn about important trade shows in major cities, check out trade publications. Your public library should have a list of trade publications that you can contact. Local wholesalers and trade associations may also be able to direct you to information about trade shows nationwide.

CASE STUDY: PET CARE

Believe it or not, some very profitable businesses have been built around animal waste. In *Fast Cash for Kids,* Bonnie and Noel Drew report that Richard Scott started a "pooper scooper" business in Seattle. Richard launched Dog Butler when he was age twenty-four. Four of his employees pick up waste from 500 dogs at 160 homes and kennels. He charges $22 per month for each pet. That adds up to revenues of $11,000 per month!

If you love animals, there are lots of money-making services you can offer. Here are some ideas:

- **Dog walker.** Many people are too busy to walk their dogs every day. But you could walk several dogs at one time! Is there a dog run in your neighborhood park? Arrange to take several neighborhood dogs to the dog run each afternoon. This is a good way to meet more busy dog owners who might need your service!

- **Cleaning aquariums.** Fish tanks are beautiful but require regular cleaning and care. This service requires some knowledge about caring for fish. A fish tank is a delicate environment. If disturbed by the wrong chemicals, fish can die. This is a good business idea, therefore, only if you already love fish and are willing to learn to take care of tanks. You will need to know how to clean both freshwater and saltwater tanks. You will also need cleaning supplies and fish food.

- **Pet sitter.** You can take care of pets for people who are on vacation. Before accepting a job, though, go to the home and meet the pet. Make sure it's an animal you feel comfortable handling by yourself. Before the owners leave, ask how to contact them in an emergency. You should also get the phone number and address of the animal's veterinarian.

- **Pet grooming.** If you love to play with animals, pet grooming can be fun and profitable. Cats and dogs need regular baths and flea treatments. If you have a good pair of clippers and have learned to use them correctly, you can also offer haircuts for dogs. Veterinarians usually offer free booklets on care and grooming of pets. A veterinarian or pet store can direct you to the safest bath and flea products to use.

RESOURCES

Book

A great primer on how to enjoy selling (and buying) at flea markets is *The Flea Market Handbook* by Robert G. Miner (Rudner, PA: Chilton Book Company, 1990).

Other Resources

To familiarize yourself with the trade show universe, visit the Web site of George Little Management, which has been producing trade shows for a century, at www.glmshows.com/home/htm.

To find trade shows near you, visit the Trade Show News Network at www.tsnn.com or TS Central at www.tscentral.com.

You might also want to subscribe to *Trade Show Week Magazine*. Contact:

Trade Show Week Magazine
249 West 17th Street
New York, NY 10011
(800) 826-7887

Chapter 21

WHAT TO DO WITH YOUR MONEY

BANKING AND INVESTING

Put not your trust in money, but put your money in trust.
—Dr. Oliver Wendell Holmes (1809–1894)
American writer and physician

RULE 1: PUT YOUR MONEY IN A SAFE PLACE (NO, NOT UNDER YOUR MATTRESS!)

Every evening, after finishing his shift at a neighborhood supermarket, Damon would race home to work on his remote control car repair business. The colorful little cars were very popular with kids in Damon's neighborhood on Manhattan's Lower East Side, but they broke down a lot—which was good for Damon!

Damon repaired about twenty cars a week and charged $6 per repair. (Quick, what was his weekly revenue? Hint: Multiply twenty by $6.) He didn't bother to open a bank account because he didn't think he needed one. He cashed his supermarket check at a local check cashing office, and he conducted his car repair business entirely in cash.

But one day, when Damon got home, all the money he'd made repairing cars that week had been stolen. Damon opened a savings account the next morning—and we suggest you do the same!

When you have a bank account, you have a safe place to store your money. People who do not have bank accounts have to carry all their money around at all times or hide it where they live. Both solutions are risky and dangerous. Stick your hard-earned cash in a bank.

Your bank deposits are protected by the Federal Deposit Insurance Corporation (FDIC). Individual accounts are protected up to $100,000. This means that even if the bank goes out of business, the FDIC will replace your money, up to $100,000.

SAVINGS ACCOUNTS

The very first bank account you will need is a **savings account.** When you deposit money in a savings account, not only is the money safe, but the bank pays you interest. Savings account interest rates are usually quite low, but there is virtually no risk that you will lose your money. A savings account is a low-risk, low-yield investment.

A savings account also provides **liquidity.** Liquidity is the ease with which you can retrieve your savings as cash. You can withdraw your money from your savings account on any banking day without having to pay the bank anything. Many savings banks offer twenty-four-hour automatic teller machines (ATMs). Be aware, though, that you might be charged a fee when you use a cash machine that is not your bank's. Some banks charge as much as $1.50 to nondepositors who use their ATMs. If you think you will be using ATMs frequently, open your account at a bank that has convenient ATMs in your area, so you can use them for free.

To open your savings account, visit your local bank and bring along the money you wish to deposit. Bring your Social Security card. You will also need identification with your photo on it, such as a driver's license, state ID, or passport.

What's in it for the bank? Very simply, banks make money by charging higher interest rates for loans than they pay for deposits. A bank might pay you 4 percent interest on your savings, but charge 14 percent interest to someone who wants to borrow money. That 10 percent difference is the bank's profit.

CHECKING ACCOUNTS

When you start a business and can start depositing money fairly regularly, you should also open a **checking account.** Paying by check, not cash, is the professional way to do business. Checks provide a written record of every business transaction you make. It is also safer to carry checks instead of cash.

When you write a check to someone, that piece of paper tells your bank to pay the person the stated amount from your checking account. Each month, the bank sends you a statement, along with the actual checks (or front-and-back photos of them) the bank has paid. These canceled checks provide you with proof that you have paid your bills. Keep them for at least seven years.

Shop around carefully before you decide where to place your checking account. Different banks have different costs and requirements. Some demand that you keep a large minimum balance in your account. Others require a minimum balance for you to write checks for free. If your balance is lower than the minimum, the bank charges you a fee for each check. Look into what different banks offer. Choose the checking account that best suits your needs, or you could wind up paying expensive bank charges.

The Check

Chart 16 shows a typical check. The circled numbers correspond to these explanations:

1. **Your name and address.** When you open your checking account, instruct the bank to preprint these lines on each batch of blank checks that you order.

2. **Bank number and branch number.**

3. **Check number.** Preprinted on the checks (often beginning with 0001). Always use your checks in numerical order.

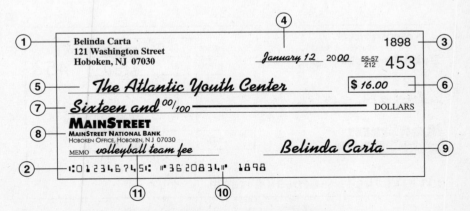

Chart 16 The Key Parts of a Check

4. **Date you made the check out to someone.**

5. **Payee.** The person or business to whom the money is to be paid.

6. **Amount of the check in numbers.** Be sure to start the amount right next to the dollar sign so no one can sneak in another number.

7. **Amount of the check in words, with the cents as a fraction of 100.** Fifty cents would be written as 50/100. Start writing at the beginning of the line. Draw a line to fill any space left after you have written the amount. These steps will prevent another person from altering the check. If the amount written in numbers differs from the amount written in words, the bank will pay the amount written in words.

8. **Drawee.** Your bank branch.

9. **Drawer.** You. The check is no good unless you sign here.

10. **Electronic scanning number.** Used by the bank to process your check.

11. **Memo.** You don't have to fill this in for the check to be valid, but it's a good place to write a reminder of the purpose of the check.

Depositing Your Money

To deposit money—cash and/or checks—in your checking account, fill out a deposit slip like the one in Chart 17. Simply write in the amount

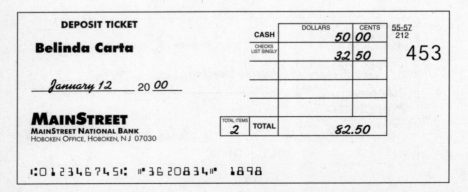

Chart 17 A Deposit Slip for Placing Cash and Checks into Your Checking Account

of cash and/or each check you are depositing, and the date of the deposit. You don't need to sign the deposit slip.

You do, however, need to sign the back of any checks you wish to deposit and write your account number on them. Your signature on the back of the check is called an endorsement. Underneath your endorsement and the account number, write "for deposit only," so no one can try to cash the check. Chart 18 shows a completed endorsement.

Writing a Check

NFTE Solutions, Inc. is a nonprofit organization established by Maximo Blake-DeCastro in the South Bronx, in January 1993, with support from NFTE and seed funding from the J. M. Foundation. Blake-DeCastro is well known for successfully putting high-risk youth to work and teaching them valuable job skills. Before founding his company, he trained New York State prison system convicts in building renovation and contracting.

When Max and I met, we realized there was a lot we could accomplish together. We started by providing his workers with an entrepreneurship education. In fact, the first lesson he taught was check writing. We include the basics of check writing here for those readers who need a brush-up.

Study the sample in the top portion of Chart 19. Then fill out the bottom check. Pretend you are paying a $37.50 phone bill to Bell Atlantic.

Before you write any checks, be sure you have enough money in your account to pay out the amount of the check. If any of your checks are rejected by your bank for having "not sufficient funds" (NSF), you

Chart 18 An Endorsed Check

	1898

January 12 20 _00_   55-57 / 212   **453**

The Atlantic Youth Center $ _16.00_

Sixteen and $^{00}/_{100}$ _____ DOLLARS

MainStreet
MainStreet National Bank
Hoboken Office, Hoboken, N J 07030
MEMO _choir dues_   Yolanda Baxter

⑆0⑈23⑈4⑉67⑈45⑆ ⑈3620834⑈ ⑈898

	1899

_____ 20 ___   55-57 / 212   **453**

$

_____ DOLLARS

MainStreet
MainStreet National Bank
Hoboken Office, Hoboken, N J 07030
MEMO _____

⑆0⑈23⑈4⑉67⑈45⑆ ⑈3620834⑈ ⑈899

Chart 19 Writing Checks Correctly Protects Your Money

will be charged a fee. If you are frequently listed as having NSF, it could negatively affect your chances to get a bank loan from your bank or any other.

ON-LINE BANKING

If you have a computer and are hooked up to the Internet, you can do all your banking—except for getting cash—from your computer. To bank on-line, you will need a **browser** that supports 128-bit **encryption.** A browser is software, such as Netscape Navigator or Microsoft Internet Explorer, that allows you to read Web documents. Encryption scrambles ordinary words and numbers using a secret code, to ensure that your on-line conversations with your bank remain private and confidential. If you are already surfing the Net, you are probably using a browser that supports 128-bit encryption. If not, you can go to Netscape's Web site and download the latest version of Netscape Navigator—for free! (Remember freeware from Chapter 15?)

The next step is to register with your bank's Web site. Most banks provide customers with a brochure that explains exactly how to do this. Be sure to find out how much the bank will charge for any on-line banking services you use. Some banks charge a monthly fee for you to pay bills on-line, for example.

To register, go to the bank's Web site and follow a series of steps. Within two weeks, you should receive your log-on ID by mail. The bank will also send your password in a separate mailing.

After you are registered, you can do many of these banking tasks on-line:

- **Pay bills.** You can arrange to pay your phone and electricity bills on-line, for example.
- **Transfer money from one account to another account.** Let's say you get home and realize you wrote a check but there's not enough money in your checking account to cover it. Yikes! With on-line banking, you can simply transfer some money from your savings account to your checking account to cover that check.
- **Send e-mail to the bank.** This is a super-fast way to get your questions answered.
- **Get information about your accounts.** See how much money you have. Which checks have been paid and which ones are still outstanding (unpaid)?

And the best thing? You don't have to wait on line when you bank on-line!

MAKE FRIENDS WITH A BANKER

Here's another great reason to open a bank account: Banks have money! Banks are a major source of business financing. You should begin a friendship with a kindly banker early in your business career. Most adults are happy to make time for a young person who turns to them for advice, and bankers are no exception.

One of my students opened a bank account when she started her lingerie business during her senior year in high school. Tanya bought lingerie from wholesalers and sold it at parties she threw for friends.

Tanya introduced herself to the manager of her bank and kept him up to date on her business as it developed. As a result, the manager recommended that she apply for a $4,000 college scholarship the bank planned to award to a local high school senior. Tanya won the scholarship, largely because she had such great recommendations from the bank manager and other adults she had met while conducting her business. If she ever needs a loan to expand her business, she probably won't have too much trouble getting one from her bank.

In *How to Get a Business Loan Without Signing Your Life Away* (Englewood Cliffs: Prentice-Hall, 1990), best-selling entrepreneurship author Joseph Mancuso says: "I recommend that you make your banker your best friend; in fact, start to think of him as the key person in your company. When you think about it, you will realize that your banker is really the key to building a good company, but too many of us do a poor job of cultivating this crucial relationship."[1]

Entrepreneur Story
Bart Breighner,
Artistic Impressions

Some people don't start their first business until they've tired of their career—but when they do, they find out how important their banker can be. Bart Breighner had spent twenty years with World Book, where he set many sales records and became executive vice president.

Breighner's hobby was collecting art. When he heard about companies that were selling original oil paintings and prints to customers through home parties, he became intrigued with the idea of entering this business but doing it on a much broader scale. He wanted to make a wider variety of art available and become the dominant company in the industry.

To finance his dream, Breighner went to his banker, whom he had known for many years. Breighner's banker raised over a million dollars in loans. He took a big risk because he hoped to reap a big reward.

Breighner started Artistic Impressions, Inc. in 1985. Today, the company's annual sales are roughly $20 million. Breighner was able to pay back the bank *and* send his kids to college!

Over 1,350 art consultants in 42 states sell art for Artistic Impressions. Because Breighner believes in entrepreneurship, his consultants are treated like the proprietors of their own small businesses. Breighner, who serves on NFTE's board of directors, has received national recognition from the Direct Selling Association for his efforts to encourage women and minorities to join his company. To underline their belief in entrepreneurship, Breighner and his consultants hold benefit art auctions for NFTE, donate a portion of their sales to us, hold a NFTE "Walk-A-Thon," and co-sponsor our Chicago program.

What About Credit Cards?

Once you hit age eighteen, you will probably be inundated with tempting **credit card** offers. Please remember that a credit card is not free money; it's a loan—usually at a sky-high interest rate. You might be tempted to use credit cards to finance your business, but this is a bad idea. A really bad idea! Why?

- Credit card companies charge very high rates of interest and you will soon find yourself trying to pay off a mountain of debt. The ideas in Chapter 19, "Financing Strategies That Work for Young Entrepreneurs" are much better.
- If you fail to make even one credit card payment, your interest rate may be jacked up even higher and the credit card company may report you as a bad credit risk. This can destroy your chances of ever getting a loan to sustain your business, to buy a house, to go to school, or even to buy a car. Very humiliating!

There is one excellent use for a credit card, however: Use it to make as many of your purchases as possible—and pay it off completely *every month*. The credit card company will send you, each month, a list of all your purchases. Use the list to keep an eye on your spending and to back up your financial records. The key phrase here, though, is "and pay it off completely *every month*." If you know you don't have the discipline to do this, don't get a credit card. Or, apply for an American Express card or another charge card that has to be paid off each month. (Thanks to Ed T. Koch and Debra DeSalvo's book, *The Complete Idiot's Guide to Investing Like a Pro*, Alpha Books, 1999, for this suggestion.)

Putting Your Money to Work . . . for You!

You know that you can work to earn money, but do you realize that money can work for you? Putting your money to work is called **investing.** Investing is putting your money somewhere because you hope to earn a rate of return.

When John D. Rockefeller was a teenager in the mid-1800s, he lent $50 to a farmer. After a year, the farmer paid him back the $50, plus $3.50 in interest. Rockefeller compared that to the $1.12 he had earned hoeing potatoes for an entire week for another farmer, and he decided he'd rather be an investor than a farmer. "From that time on I was determined to make money work for me," Rockefeller wrote in his autobiography, *Random Reminiscences.*

Rockefeller soon discovered that he could make his money grow really fast if he reinvested his returns. This is called compounding. **Compound interest** is the interest you earn on your interest.

If you put $100 in an investment that earns 10 percent, for example, you will have $110 at the end of a year. At that point, you have a choice: You can spend the $10 you earned, or you can reinvest it.

- If you spend the $10, you will once again have $110 at the end of the year.
- If you reinvest the $10, you will earn 10 percent on $110. This comes out to $11, so, by the end of the second year, you will have $110 + $11= $121.

If you keep reinvesting your earnings for 10 years, your original $100 will grow to $259.37. To see how we figured that out, check out Chart 20, which shows how much $1 will grow, depending on the rate of return and how many years it has been invested. If you look under 10 percent and across to 10 years, you will see the number 2.5937. One dollar, therefore, would grow to $2.5937 after being invested for 10 years at 10 percent. If you've invested $100, multiply $2.5937 by 100. Wow, now we're growing some money, using the magic of compounding!

Getting Started with Mutual Funds

Many types of investments are available, but stocks are among the most profitable over the long run. Stocks, as you learned in Chapter 17,

Periods (in years)	1%	2%	3%	4%	5%	6%	7%	8%	9%	10%	11%	12%
1	1.0100	1.0200	1.0300	1.0400	1.0500	1.0600	1.0700	1.0800	1.0900	1.1000	1.1100	1.1200
2	1.0201	1.0404	1.0609	1.0816*	1.1025	1.1236	1.1449	1.1664	1.1881	1.2100	1.2321	1.2544
3	1.0303	1.0612	1.0927	1.1249	1.1576	1.1910	1.2250	1.2597	1.2950	1.3310	1.3676	1.4049
4	1.0406	1.0824	1.1255	1.1699	1.2155	1.2625	1.3108	1.3605	1.4116	1.4641	1.5181	1.5735
5	1.0510	1.1041	1.1593	1.2167	1.2763	1.3382	1.4026	1.4693	1.5386	1.6105	1.6851	1.7623
6	1.0615	1.1261	1.1941	1.2653	1.3401	1.4185	1.5007	1.5869	1.6771	1.7716	1.8704	1.9738
7	1.0721	1.1487	1.2299	1.3159	1.4071	1.5036	1.6058	1.7138	1.8280	1.9487	2.0762	2.2107
8	1.0829	1.1717	1.2668	1.3686	1.4775	1.5939	1.7182	1.8509	1.9926	2.1436	2.3045	2.4760
9	1.0937	1.1951	1.3048	1.4233	1.5513	1.6895	1.8385	1.9990	2.1719	2.3580	2.5580	2.7731
10	1.1046	1.2190	1.3439	1.4802	1.6209	1.7909	1.9672	2.1589	2.3674	2.5937	2.8394	3.1059
11	1.1157	1.2434	1.3842	1.5395	1.7103	1.8983	2.1049	2.3316	2.5084	2.8531	3.1518	3.4786
12	1.1268	1.2682	1.4258	1.6010	1.7959	2.0122	2.2522	2.5182	2.8127	3.1384	3.4985	3.8960
13	1.1381	1.2936	1.4685	1.6651	1.8057	2.1329	2.4098	2.7196	3.0658	3.4523	3.8833	4.3635
14	1.1495	1.3195	1.5126	1.7317	1.9799	2.2609	2.5785	2.9372	3.3417	3.7975	4.3104	4.8871
15	1.1610	1.3459	1.5580	1.8009	2.0789	2.3966	2.7590	3.1722	3.6425	4.1773	4.7846	5.4736

To find the future value, take a given interest rate, go down the column to the correct number of periods, then multiply by the number you find.

*If you invest $1 at 4 percent for two years, it will be worth $1.08 at the end of that period.

Chart 20 The Future Value of $1 After "n" Periods

represent shares of ownership of corporations, but stocks can be risky, unless you can afford to buy a wide variety of stocks from many different high-quality companies. If you put all your money in General Motors stock, for example, and General Motors goes out of business, there goes all your money.

For this reason, many small investors buy into **mutual funds.** A mutual fund is a company that invests in a wide variety of stocks or other securities and then sells shares of *itself* to other investors. Buying into a mutual fund provides you with excellent **diversification.** Diversification makes investing less risky because your money is spread among many different investments. You would find it difficult to manage the amount of investments that most mutual funds make, so they are a convenient service as well.

Over the past seventy years, the Standard & Poor's 500 Stock Index, which tracks 500 stocks in the American stock market, has earned an average rate of return of 11 percent. If you had invested $1,000 in a mutual fund that bought those 500 stocks forty years ago, you would have $65,000 today—without having lifted a finger.

Author Barbara Beshel notes that if you invest $1 a day in an investment yielding 12 percent, you will have a million dollars in fifty years. Your total investment would be only $18,000! Her book, *Dollars To Dividends: How Any Young Adult Can Become A Millionaire By Investing Just $1 A Day* (Beshel, 1999), explains the details.

The Rule of 72

Use The Rule of 72 to figure out how long an investment will take to double. Simply divide 72 by the annual interest rate your investment is earning. An investment earning 10 percent, for example, will double in 7.2 years. If you invest $1,000 at 10 percent, you will have $2,000 in 7.2 years.

TIME IS ON YOUR SIDE, KID

You are especially lucky; you have time on your side. The sooner you start investing, the more magic compounding can work on your money. (Remember how powerful compound interest is!) The difference, in fact, between someone who invests briefly, beginning at age eighteen (Investor A in Chart 21) and someone who waits until age twenty-four and then invests annually (Investor B) is amazing.

Age	Investor A Investment	Investor B Investment
18	$2,000	$0
19	2,000	0
20	2,000	0
21	2,000	0
22	2,000	0
23	2,000	0
24		2,000
26		2,000
27		2,000
28		2,000
29		2,000
30		2,000
31		2,000
32		2,000
33		2,000
34		2,000
35		2,000
36		2,000
37		2,000
38		2,000
39		2,000
40		2,000
41		2,000
42		2,000
43		2,000
44		2,000
45		2,000
46		2,000
47		2,000
48		2,000
49		2,000
50		2,000
51		2,000
52		2,000
53		2,000
54		2,000
55		2,000
56		2,000
57		2,000
58		2,000
59		2,000

Total invested: $12,000
Total at age 60: $959,793

Total invested: $70,000
Total at age 60: $966,926

Chart 21 Comparative Patterns of Investing and Their Yield at Age Sixty

- **Investor A:** You get out of high school at age eighteen and start a small business. You're doing pretty well, and you manage to stick $2,000 per year into a mutual fund that earns 12 percent. You do this for six successive years, so your total investment is $12,000. By age sixty, your $12,000 investment will have grown to almost a million dollars ($959,793 to be exact)!

- **Investor B:** You get out of high school and goof off for a few years. You spend all your money on new clothes and going to clubs. Finally, at age twenty-four, you start investing $2,000 a year at 12 percent. You repeat that investment every year for thirty-five years. Your total investment is $70,000.

OK, here's the shocker: Your $70,000 investment will grow to $966,926 by age sixty. That's just about the same amount you would have had if you'd started at age eighteen and invested $58,000 less!! That's a lot of pizza.

Start investing as soon as you possibly can. Let your youth work for you, and your investments could grow tremendously! Investment advisers recommend that you invest at least 10 percent of your income. Get into the habit of doing that and you won't spend your life worrying about money.

Mutual funds will be delighted to send you information about investing in their funds. They can even set up programs that automatically deduct $50 or $100 from your savings account every month, so you don't even have to think about it. Here are a few contacts to get you started:

- Vanguard Funds: (800) 662-7447
- T.Rowe Price: (800) 638-5660
- Janus: (800) 525-8983

All the calls are free, but if you are under age eighteen, you will need a parent or guardian to approve any investments you make.

CASE STUDY: RESTAURANT DELIVERY SERVICE

From an investment point of view, you can evaluate every decision you make by asking one simple question: "If I invest this money [or time] this way, will my return on my investment be satisfying?" Going to college is an investment that can be analyzed this way. You spend your time and your money (or your parents' money) to get an education because you expect that this investment will increase your ability to make money in the future.

Some young entrepreneurs, however, have decided to skip or postpone college and invest in starting businesses instead. Kenneth Johnson's parents were not happy when he dropped out of Wichita State University, but now that his restaurant delivery business, Dial-A-Waiter, pulls in revenues of over $750,000 a year, they feel better!

Johnson noticed that few of the restaurants in Wichita delivered. He persuaded six Wichita restaurants to let him provide a delivery service for them. Today, he has ten drivers delivering food for forty Wichita restaurants. Johnson charges customers the menu price plus $6 per delivery. He also gets a 30 to 35 percent discount from the restaurants, so he gets to keep the difference between the menu price and the discount price.

Johnson is even developing a franchise—he charges $7,500 to show entrepreneurs in other cities how to start Dial-A-Waiter businesses. "I sort of created my own career," Johnson told *Forbes* ("The Tyranny Of The Diploma," December 28, 1998).

Other entrepreneurs have started successful businesses but still decided to go to college. John Magennis, 17, founded Internet Exposer Corporation, an Internet marketing company, when he was only 14. Although he earns $65,000 a year, he decided to go to Babson College to major in entrepreneurial studies. Why? "You need to have a minimum amount of certifications and credentials behind you," John told *Forbes*.

RESOURCES

Books

The Complete Idiot's Guide To Investing Like A Pro by Edward T. Koch and Debra DeSalvo (Alpha Books, 1999) is a very comprehensive resource for anyone just getting started with investing. Other good books on investing include:

The Only Investment Guide You'll Ever Need by Andrew Tobias (Harcourt Brace, 1996)

Investing For Dummies by Eric Tyson (IDG Books, 1997)

Barbara Beshel's book *Dollar To Dividends: How Any Young Adult Can Become A Millionaire By Investing Just $1 A Day* (Beshel, 1999) has great advice on picking mutual funds and developing an investment strategy.

These books explain how banks borrow and lend money and how compound interest works: *Capitalism for Kids* by Karl Hess (Chicago: Dearborn Financial Publishing, 1992); and *Making Cents: Every Kid's Guide to Money* by Elizabeth Wilkinson (Boston: Little, Brown & Co., 1989).

Other Resources

Don't forget *The Wall Street Journal!* As a budding entrepreneur, you should be reading it anyway, but it's also loaded with investment advice. To subscribe, call (800) 521-2170, ext. 247, or visit www.wsj.com.

If you are ready to apply for a bank loan, check out the list of the 187 most "small-business-friendly banks," in the July 1999 issue of *Entrepreneur* magazine. Your local library should have a copy.

Chapter 22

THE ENTREPRENEUR'S
GUIDE TO TAXES

HOW TO FILE THE APPROPRIATE TAXES FOR YOUR BUSINESS

To tax and to please, no more than to love and to be wise, is not given to men.

—Edmund Burke (1729–1797)
Irish philosopher and statesman

YOUR LEGAL OBLIGATION AS A SUCCESSFUL BUSINESS OWNER

Paying taxes is the last thing a struggling new business owner may want to think about. Neglecting your taxes, however, may cost you not only your business, but your business career.

David opened a small café near a college when he was twenty-two. He didn't set up his accounting system or apply for a tax ID number right away. He figured he'd have more time to do it once he got the business off the ground. Unfortunately, after his business had been open a few months, the State Department of Revenue (DOR) did a spot check and found that he was not collecting meals tax. The DOR closed his business and put liens on his personal assets. This meant the DOR could seize his personal belongings and sell them if David did not pay his tax bill. This derailed David's business career before he had gotten a firm start.

A **tax** is the percentage of your profit or income that you are required by law to pay to the government. The government uses taxes to support schools, the military, police and fire departments, and many other public services.

Most states impose an income tax. City and other local governments are supported primarily by taxes on property. The federal government is financed by personal and corporate income taxes.

SALES TAX

States usually raise money from a **sales tax** on the sale of goods (but generally not services). The sales tax is a percentage of the cost of the item sold and is included in the amount paid. In New York State, the sales tax is 8.25 percent. Tax on a $10.00 item is $0.83, so the total paid by the consumer is $10.83.

A SOLE PROPRIETOR PAYS INCOME TAX AND SELF-EMPLOYMENT TAX

You may already be paying income tax if you have a job. If your small business earns more than $400 a year, you will have to pay self-employment tax on your business income.

Income Tax

Tax forms are available at your local post office or bank. Forms can also be ordered from the Internal Revenue Service (IRS), which is the federal government agency responsible for collecting federal taxes. The IRS can charge you penalties and even put you in jail for **tax evasion**, if you fail to file tax returns.

You can call the IRS at 1-800-829-3676 to order forms, or visit the IRS Web site at www.irs.ustreas.gov/plain/. Your forms must be filed— sent to the IRS with your payment—by April 15 each year. You can file your tax return electronically with the IRS at www.irs.ustreas.gov /prod/elec_svs/index.html. Another option is to use one of the tax preparation software programs, such as TurboTax, which includes all necessary forms and enables you to file electronically. Another advantage of using tax preparation software is that if you use Quicken or another bookkeeping software, you can usually transfer data easily from your books directly to the tax preparation software.

Form 1040EZ

You will probably want to use Form 1040EZ for filing your income tax return. It is the simplest tax form to complete (see Chart 22 on pp. 290–291). To qualify for Form 1040EZ, you must:

- Be single and younger than age sixty-five.
- Have only one dependent (yourself) or be claimed as a dependent by your parents.
- Earn less than $50,000 gross income.
- Earn less than $400 in interest income.

Self-Employment Tax (Schedule SE)

When you work for an employer, the employer pays into your Social Security fund 7.65 percent of the amount of your income. When you retire, or if you become disabled and can no longer work, your employer's contributions to your Social Security fund allow you to receive an amount each month.

The federal government takes another 7.65 percent out of your earnings, as your contribution to your own Social Security fund. Between your contributions and those of your employer, your Social Security fund is paid 15.3 percent of your income each year.

If you are self-employed—running your own business, for instance—there is no employer to make Social Security contributions. You must make up the difference by paying self-employment tax. If you have net income from self-employment of over $400 a year, you are required to pay 15.3 percent of your business income to Social Security as self-employment tax. The tax form, shown in Chart 23 on pages 292–293, is called Schedule SE.

Profit or Loss from Business (Schedule C-EZ or Schedule C)

In addition to self-employment tax, you will pay income tax on your entrepreneurship income. If you had a profit, you can file Schedule C-EZ, shown as Chart 24 on pages 294–295. Alternatively, or if you are declaring a loss, you should file Schedule C, shown as Chart 25 on pages 296–297.

Form **1040EZ**

Income Tax Return for Single and Joint Filers With No Dependents (99) **1998**   OMB No. 1545-0675

Use the IRS label here

Your first name and initial   Last name

If a joint return, spouse's first name and initial   Last name

Home address (number and street). If you have a P.O. box, see page 7.   Apt. no.

City, town or post office, state, and ZIP code. If you have a foreign address, see page 7.

Your social security number

Spouse's social security number

▲ **IMPORTANT!** ▲
You **must** enter your SSN(s) above.

Presidential Election Campaign (See page 7.)

Note: *Checking "Yes" will not change your tax or reduce your refund.*

Do you want $3 to go to this fund? ▶ Yes ☐ No ☐

If a joint return, does your spouse want $3 to go to this fund? ▶ Yes ☐ No ☐

Dollars   Cents

Income

Attach Copy B of Form(s) W-2 here. Enclose, but do not staple, any payment.

1 Total wages, salaries, and tips. This should be shown in box 1 of your W-2 form(s). Attach your W-2 form(s).   1

2 Taxable interest income. If the total is over $400, you cannot use Form 1040EZ.   2

3 Unemployment compensation (see page 8).   3

4 Add lines 1, 2, and 3. This is your **adjusted gross income.** If under $10,030, see page 9 to find out if you can claim the earned income credit on line 8a.   4

Note: *You **must** check Yes or No.*

5 Can your parents (or someone else) claim you on their return?

Yes. Enter amount from worksheet on back. ☐

No. If **single,** enter 6,950.00. If **married,** enter 12,500.00. See back for explanation. ☐   5

6 Subtract line 5 from line 4. If line 5 is larger than line 4, enter 0. This is your **taxable income.** ▶ 6

Payments and tax

7 Enter your Federal income tax withheld from box 2 of your W-2 form(s).   7

8a Earned income credit (see page 9).
b Nontaxable earned income: enter type and amount below.

Type ___ $ ___   8a

9 Add lines 7 and 8a. These are your **total payments.**   9

10 Tax. Use the amount on **line 6 above** to find your tax in the tax table on pages 20–24 of the booklet. Then, enter the tax from the table on this line.   10

Refund

Have it directly deposited! See page 12 and fill in 11b, 11c, and 11d.

11a If line 9 is larger than line 10, subtract line 10 from line 9. This is your **refund.**   11a

b Routing number

c Type: Checking ☐   Savings ☐

d Account number

Amount you owe

12 If line 10 is larger than line 9, subtract line 9 from line 10. This is the **amount you owe.** See page 14 for details on how to pay.   12

For Official Use Only

1 2 3 4 5
6 7 8 9 10

Sign here

I have read this return. Under penalties of perjury, I declare that to the best of my knowledge and belief, the return is true, correct, and accurately lists all amounts and sources of income I received during the tax year.

Keep copy for your records.

Your signature   Spouse's signature if joint return. See page 7.

Date   Your occupation   Date   Spouse's occupation

For Disclosure, Privacy Act, and Paperwork Reduction Act Notice, see page 18.   Cat. No. 11329W   1998 Form 1040EZ

Chart 22 1040EZ: Use This Form to File Your Income Tax Return Before April 15

1998 Form 1040EZ page 2

Use this form if

- Your filing status is single or married filing jointly.
- You do not claim any dependents.
- You do not claim a student loan interest deduction or an education credit. See page 3.
- You had **only** wages, salaries, tips, taxable scholarship or fellowship grants, unemployment compensation, or Alaska Permanent Fund dividends, and your taxable interest income was not over $400. **But** if you earned tips, including allocated tips, that are not included in box 5 and box 7 of your W-2, you may not be able to use Form 1040EZ. See page 8.
- You (and your spouse if married) were under 65 on January 1, 1999, and not blind at the end of 1998.
- Your taxable income (line 6) is less than $50,000.
- You did not receive any advance earned income credit payments.

If you are not sure about your filing status, see page 7. If you have questions about dependents, use TeleTax topic 354 (see page 17). If you **cannot use this form,** use TeleTax topic 352 (see page 17).

Filling in your return

For tips on how to avoid common mistakes, see page 25.

Enter your (and your spouse's if married) social security number on the front. Because this form is read by a machine, please print your numbers inside the boxes like this:

9 8 7 6 5 4 3 2 1 0   Do not type your numbers. Do not use dollar signs.

If you received a scholarship or fellowship grant or tax-exempt interest income, such as on municipal bonds, see the booklet before filling in the form. Also, see the booklet if you received a Form 1099-INT showing Federal income tax withheld or if Federal income tax was withheld from your unemployment compensation or Alaska Permanent Fund dividends.

Remember, you must report all wages, salaries, and tips even if you do not get a W-2 form from your employer. You must also report all your taxable interest income, including interest from banks, savings and loans, credit unions, etc., even if you do not get a Form 1099-INT.

Worksheet for dependents who checked "Yes" on line 5

Use this worksheet to figure the amount to enter on line 5 if someone can claim you (or your spouse if married) as a dependent, even if that person chooses not to do so. To find out if someone can claim you as a dependent, use TeleTax topic 354 (see page 17).

A. Amount, if any, from line 1 on front _____

              +   250.00 Enter total ▶ A. _____

B. Minimum standard deduction . . . . B. _____ 700.00

C. Enter the LARGER of line A or line B here . . . . C. _____

D. Maximum standard deduction. If **single,** enter 4,250.00; if **married,** enter 7,100.00 . . . . D. _____

E. Enter the SMALLER of line C or line D here. This is your standard deduction . . . . E. _____

F. Exemption amount.
   - If single, enter 0.
   - If married and—
     —both you and your spouse can be claimed as dependents, enter 0.
     —only one of you can be claimed as a dependent, enter 2,700.00.   F. _____

G. Add lines E and F. Enter the total here and on line 5 on the front . . G. _____

If you checked "No" on line 5 because no one can claim you (or your spouse if married) as a dependent, enter on line 5 the amount shown below that applies to you.

- Single, enter 6,950.00. This is the total of your standard deduction (4,250.00) and your exemption (2,700.00).
- Married, enter 12,500.00. This is the total of your standard deduction (7,100.00), your exemption (2,700.00), and your spouse's exemption (2,700.00).

Mailing return

Mail your return by **April 15, 1999.** Use the envelope that came with your booklet. If you do not have that envelope, see page 28 for the address to use.

Paid preparer's use only

See page 14.

Under penalties of perjury, I declare that I have examined this return, and to the best of my knowledge and belief, it is true, correct, and accurately lists all amounts and sources of income received during the tax year. This declaration is based on all information of which I have any knowledge.

Preparer's signature ▶		Date	Check if self-employed ☐	Preparer's SSN
Firm's name (or yours if self-employed) and address ▶			EIN	
			ZIP code	

✆

Chart 22 (Continued)

SCHEDULE SE (Form 1040) Department of the Treasury Internal Revenue Service	**Self-Employment Tax** ▶ See Instructions for Schedule SE (Form 1040). ▶ Attach to Form 1040.	OMB No. 1545-0074 **1998** Attachment Sequence No. **17**

Name of person with **self-employment** income (as shown on Form 1040)	Social security number of person with **self-employment** income ▶

Who Must File Schedule SE

You must file Schedule SE if:

- You had net earnings from self-employment from **other than** church employee income (line 4 of Short Schedule SE or line 4c of Long Schedule SE) of $400 or more, **OR**

- You had church employee income of $108.28 or more. Income from services you performed as a minister or a member of a religious order **is not** church employee income. See page SE-1.

Note: *Even if you had a loss or a small amount of income from self-employment, it may be to your benefit to file Schedule SE and use either "optional method" in Part II of Long Schedule SE. See page SE-3.*

Exception. If your only self-employment income was from earnings as a minister, member of a religious order, or Christian Science practitioner **and** you filed Form 4361 and received IRS approval not to be taxed on those earnings, **do not** file Schedule SE. Instead, write "Exempt–Form 4361" on Form 1040, line 50.

May I Use Short Schedule SE or MUST I Use Long Schedule SE?

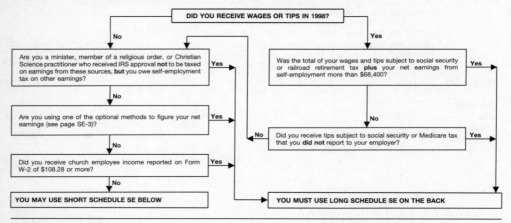

Section A—Short Schedule SE. Caution: *Read above to see if you can use Short Schedule SE.*

1	Net farm profit or (loss) from Schedule F, line 36, and farm partnerships, Schedule K-1 (Form 1065), line 15a	**1**
2	Net profit or (loss) from Schedule C, line 31; Schedule C-EZ, line 3; Schedule K-1 (Form 1065), line 15a (other than farming); and Schedule K-1 (Form 1065-B), box 9. Ministers and members of religious orders, see page SE-1 for amounts to report on this line. See page SE-2 for other income to report	**2**
3	Combine lines 1 and 2	**3**
4	**Net earnings from self-employment.** Multiply line 3 by 92.35% (.9235). If less than $400, **do not** file this schedule; you do not owe self-employment tax . . . . ▶	**4**
5	**Self-employment tax.** If the amount on line 4 is: • $68,400 or less, multiply line 4 by 15.3% (.153). Enter the result here and on **Form 1040, line 50.** • More than $68,400, multiply line 4 by 2.9% (.029). Then, add $8,481.60 to the result. Enter the total here and on **Form 1040, line 50.**	**5**
6	**Deduction for one-half of self-employment tax.** Multiply line 5 by 50% (.5). Enter the result here and on **Form 1040, line 27**	**6**	

For Paperwork Reduction Act Notice, see Form 1040 instructions.   Cat. No. 11358Z   Schedule SE (Form 1040) 1998

Chart 23 As a Self-Employed Entrepreneur, You File Your Social Security Tax on Schedule SE

Schedule SE (Form 1040) 1998   Attachment Sequence No. **17**   Page **2**

Name of person with **self-employment** income (as shown on Form 1040)	Social security number of person with **self-employment** income ▶	

Section B—Long Schedule SE

Part I   Self-Employment Tax

Note: *If your only income subject to self-employment tax is **church employee income**, skip lines 1 through 4b. Enter -0- on line 4c and go to line 5a. Income from services you performed as a minister or a member of a religious order **is not** church employee income. See page SE-1.*

A   If you are a minister, member of a religious order, or Christian Science practitioner **and** you filed Form 4361, but you had $400 or more of **other** net earnings from self-employment, check here and continue with Part I. . . . . . . ▶ ☐

1	Net farm profit or (loss) from Schedule F, line 36, and farm partnerships, Schedule K-1 (Form 1065), line 15a. **Note:** *Skip this line if you use the farm optional method. See page SE-4*	**1**	
2	Net profit or (loss) from Schedule C, line 31; Schedule C-EZ, line 3; Schedule K-1 (Form 1065), line 15a (other than farming); and Schedule K-1 (Form 1065-B), box 9. Ministers and members of religious orders, see page SE-1 for amounts to report on this line. See page SE-2 for other income to report. **Note:** *Skip this line if you use the nonfarm optional method. See page SE-4* .	**2**	
3	Combine lines 1 and 2	**3**	
4a	If line 3 is more than zero, multiply line 3 by 92.35% (.9235). Otherwise, enter amount from line 3	**4a**	
b	If you elected one or both of the optional methods, enter the total of lines 15 and 17 here . .	**4b**	
c	Combine lines 4a and 4b. If less than $400, **do not** file this schedule; you do not owe self-employment tax. **Exception.** If less than $400 and you had **church employee income,** enter -0- and continue ▶	**4c**	
5a	Enter your **church employee income** from Form W-2. **Caution:** *See page SE-1 for definition of church employee income* **5a**		
b	Multiply line 5a by 92.35% (.9235). If less than $100, enter -0- . .	**5b**	
6	**Net earnings from self-employment.** Add lines 4c and 5b . . .	**6**	
7	Maximum amount of combined wages and self-employment earnings subject to social security tax or the 6.2% portion of the 7.65% railroad retirement (tier 1) tax for 1998	**7**	68,400 00
8a	Total social security wages and tips (total of boxes 3 and 7 on Form(s) W-2) and railroad retirement (tier 1) compensation **8a**		
b	Unreported tips subject to social security tax (from Form 4137, line 9) **8b**		
c	Add lines 8a and 8b	**8c**	
9	Subtract line 8c from line 7. If zero or less, enter -0- here and on line 10 and go to line 11 . ▶	**9**	
10	Multiply the **smaller** of line 6 or line 9 by 12.4% (.124)	**10**	
11	Multiply line 6 by 2.9% (.029)	**11**	
12	**Self-employment tax.** Add lines 10 and 11. Enter here and on **Form 1040, line 50**	**12**	
13	**Deduction for one-half of self-employment tax.** Multiply line 12 by 50% (.5). Enter the result here and on **Form 1040, line 27** **13**		

Part II   Optional Methods To Figure Net Earnings (See page SE-3.)

Farm Optional Method. You may use this method **only** if:
- Your gross farm income[1] was not more than $2,400, **or**
- Your gross farm income[1] was more than $2,400 and your net farm profits[2] were less than $1,733.

14	Maximum income for optional methods	**14**	1,600 00
15	Enter the **smaller** of: two-thirds (⅔) of gross farm income[1] (not less than zero) **or** $1,600. Also, include this amount on line 4b above	**15**	

Nonfarm Optional Method. You may use this method **only** if:
- Your net nonfarm profits[3] were less than $1,733 and also less than 72.189% of your gross nonfarm income,[4] **and**
- You had net earnings from self-employment of at least $400 in 2 of the prior 3 years.

Caution: *You may use this method no more than five times.*

16	Subtract line 15 from line 14	**16**	
17	Enter the **smaller** of: two-thirds (⅔) of gross nonfarm income[4] (not less than zero) **or** the amount on line 16. Also, include this amount on line 4b above	**17**	

[1]From Sch. F, line 11, and Sch. K-1 (Form 1065), line 15b.   [3]From Sch. C, line 31; Sch. C-EZ, line 3; Sch. K-1 (Form 1065), line 15a; and Sch. K-1 (Form 1065-B), box 9.
[2]From Sch. F, line 36, and Sch. K-1 (Form 1065), line 15a.   [4]From Sch. C, line 7; Sch. C-EZ, line 1; Sch. K-1 (Form 1065), line 15c; and Sch. K-1 (Form 1065-B), box 9.

⊛

Chart 23 (Continued)

SCHEDULE C-EZ
(Form 1040)

Department of the Treasury
Internal Revenue Service   (99)

Net Profit From Business

(Sole Proprietorship)

▶ Partnerships, joint ventures, etc., must file Form 1065 or 1065-B.

▶ Attach to Form 1040 or Form 1041. ▶ See instructions on back.

OMB No. 1545-0074

1999

Attachment
Sequence No. **09A**

Name of proprietor

Social security number (SSN)

Part I   General Information

You May Use
Schedule C-EZ
Instead of
Schedule C
Only If You:

- Had business expenses of $2,500 or less.
- Use the cash method of accounting.
- Did not have an inventory at any time during the year.
- Did not have a net loss from your business.
- Had only one business as a sole proprietor.

And You:

- Had no employees during the year.
- Are not required to file **Form 4562**, Depreciation and Amortization, for this business. See the instructions for Schedule C, line 13, on page C-3 to find out if you must file.
- Do not deduct expenses for business use of your home.
- Do not have prior year unallowed passive activity losses from this business.

A Principal business or profession, including product or service

B Enter code from pages C-8 & 9
▶

C Business name. If no separate business name, leave blank.

D Employer ID number (EIN), if any

E Business address (including suite or room no.). Address not required if same as on Form 1040, page 1.

City, town or post office, state, and ZIP code

Part II   Figure Your Net Profit

1   **Gross receipts. Caution:** *If this income was reported to you on Form W-2 and the "Statutory employee" box on that form was checked, see **Statutory Employees** in the instructions for Schedule C, line 1, on page C-2 and check here* . . . . ▶ ☐ | **1**

2   **Total expenses.** If more than $2,500, you **must** use Schedule C. See instructions . . . . . | **2**

3   **Net profit.** Subtract line 2 from line 1. If less than zero, you **must** use Schedule C. Enter on **Form 1040, line 12,** and ALSO on **Schedule SE, line 2.** (Statutory employees **do not** report this amount on Schedule SE, line 2. Estates and trusts, enter on Form 1041, line 3.) . . . . . | **3**

Part III   **Information on Your Vehicle.** Complete this part **ONLY** if you are claiming car or truck expenses on line 2.

4   When did you place your vehicle in service for business purposes? (month, day, year) ▶ ..../......../........ .

5   Of the total number of miles you drove your vehicle during 1999, enter the number of miles you used your vehicle for:

a Business .... b Commuting .... c Other ....

6   Do you (or your spouse) have another vehicle available for personal use? . . . .   ☐ Yes ☐ No

7   Was your vehicle available for use during off-duty hours? . . . .   ☐ Yes ☐ No

8a Do you have evidence to support your deduction? . . . .   ☐ Yes ☐ No

b If "Yes," is the evidence written? . . . .   ☐ Yes ☐ No

For Paperwork Reduction Act Notice, see Form 1040 instructions.   Cat. No. 14374D   **Schedule C-EZ (Form 1040) 1999**

Chart 24 Use This Schedule for a Sole Proprietorship

Instructions

You may use Schedule C-EZ instead of Schedule C if you operated a business or practiced a profession as a sole proprietorship and you have met all the requirements listed in Part I of Schedule C-EZ.

Line A

Describe the business or professional activity that provided your principal source of income reported on line 1. Give the general field or activity and the type of product or service.

Line B

Enter the six-digit code that identifies your principal business or professional activity. See pages C-8 and C-9 for the list of codes.

Line D

You need an employer identification number (EIN) only if you had a Keogh plan or were required to file an employment, excise, estate, trust, or alcohol, tobacco, and firearms tax return. If you need an EIN, file **Form SS-4,** Application for Employer Identification Number. If you do not have an EIN, leave line D blank. **Do not** enter your SSN.

Line E

Enter your business address. Show a street address instead of a box number. Include the suite or room number, if any.

Line 1

Enter gross receipts from your trade or business. Include amounts you received in your trade or business that were properly shown on **Forms 1099-MISC.** If the total amounts that were reported in box 7 of Forms 1099-MISC are more than the total you are reporting on line 1, attach a statement explaining the difference. You must show all items of taxable income actually or constructively received during the year (in cash, property, or services). Income is constructively received when it is credited to your account or set aside for you to use. Do not offset this amount by any losses.

Line 2

Enter the total amount of all deductible business expenses you actually paid during the year. Examples of these expenses include advertising, car and truck expenses, commissions and fees, insurance, interest, legal and professional services, office expense, rent or lease expenses, repairs and maintenance, supplies, taxes, travel, the allowable percentage of business meals and entertainment, and utilities (including telephone). For details, see the instructions for Schedule C, Parts II and V, on pages C-3 through C-7. If you wish, you may use the optional worksheet below to record your expenses.

If you claim car or truck expenses, be sure to complete Part III of Schedule C-EZ.

Optional Worksheet for Line 2 (keep a copy for your records)

a Business meals and entertainment	**a**				
b Enter nondeductible amount included on line **a** (see the instructions for lines 24b and 24c on page C-5)	**b**				
c Deductible business meals and entertainment. Subtract line **b** from line **a**	**c**				
d	**d**				
e	**e**				
f	**f**				
g	**g**				
h	**h**				
i	**i**				
j **Total.** Add lines **c** through **i.** Enter here and on line 2	**j**				

Schedule C-EZ (Form 1040) 1999

⊛

Chart 24 (Continued)

SCHEDULE C
(Form 1040)

Department of the Treasury
Internal Revenue Service   (99)

Profit or Loss From Business

(Sole Proprietorship)

▶ Partnerships, joint ventures, etc., must file Form 1065 or Form 1065-B.

▶ Attach to Form 1040 or Form 1041.   ▶ See Instructions for Schedule C (Form 1040).

OMB No. 1545-0074

19**98**

Attachment
Sequence No. **09**

Name of proprietor

Social security number (SSN)

A	Principal business or profession, including product or service (see page C-1)	**B** Enter NEW code from pages C-8 & 9 ▶
C	Business name. If no separate business name, leave blank.	**D** Employer ID number (EIN), if any

E Business address (including suite or room no.) ▶ ....
City, town or post office, state, and ZIP code

F Accounting method: **(1)** ☐ Cash **(2)** ☐ Accrual **(3)** ☐ Other (specify) ▶ ....

G Did you "materially participate" in the operation of this business during 1998? If "No," see page C-2 for limit on losses   ☐ Yes ☐ No

H If you started or acquired this business during 1998, check here . . . . ▶ ☐

Part I   Income

1	Gross receipts or sales. **Caution:** If this income was reported to you on Form W-2 and the "Statutory employee" box on that form was checked, see page C-3 and check here . . . . ▶ ☐	1
2	Returns and allowances	2
3	Subtract line 2 from line 1	3
4	Cost of goods sold (from line 42 on page 2)	4
5	**Gross profit.** Subtract line 4 from line 3	5
6	Other income, including Federal and state gasoline or fuel tax credit or refund (see page C-3) . . .	6
7	**Gross income.** Add lines 5 and 6 . . . . ▶	7

Part II   Expenses. Enter expenses for business use of your home **only** on line 30.

8	Advertising	8		19 Pension and profit-sharing plans	19
9	Bad debts from sales or services (see page C-3) . .	9		20 Rent or lease (see page C-5):	
				a Vehicles, machinery, and equipment .	20a
10	Car and truck expenses (see page C-3)	10		b Other business property . .	20b
11	Commissions and fees . . .	11		21 Repairs and maintenance . .	21
12	Depletion	12		22 Supplies (not included in Part III) .	22
13	Depreciation and section 179 expense deduction (not included in Part III) (see page C-4) . .	13		23 Taxes and licenses	23
				24 Travel, meals, and entertainment:	
				a Travel	24a
14	Employee benefit programs (other than on line 19) . . .	14		b Meals and entertainment . .	
15	Insurance (other than health) .	15		c Enter 50% of line 24b subject to limitations (see page C-6) .	
16	Interest:				
a	Mortgage (paid to banks, etc.) .	16a		d Subtract line 24c from line 24b	24d
b	Other	16b		25 Utilities	25
17	Legal and professional services	17		26 Wages (less employment credits) .	26
18	Office expense	18		27 Other expenses (from line 48 on page 2)	27

28	**Total expenses** before expenses for business use of home. Add lines 8 through 27 in columns ▶	28
29	Tentative profit (loss). Subtract line 28 from line 7	29
30	Expenses for business use of your home. Attach **Form 8829**	30
31	**Net profit or (loss).** Subtract line 30 from line 29.	
	• If a profit, enter on **Form 1040, line 12,** and ALSO on **Schedule SE, line 2** (statutory employees, see page C-6). Estates and trusts, enter on Form 1041, line 3.	31
	• If a loss, you MUST go on to line 32.	
32	If you have a loss, check the box that describes your investment in this activity (see page C-6).	
	• If you checked 32a, enter the loss on **Form 1040, line 12,** and ALSO on **Schedule SE, line 2** (statutory employees, see page C-6). Estates and trusts, enter on Form 1041, line 3.	32a ☐ All investment is at risk. 32b ☐ Some investment is not at risk.
	• If you checked 32b, you MUST attach **Form 6198.**	

For Paperwork Reduction Act Notice, see Form 1040 instructions.   Cat. No. 11334P   Schedule C (Form 1040) 1998

Chart 25 Your Profit or Loss from Your Single-Owner Business Is Recorded on Schedule C and Filed with Your Tax Return

Schedule C (Form 1040) 1998   Page **2**

Part III	Cost of Goods Sold (see page C-7)

33 Method(s) used to
value closing inventory: **a** ☐ Cost   **b** ☐ Lower of cost or market   **c** ☐ Other (attach explanation)

34 Was there any change in determining quantities, costs, or valuations between opening and closing inventory? If
"Yes," attach explanation . . . . ☐ **Yes**   ☐ **No**

35	Inventory at beginning of year. If different from last year's closing inventory, attach explanation . .	**35**	
36	Purchases less cost of items withdrawn for personal use	**36**	
37	Cost of labor. Do not include any amounts paid to yourself	**37**	
38	Materials and supplies	**38**	
39	Other costs	**39**	
40	Add lines 35 through 39	**40**	
41	Inventory at end of year	**41**	
42	**Cost of goods sold.** Subtract line 41 from line 40. Enter the result here and on page 1, line 4 . .	**42**	

Part IV	Information on Your Vehicle. Complete this part **ONLY** if you are claiming car or truck expenses on line 10 and are not required to file Form 4562 for this business. See the instructions for line 13 on page C-4 to find out if you must file.

43 When did you place your vehicle in service for business purposes? (month, day, year) ▶ ..../.........../.......... .

44 Of the total number of miles you drove your vehicle during 1998, enter the number of miles you used your vehicle for:

a Business ....   **b** Commuting ....   **c** Other ....

45 Do you (or your spouse) have another vehicle available for personal use? . . . . ☐ **Yes**   ☐ **No**

46 Was your vehicle available for use during off-duty hours? . . . . ☐ **Yes**   ☐ **No**

47a Do you have evidence to support your deduction? . . . . ☐ **Yes**   ☐ **No**

  b If "Yes," is the evidence written? . . . . ☐ **Yes**   ☐ **No**

Part V	Other Expenses. List below business expenses not included on lines 8–26 or line 30.

....		
....		
....		
....		
....		
....		
....		
48 **Total other expenses.** Enter here and on page 1, line 27	**48**	

✲

Chart 25 (Continued)

THE IRS CAN HELP

The tax code is very complex. The IRS offers booklets and telephone service to help answer questions. Help with the Form 1040 is available from 1-800-424-1040. You can also go to the IRS office in your town and meet with an IRS agent, who will guide you through the forms for free. You must obtain new forms and booklets each year. Rules, rates, and forms change from one year to the next.

HELP YOURSELF BY KEEPING GOOD RECORDS

You can make filing your taxes easier by keeping good records throughout the year. You will have to determine your net income. If you have kept your ledger of income and expenses up to date, this should not be too difficult.

When in doubt, call the IRS or visit an accountant or tax preparation office, such as H&R Block. Mistakes on your tax return could cause the IRS to **audit** you. That means the IRS will send an agent to your business to examine your ledgers, receipts, and invoices and to make sure your taxes were filed correctly.

Always fully comply with the IRS by keeping good records and filing your return and paying your taxes on time. Audits are nerve-wracking and time-consuming.

EVALUATING TAXES

Tax forms and laws are confusing, and they change frequently. People do not agree on who should pay taxes and what government programs and services taxes should support. As a taxpayer, you have the right to ask these questions:

- Where are my tax dollars going?
- Are my tax dollars supporting services that will benefit me and my community?
- Am I paying taxes to support services that could be better supplied by private industry than by the government?
- Are the tax rates fair?

Taxpayers demand answers to these questions from the politicians who represent them in city councils, state legislatures, and the U.S. Congress. One of the most important jobs politicians do each year is figure government budgets and then determine how much to tax people to finance those budgets. They also pass laws to change the tax code.

ARGUMENTS FOR LOWER TAXES AND FOR SIMPLIFYING THE TAX CODE

Many Americans believe taxes are too high and tax rates are unfair. They are putting pressure on politicians to respond to these concerns.

Many business owners argue that the tax laws are so complicated and the rates are so high that people are afraid to start new businesses. The U.S. tax code now runs to 38,000 pages. The tax code also changes all the time, making it difficult for small business owners to handle their taxes without the expensive aid of accountants. This is one of my pet peeves, too. I believe the complexity of the tax code, combined with high tax rates, discourages low- to middle-income people from starting new businesses. It encourages others to start businesses but keep them underground. I have testified before the National Commission on Economic Growth and Tax Reform, headed by Jack Kemp and Ted Forstmann, on this subject. I told the Commission that both the complexity of the tax code and the high rates of taxation do more to prevent people from rising out of poverty through entrepreneurship than almost anything else.

Some business owners argue that many of the services that various levels of government provide—such as the U.S. Postal Service, or garbage collection—could be supplied more efficiently by private industry. This transfer would lower taxes. Business owners also argue that the government should make the tax code easier to understand and should make it easier for would-be entrepreneurs to license their businesses and pay their taxes.

CASE STUDY: WEB CONSULTING

Tom Whitnah never thought he'd make money doing something he loves so much—working with computers. At age seventeen, Whitnah turned his passion for computers into a home-based consulting company, Vision Net Consulting. As a consultant, Whitnah teaches computer skills to adults and senior citizens. He also designs and maintains Web sites for local small businesses and nonprofit organizations.

Whitnah spread the word about his new business by volunteering his services to several community organizations. Through volunteering, he gained experience and built a client base. He designed Web sites for the City of San Carlos Youth Advisory Council and the San Carlos Senior Center. Whitnah's work on his high school's Web site even led to a job at a search engine company.

To learn more about running his business, Whitnah attended the NFTE BizCamp at Stanford University during the summer of 1998. There he met people who could help him with issues such as how to set up his record-keeping system and deal with taxes. At the BizCamp, Whitnah was introduced to the Microsoft/BizTech Online Program. He loved learning on-line and finished all twenty-five chapters in one night. Whitnah's obvious proficiency led NFTE to offer him a position as a NFTE instructor's teaching assistant.

Whitnah also loved Stanford University, and decided to study computer science there. His story reminds us that starting a small business can lead to brand new worlds with all kinds of exciting opportunities and challenges.

Taxes are just one of many complicated regulatory challenges an entrepreneur faces. Always take advantage of any opportunities you have—from taking an entrepreneurship course to attending seminars and volunteering. Odds are, you'll meet people who will become invaluable advisers for your business.

Tip

When you are self-employed, you are required to pay your taxes quarterly. Do it—it prevents you from building up a huge tax bill you can't afford.

RESOURCES

Books

There are lots of excellent books to help you with your taxes, including:

J.K. Lasser's Tax Reductions for Small Businesses (2nd Edition) by Barbara Weltman (Macmillan, 1997).

Doing Business Tax-Free: Perfectly Legal Techniques for Reducing or Eliminating Your Federal Business Taxes by Robert Cooke (Wiley, 1995).

Finance and Taxes for the Home Based Business by Charles Lickson (Crips Publications, 1997).

Other Resources

To tap into the Internal Revenue Service's massive and very helpful Web site, visit www.irs.ustreas.gov./plain/. There are even tax tips for small business owners!

For just about any other federal government document you could ever want to see, visit the FedWorld Information Network Home Page at www.fedworld.gov.

Chapter 23

REPLICATING YOUR BUSINESS IDEA

FRANCHISING AND LICENSING

Nothing in the world can take the place of persistence. Talent will not; nothing is more common than unsuccessful men with talent. Genius will not; the world is full of educated derelicts. Persistence and determination alone are omnipotent.

—Ray Kroc (1902–1984)
Founder of McDonald's

FRANCHISING

As an entrepreneur, you might develop a business that could be reproduced or replicated. In that event, you could franchise your business and reap the rewards of all your hard work. A **franchise** is a business that markets a product or service in the manner prescribed by the person who developed the business.

Cloning an Organization: McDonald's

McDonald's restaurants are examples of franchises. McDonald's was developed by Ray Kroc, who had persuaded the McDonald brothers to let him become the franchising agent for their highly successful hamburger restaurant in San Bernardino, California. Kroc's great insight was to realize that the **franchisees**—the people who bought McDonald's franchises—needed extensive training and support in order to make the food taste just like the food from the original restaurant. Kroc timed everything. McDonald's franchisees are taught exactly how many minutes to fry potatoes and when to turn a burger. They are also taught precisely how to greet customers and handle orders.

A McDonald's franchisee owns the restaurant, but agrees to market the food, under the McDonald's name and trademark, in the exact fashion developed by Kroc. This is spelled out in the franchise agreement. In return, the franchisee knows he or she is investing in a proven, successful business concept. The franchisee also benefits from use of the McDonald's trademark, and from McDonald's management training, marketing, national advertising, and promotional assistance. McDonald's receives a franchise fee and royalties. A **royalty** is a percentage of the revenue generated by the sale of each unit.

Here are some sample fees, startup costs, and royalty fees for some popular franchises:

Franchise	Franchise Fee	Startup Costs	Royalty Fee
McDonald's	$22,000	various	4%
Arby's Inc.	$25,000–$37,500	$550,000–$887,500	4%
General Nutrition Franchising, Inc.	$17,500	$58,700–$137,500	5%
Hardee's	$15,000	$699,900–$1.7 million	4%

The Franchise Boom

Although franchising has been around since the Singer Sewing Machine Company first used it in the 1850s, its popularity has exploded in recent years. Many different kinds of businesses have been franchised—fast-food restaurants, auto repair shops, motels, health clubs, and hair salons.

Women and minorities have been especially drawn to franchises as a low-capital way to become entrepreneurs. Recognizing this, Burger King, Pizza Hut, Taco Bell, Kentucky Fried Chicken (KFC), and Baskin-Robbins all offer special financing and other incentives to recruit minority franchise owners. Other franchise programs have focused, with great success, on recruiting women.

Through franchising, Ray Kroc turned a simple idea—the fast production of inexpensive hamburgers—into an internationally recognized symbol of American enterprise. Today, franchising accounts for more than $800 billion in annual sales in a wide variety of industries.

A Word of Caution

Before you get involved in either franchising your business or becoming a franchisee, consult with a franchise attorney and do extensive research. Some eager franchisees have had bad experiences with franchisors who open too many franchises in an area or fail to honor the franchise contract. Before investing in a franchise, talk to other franchisees of the company you are researching. Ask questions such as: Are they happy with their sales? Are they satisfied with the level of support, training, and advertising provided by the franchisor? Get the answers to all your questions before you agree to become a franchisee.

LICENSING

Another way for an entrepreneur to profit from a business idea is through licensing. The difference between **licensing** and franchising is one of control. The franchisor controls every aspect of how the franchisee runs the franchise. It's all spelled out in the franchise agreement.

In contrast, the **licensor** grants the **licensee** the right to use the licensor's name on a product or service but has less control of how the licensee does business. The licensee simply pays a fee for the license and pays royalties to the licensor.

Licensing is only effective when the licensor is confident that his or her company name won't be tarnished by how the licensee uses it. When Coca-Cola licenses its name to a T-shirt maker, there's not much the T-shirt maker can do to tarnish the reputation of Coca-Cola. Coca-Cola gets free advertising, as well as royalties.

Coca-Cola would not license its name to a soft-drink manufacturer, however, because the licensing agreement would not guarantee that the manufacturer would make a product of the same quality as Coca-Cola's. If Coca-Cola wanted to expand in this fashion, it would be better served by a franchising agreement.

Fashion designers and celebrities have made millions by licensing their famous names for use on perfumes, athletic shoes, and other products. Licensing is subject to fewer government regulations than franchising.

CASE STUDY: ARTIST MANAGEMENT

Licensing is an important aspect of business for UP JAM Entertainment, a music management and production company that works primarily with hip-hop, rap, and R&B artists. UP JAM has secured product endorsement deals for its artists with NY, Lugz, Converse Sneakers, Oakley, Reebok, and Fox Racing.

UP JAM was founded in Philadelphia in 1989 by Jimmy Mac, 22. As a youngster, Jimmy excelled at bicycle racing and running. His success in these sports led to endorsement contracts with many top sporting goods companies. After high school, Jimmy began to pursue sports marketing and management as a career. His love of music, however, led him to realize that he could apply what he'd learned about sports marketing and management to management of artists.

Before he could do that, though, he knew he needed to learn more about starting and operating a business. He enrolled in the Young Entrepreneurs Program taught by NFTE at the Wharton School of Business. After achieving moderate success working with Philadelphia musicians, Jimmy decided to take his sharpened business skills to New York City. There, Jimmy began teaching and mentoring for NFTE.

While volunteering as a mentor/teacher with New York's Fresh Air Fund, he became friends with a fellow counselor. Joel, 23, had left IBM to pursue a career as a music industry executive. He was working his way up through the ranks at HUSH Productions, one of the top five African American entertainment firms in the country.

Joel and Jimmy formed a partnership and quickly began landing freelance work with HUSH. Soon, HUSH offered UP JAM its present subsidiary status. Under the deal, Jimmy and Joel not only oversee HUSH's rap and R&B divisions, they also have the freedom to sign and develop acts independently under the umbrella of their own company, which they have renamed Bulldog Entertainment. Their tremendous success illustrates some of the key concepts I have tried to get across in this book: Do what you love, educate yourself about entrepreneurship, and give back to your community through volunteering, teaching, or philanthropy. You never know whom you might meet!

RESOURCES

Books

The most complete reference book on franchising is the *Franchise Opportunities Handbook,* a U.S. government publication. It costs $15 and can be ordered by calling or writing:

> Superintendent of Documents
> U.S. Government Printing Office
> 710 North Capital Street, N.W.
> Washington, DC 20402-9325
> (202) 783-3238

Information Press publishes a directory of around 3,000 franchises. Contact:

> Information Press
> 728 Center Street
> P.O. Box 550
> Lewiston, NY 14092
> (716) 754-4669

NFTE's legal counsel, Andrew Sherman, happens to be an expert in the field of franchising and licensing. His well-known book, *Franchising and Licensing: Two Ways to Build Your Business* (New York: AMACOM, 1991), is an important resource.

Magazines

Entrepreneur magazine publishes an annual "Franchising Directory." Contact:

> *Entrepreneur*
> 2311 Pontius Avenue
> Los Angeles, CA 90064
> (213) 477-1011

Chapter 24

DOING GOOD IS GOOD BUSINESS

WHY SOCIAL ENTERPRISE WORKS

> Men who leave vast sums [at death] may fairly be thought
> men who would not have left it at all had they been able to
> take it with them. The man who dies thus rich dies disgraced.
>
> —Andrew Carnegie
> The richest man in the world in 1901, who gave away
> $350 million before dying in 1919

THE GOLDEN RULE

Are you suspicious of business owners? Do you sometimes wonder whether the price you are being charged for your sneakers or for a meal at a restaurant is fair? When you feel that a business has overcharged you or treated you badly, do you go back? Probably not.

Business success is not built by luring a customer in and taking as much of his or her money as possible. Success comes from **repeat business**—customers who come back again and again and tell their friends how wonderful your business is.

Ethical business behavior is not only morally right, it's good for business. Ethics are rules you can use to guide your behavior. The Golden Rule, "Do unto others as you would have others do unto you," is a famous ethic from the Bible. It can help you with any decision you face.

A few years ago, I was shocked to learn from a survey that most NFTE students from inner cities thought the entrepreneurs in their neighborhoods made ninety cents profit for every dollar that they took in. When my students learned that the profit earned by these shop-keepers and store owners was more like five to ten cents to the dollar, they realized how hard these people were working to earn a living.

Most successful entrepreneurs apply the Golden Rule. They are careful to run their businesses honestly and to treat their customers with respect—not only because it's the right thing to do but because it builds repeat business. However, many entrepreneurs have taken this concept a step further. They try to be good citizens in their communities by giving money and time to organizations that help people help themselves.

THE CONNECTION BETWEEN ENTREPRENEURS AND PHILANTHROPY

There is a long, proud connection in the United States between entrepreneurs and **philanthropy.** Philanthropy is concern for other beings, expressed through giving money to charities or foundations. Foundations are organizations that manage donated money and use it to finance programs that help people.

Each foundation has a mission. NFTE, for example, stands for the National Foundation for Teaching Entrepreneurship, and its mission is to teach young people how to become entrepreneurs. Companies that believe in our mission help us by donating money and expertise. Microsoft, for example, is helping us develop our on-line curriculum, BizTech, at www.nfte.com. Microsoft has donated both money and computer programming experts to this project.

Why would Microsoft do this? For two reasons:

1. Bill Gates believes in NFTE's mission and wants to help. The on-line program will make it much easier to teach entrepreneurship to young people around the country.
2. Supporting this program is an intelligent business move for Microsoft. Microsoft will gain **good will.** Good will is made up of intangible assets, such as reputation, name recognition, and customer relations, that give a company an advantage over its competitors.

Most philanthropic foundations in this country were created by entrepreneurs who wanted to give back to their communities some of the wealth they had earned. Many of our great museums, libraries, universities, and other valuable institutions have been financed by philanthropists' generosity. The Rockefeller Foundation, The Coleman Foundation, Inc., The Charles G. Koch Foundation, The Ford Foundation, and The Carnegie Corporation are among the famous foundations created by entrepreneurs.

Ironically, some of the most aggressive entrepreneurs in American history—for example, Andrew Carnegie—have also been the most generous. In 1901, after a long and sometimes ruthless business career, Carnegie sold his steel company to J.P. Morgan for $420 million. Overnight, Carnegie became one of the richest men in the world. After retiring, Carnegie spent most of his time giving away his wealth to libraries, colleges, museums, and other worthwhile institutions that still benefit people today.

Carnegie often said that a rich man dies disgraced. By the time of his death from pneumonia, in Lenox, Massachusetts, on August 11, 1919, the 84-year-old Carnegie had given away $350 million.

APPLYING ETHICS TO YOUR BUSINESS

You may not have a million dollars to give to your favorite charity, but there are still many ways that, as a business owner, you can do good in your community. First and foremost, run your business ethically:

- **Treat your customers like gold.** In *How To Sell Yourself* (New York: Warner Books, 1988), Joe Girard, one of the world's top salesmen, describes a great rule he calls "The Rule of 250." Girard notes that every person knows about 250 other people who would attend his or her funeral. This is each person's circle of influence. If you treat just one customer badly, 250 people could hear about it! Treat one customer like gold, and you can bet that his or her friends will flock to your business.

- **Treat your employees like family.** In Japan, employees are considered members of the business owner's family. The owner does everything possible to ensure that employees will be able to keep their jobs, and he or she treats them very well. In turn, the employees are very motivated and do great work. You can motivate your employees in four ways:

  1. **Treat them fairly and considerately.** Apply The Golden Rule!

2. **Make them feel like owners of the company, too.** You work long hours because you own and love your business. Suppose you could inspire that feeling in your employees. Wow! Many employers offer their employees stock in the company at low prices, or they give employees *bonuses* (sums of money at the end of each year, based on the company's performance). This motivates employees to do their best so that the company will do well and they will make more money. Bill Gates used this strategy early in Microsoft's history because he knew he would be asking computer programmers to work long hours on very difficult tasks. As a result, many Microsoft employees became millionaires—and they still want to work for Microsoft!

3. **Help them with training and educational expenses.** The best companies pay for their employees to go to seminars and conferences, or even to school. You may not be in a position to do that, but you can make an extra effort to teach your employees as many skills as possible.

4. **Create an environment that makes your employees want to stay.** The longer they stay with you, the more committed they become to your company and the more knowledge and experience they have. This attitude is leading major corporations—many of which lost brilliant female executives to motherhood because they failed to provide adequate maternity leave, day care, and flexible scheduling—to retool their maternity policies.[1]

- **Treat *yourself* like your most precious asset.** Running a business is tough, demanding work. You can't afford to get sick. Stay healthy by eating good food instead of junk food and by exercising. Exercise keeps you strong and, as a good antidote to stress, is a very important activity for entrepreneurs! Candy, soda, and other junk foods can give you quick jolts of energy but will leave you feeling depressed a few hours later. As an entrepreneur, you need a steady stream of energy. Drink water or juice, and snack on fruit, yogurt, or granola bars instead of candy and chips.

- **Treat other entrepreneurs and business contacts like best friends.** If you practice good business, other entrepreneurs and business contacts will be willing to share valuable business information with you—for instance, which suppliers are the most reliable, or which wholesalers give the best deals. Whenever you can, share information and contacts with another entrepreneur or businessperson. This exchange is called **networking.** It creates goodwill and can really help your business grow.

MENTORING WORKS

There's another way you can help both your community and your business—get involved with a mentor program. The word **mentor** comes from a character in the Greek classic, "The Odyssey." The character Mentor is described as a "wise and trusted friend." When Odysseus leaves home to fight in the Trojan War, he asks Mentor to guard his house and family for him.

Today, the word *mentor* describes a person who agrees to share his or her expertise and caring in an ongoing relationship with another person who could use this help. A teacher who takes extra time after class to help you with a science project, or who inspires you to become a writer and helps you apply to colleges with good writing programs, is a mentor. So is a more experienced entrepreneur who helps a newer entrepreneur to meet business contacts or to resolve cash flow problems.

Jimmy McNeal is a young entrepreneur who took a year off to teach entrepreneurship after closing his first business. While teaching for NFTE, he met Peter Jannsen, one of the top young investment bankers in New York City. Peter was putting together the financing for a company called United States Bicycle Corporation, which intends to purchase brand names of bicycle companies that have not done well and recreate them under one umbrella company.

Because Jimmy is a professional bike racer who hopes to create his own bike brand, Bulldog Bikes, Peter introduced him to the owner of U.S. Bicycle and is helping negotiate a potentially lucrative deal to develop Bulldog Bikes as a subsidiary of U.S. Bicycle.

Ideally, Jimmy will maintain majority ownership of Bulldog Bikes and will sell 49 percent of the ownership to U.S. Bicycles. In return, U.S. Bicycles will completely finance the costs and expenses of Bulldog Bikes and pay Jimmy a substantial salary. Jimmy remains chief executive officer of Bulldog Bikes and will sit on the board of directors of U.S. Bicycle. For selling 49 percent of Bulldog Bikes to U.S. Bicycle, Jimmy hopefully will also receive an ownership stake in U.S. Bicycle and, of course, a stake in the income earned by Bulldog Bikes.

This is how mentoring works—the right mentor can provide contacts and hands-on guidance that can help you take your business forward beyond your wildest dreams.

America's Promise—The Alliance For Youth

General Colin Powell is the chairman of a foundation called America's Promise—The Alliance For Youth. This foundation's mission is to help young Americans succeed. One of its goals, according to General Powell, is to provide every young person in the United States with "an ongoing relationship with a caring adult," or a mentor. To make this happen, America's Promise has helped to arrange for Big Brothers and Big Sisters of America, a prominent mentoring organization, to start working with the Boys & Girls Clubs of America. Big Brothers and Sisters will provide trained mentors, and the Boys & Girls Clubs will provide safe places for mentors and mentees to meet.

How can you find a mentor to help you with your brand new business? You may already have a mentor in your life. Is there an adult who has shown an interest in your business and has helped you with advice or contacts? Perhaps he or she would be willing to become your mentor. If you don't have a mentor, you can start to find one by visiting The National Mentoring Partnership at www.mentoring.org and by looking for mentor programs in your area. Another good idea: Find out how to attend meetings and events held by any professional organizations in your field.

Become a Mentor

If you are over age eighteen, you could become a mentor yourself. If you're worried that you won't be able to find the time, remember that some of the busiest people in the world still find time for mentoring. Six-time Olympic medal winner and track star Jackie Joyner-Kersee finds time to counsel young people. "Mentoring," she said in the *Newsweek*/Kaplan guide, "How To Be A Great Mentor," "is so important to success because it can broaden your horizons and introduce you to a whole new world."

That goes for both mentor and mentee. If you join Big Brothers and Big Sisters, for example, you might be assigned to a child from a background completely different from your own. You will probably learn as much from this mentoring relationship as your mentee!

When you become a more experienced entrepreneur, consider mentoring someone who is just starting his or her own business. Not only will you feel great about being an adviser, but, through sharing your mentor's experience, you will learn even more about business and will meet more contacts. Another plus: You will forge, with your mentee, a positive bond that may last a long time.

ENLIGHTENED CAPITALISM

Anita Roddick of The Body Shop, Inc. and Ben Cohen and Jerry Greenfield of Ben & Jerry's ice cream company are entrepreneurs who take business ethics a step further. They believe that they should use their businesses to make the world a better place. Roddick has dubbed this approach "enlightened capitalism."

ENTREPRENEUR STORY
ANITA RODDICK, THE BODY SHOP

Roddick treats her company, The Body Shop, as a force for social change. Each Body Shop store is expected to get involved with a local community project. The store staff is encouraged to do volunteer work at the project on company time. "I pay my staff to be active citizens," Roddick has said.

Roddick had never expected to be wealthy; she opened the first Body Shop to support herself and her children while her husband was away in South America on an expedition. In 1984, however, The Body Shop stock went on sale and quickly rose in price until the company was worth £8 million (British pounds). The Roddicks were millionaires.

Anita and her husband Gordon discussed their future. Suddenly, they had power and wealth, which they wanted to use wisely. Anita had already been campaigning against animal testing of cosmetics; now she had the clout to make her voice heard.

Outreach on Company Time

She and Gordon decided to use their shops to educate people about social and environmental issues. In 1985, they paid for Greenpeace, an environment preservation group, to put up posters protesting the dumping of hazardous waste into the North Sea. Customers could join Greenpeace at Body Shop stores. The next year, The Body Shop protested the slaughter of sperm whales for their oil. The Body Shop uses jojoba oil, a desert plant wax, instead of sperm oil in its products. Greenpeace designed posters and leaflets for the stores.

The Body Shop worked next with Friends of the Earth on campaigns that protested against acid rain and fostered awareness of the dangers to the ozone layer from aerosol sprays. During these campaigns, the Roddicks learned to keep the message clear and to provide plenty of easy-to-understand information to Body Shop employees and customers.

The Reach of Body Shop Campaigns

The environmental campaigning attracted media attention as well as customers. Roddick has estimated that the publicity generated by Body Shop campaigns has been worth millions in free advertising. The campaigns have also made Body Shop employees happier and more motivated. Their jobs have offered them an opportunity to learn about new things and change the world.

Some campaigns have been highly successful. In 1989, the European Community proposed that all cosmetics be tested on animals. More than five million people signed The Body Shop's petition against this testing, and the proposal was withdrawn. More recently, a campaign for Amnesty International resulted in the release of fifteen political prisoners in response to letters from Body Shop customers. As Anita said in a speech in New York in 1993: "That is the relevancy of what business should be doing in the marketplace."

Another important campaign was "Stop the Burning," which focused public attention on the destruction of the Brazilian rain forest. Anita traveled to Brazil to meet with tribal leaders as part of The Body Shop's "Trade Not Aid" program. She lived with Brazil's Kayapo Indians, exploring how she could trade without destroying their culture. The Body Shop now buys brazil nut oil and vegetable dye beads from the tribe and is committed to helping them survive.

"Trade Not Aid" stemmed from the Roddicks' belief—which I share—that the best way to help people in poor areas is to help them establish their own small businesses. "We avoid governments and go straight to the people in the countries," Anita says.

Although the Roddicks are deeply committed to using their business to help people and protect the environment, Anita says, "I am not rushing around the world as some kind of loony do-gooder; first and foremost, I am a trader looking for trade."

Anita and I both belong to the Social Venture Network, an organization for business leaders seeking solutions to social problems. Although I have my differences with organizations such as Greenpeace, because they consider government ownership one possible solution to environmental problems, I think Anita's emphasis on helping to solve social and environmental problems through entrepreneurship is a real breakthrough.

Cause-Related Marketing

Marketing that is inspired by a commitment to a social, environmental, or political cause is called **cause-related marketing.** Socially responsible entrepreneurs like Roddick have inspired huge corporations to get involved with cause-related marketing. AT&T, for example, announced in 1998 that it will pay employees to devote one day a month to community service.

You couldn't do anything better for your business than align it with a charity dear to your heart. Not only will this be good for employee morale, help society, and reduce the government's burden, but being associated with charity attracts tremendous media attention and can help establish your business's name in your community.

Doing good will make you happier, too, and that's the whole point of entrepreneurship—to create a life that makes you happy!

CASE STUDY: SPORTING GOODS STORE

Even if your business is small, you can do a lot of good that will be good for your business. Frank Alameda runs a sporting goods store, called East Side Sports, on Manhattan's Lower East Side. He runs an ad in The Yellow Pages, but says his most valuable promotion is community service. Each year, Frank sponsors twenty-two local baseball and basketball teams in his neighborhood by providing them with uniforms and balls. This fills his store with kids and makes him very popular with the parents in the neighborhood, too!

Frank learned the importance of nurturing one's community at the Boys Club where he studied entrepreneurship. When he was age eighteen, Frank attended a NFTE course at the first Boys Club that was ever established, on Tenth Street on New York's Lower East Side.

Before taking the entrepreneurship course, Frank had wanted to be a gym teacher. After learning about entrepreneurship, Frank channeled his love of sports into his first business: making custom uniforms for local teams. Soon, he had enough money saved to rent a storefront on a busy street not far from the Boys Club. At the time, Frank was attending college and working part-time at the Boys Club. "I started the business with under $10,000," Frank says, "so I slept four hours a night for about six months because I had no capital to renovate the store. I did all the fixing and remodeling myself."

Because Frank was very young and had no business experience, wholesalers were unwilling to let him buy on credit until he'd been in business for two years. "Doing all the business without credit for that long got really hectic," Frank says, "because I did some big orders." On the sporting goods he purchases from the wholesalers, Frank's typical markup is 80 to 100 percent for resale in his store.

By paying his bills on time and developing a great reputation in the community, Frank was able to establish credit with wholesalers and other suppliers, despite his youth and inexperience. His next goal is to build a custom workshop in his store. "I do a lot of custom work, and if I had a shop in the store I could deliver my custom orders much more quickly," he notes.

Tips

- **Location, location, location!** Frank says he knew his business would succeed because he's located on a busy street in a neighborhood full of kids and teenagers. He made his location even more attractive by getting involved with so many local teams. Today, East Side Sports is a neighborhood fixture.

- **Support a cause that makes sense for your business.** Frank aligned himself with a cause—sponsoring local sports teams—that works with the comparative advantage of his business, which is his location. This makes a lot more sense for his business than, say, giving his time or money to an organization that cares for the elderly.

RESOURCES

Books

Ben & Jerry's: The Inside Scoop—How Two Real Guys Built a Business with a Social Conscience and a Sense of Humor by Fred Lager (Crown, New York, 1994) is a funny, intimate picture of Ben & Jerry's, written by the former CEO of the company.

Anita Roddick tells the story of The Body Shop, Inc. in *Body & Soul* (Crown Publishers, Inc., New York: 1991).

A *Training Guide for Mentors*, by Jay Smink, is available from the National Dropout Prevention Center, which can be reached at www.dropoutprevention.org.

Other Resources

To learn more about General Colin Powell's commitment to America's Promise—The Alliance For Youth, visit www.Americaspromise.org, or use AOL Keyword: America's Promise.

Visit The National Mentoring Partnership at http://www.mentoring.org.

The Boys & Girls Clubs of America can be reached by calling (800) 854-CLUB or visiting www.bgca.org.

If you live in New York City, contact The NYC Mentoring Program of the New York City Board of Education, at (718) 935-4520. Volunteers mentor students through work and educational goals.

Earl Graves, publisher of *Black Enterprise* magazine, is one of many influential members of 100 Black Men, a group of volunteers who mentor African American youth. Contact 100 Black Men at www.100bm.org or call (404) 688-5100.

Chapter 25

HOW TO WRITE A SUPER BUSINESS PLAN

THE KEY TO BOTH FINANCING AND OPERATING YOUR BUSINESS

LET'S GET STARTED!

If you've read the first twenty-four chapters, you are definitely ready to write a business plan that could help you raise money to start your own small business. Just behind this chapter you'll find a sample business plan you can use as a model. Following the sample business plan is a blank Business Plan Workbook packed with worksheets that you can use to write your own plan.

This chapter tells you exactly how to fill out each worksheet. Use it as a reference as you work on your business plan.

DEFINING YOUR BUSINESS IDEA

On the first worksheet, describe your business idea clearly and concisely. What is your product or service? Who will want to buy it? Where will you sell it? Explain your competitive advantage—what you can do better than another businessperson with a similar business, and why. What gives you an advantage over your competitors?

THE ECONOMICS OF ONE UNIT

Your first decision focuses on the kind of business you are planning to run. Is it a retail, wholesale, manufacturing, or service business? After you decide, turn to the appropriate worksheet for calculating the economics of one unit.

You'll need to define one unit of your business before you can determine costs and profit. If you are selling just one product—ties, for example—one unit is one tie. The unit price would be the price of one tie. The cost of goods sold would be the cost of producing one tie. If you are selling a variety of products, define your unit as the average sale per customer. McDonald's, for example, defines its unit of sale as a $5 sale, which is roughly the cost of one sandwich, fries, and a soda.

If you are selling a service, the economic unit is usually one hour of service. Or, you could define your unit as the completion of one job.

Base your unit selling price on your cost of goods sold. It's a good idea for the selling price to "keystone," or be double the cost of producing one unit. To determine gross profit per unit, subtract your unit cost from your unit selling price. (The worksheet will take you through this process.)

Market Research

It is crucial that you research your market before developing a product or service. The worksheets offer good questions to ask about your market. Check out your competitors, too. How are they serving your market? What price are they charging? What are their costs?

For a review of market research, see Chapter 14.

Your Customer

Close your eyes and picture your ideal customer. Is it a man or a woman? How old is the customer? Where does he or she live? Work? What does he or she eat for breakfast? Try to follow this person mentally through an entire day. You'll get all kinds of ideas for how to reach your customer.

List your promotional and advertising ideas. Posters, flyers, and business cards are inexpensive, but effective.

Take the time to write a sales pitch to your target customer. Write down some potential wholesalers or suppliers you could contact.

To review promotion and advertising, please see Chapter 13. For more on sales, see Chapter 12.

YOUR MARKETING PLAN

Use the marketing plan chart to plot the strategy that will most successfully market your product or service.

LEGAL STRUCTURE

Most small businesses start as sole proprietorships or partnerships. Before registering your business, research fees, permits, and licensing requirements.

If you form a partnership, be sure to write out a formal agreement with your partner. State each partner's financial and work obligations toward the business. As soon as you can afford to spend $500 to incorporate, you should consider doing so to protect your personal assets from any debts incurred by the business. A small business with fewer than seventy-five employees can incorporate as a Subchapter S corporation.

When incorporating or forming a partnership, see a lawyer for advice. Some lawyers are willing to work with a young person for free, or for a reduced fee.

Chapter 17 offers more information on business legal structures.

FINANCING AND BUDGETING YOUR BUSINESS

Your first concern is your startup costs—the costs of items you need to purchase in order to make your first sale. Talk to a friend or mentor. He or she may think of some costs you didn't anticipate.

List where you plan to obtain the money to cover your startup costs. List the amount you expect to get from personal savings, relatives, friends, investors, or other sources. Put a check mark ($\sqrt{}$) in the appropriate column to indicate whether the financing is equity, debt, or a gift. How much ownership are you willing to give up in exchange for equity financing? If you go with debt, what's the highest interest rate you are willing to pay?

Next, calculate your operating costs, both fixed and variable. Fixed costs are costs that do not change over a range of sales your business may make. Rent is a fixed cost; you pay the same rent whether you sell five units or fifty.

Variable costs change with the amount of sales your business makes. Sales commission is an example of a variable cost. The amount of sales commission the business owner pays rises when sales rise and falls when sales fall.

Typically, young entrepreneurs' businesses have only fixed costs, but you should have a friend or mentor look at your list of costs. You may have missed some operating costs.

At this point, you are ready to prepare your monthly budget. The goal of the monthly budget is to guess accurately how many units you can sell at the selling price you've designated. You'll need to estimate the following amounts and enter them into your calculations.

1. Total Sales

- Units Sold: How many units do you expect to sell each month? Enter your estimates for each month in the top row of the monthly budget chart. Remember: "Row" means across the chart, "column" means down.

- Unit Selling Price: For what price do you plan to sell one unit? Enter that *same* price for each month across the second row of the chart.

- Total Sales: Multiply Units Sold by Unit Selling Price to get Total Sales for each month:

$$\text{Total Sales} = \text{Units Sold} \times \text{Unit Selling Price}$$

Because Units Sold will probably differ for each month, do this calculation for every month and enter the results in the Total Sales row.

2. Total Cost of Goods (or Services) Sold

- Cost of Goods (or Services) Sold: Enter your Cost of Goods (or Services) Sold per Unit across this row. (You figured out this cost earlier.)

- Total Cost of Goods (or Services) Sold: Multiply Cost of Goods (or Services) Sold per Unit by Units Sold for each month.

$$\text{Total Cost of Goods (or Services) Sold} = \text{Units Sold} \times \text{Cost of Goods (or Services) Sold per Unit}$$

Do this calculation for each month. Enter the results in the Total Cost of Goods (or Services) row.

3. Gross Profit

To calculate Gross Profit, subtract Total Cost of Goods (or Services) Sold from Total Sales. Do this calculation for each month. Enter the results in the Gross Profit row.

$$\text{Gross Profit} = \text{Total Sales} - \frac{\text{Total Cost of Goods}}{\text{(or Services) Sold}}$$

4. Operating Costs

- Monthly Fixed Costs: Enter your estimate of monthly Fixed Costs from your Operating Costs worksheet.
- Monthly Variable Costs: Enter your estimate of monthly Variable Costs from your Operating Costs worksheet.

To calculate Operating Costs, add Monthly Fixed Costs to Monthly Variable Costs.

$$\text{Operating Costs} = \text{Monthly Fixed Costs} + \text{Monthly Variable Costs}$$

5. Profit/(Loss) Before Taxes

To calculate Profit/(Loss), subtract Operating Costs from Gross Profit.

$$\text{Profit/(Loss)} = \text{Gross Profit} - \text{Operating Costs}$$

6. Total

To fill in the Total column for most of the entries, simply add together the numbers across a row. For example, if your Units Sold row contains twelve numbers, indicating sales in all twelve months, you get the total by adding up all twelve numbers. Your arithmetic might be: (40 + 35 + 60 + 75 + 80 + 85 + 90 + 90 + 85 + 100 + 75 + 90), or 905. You would then write 905 in the Total column at the end of the Units Sold row. Repeat this addition process to fill in the totals for all of the other rows **except** the Unit Selling Price and Cost of Goods Sold rows. *Do not add* *together the numbers in these rows!* Simply enter the same number all the way across *and* in the Total column.

7. Net Profit

If your total in the Profit/(Loss) row is positive, your business is showing a projected profit before taxes. To calculate Net Profit, you will have to subtract taxes. For our purposes, let's assume that taxes will be 25 percent of Profit. (Your actual taxes could be higher or lower.)

To calculate taxes, multiply Profit by .25.

$$\text{Taxes} = \text{Profit} \times .25$$

Profit minus taxes gives you Net Profit.

$$\text{Net Profit} = \text{Profit} - \text{Taxes}$$

YOUR YEARLY INCOME STATEMENT

A yearly income statement will fall neatly out of the monthly projected income statement you have just created. Look at the last ("Total") column of the monthly statement. There you will find the numbers to plug into your yearly income statement.

SAMPLE BUSINESS PLAN

The sample business plan that follows will show you, step by step, how to prepare a business plan for a small business. Be sure you understand each step before you go on to the next one. You can then use the Business Plan Workbook, in the next section, for the business plan that will launch your own venture.

Good luck, and have fun!

Your Business Idea

....

Describe your business idea:

My business idea is to clean and maintain home aquariums. I would clean each aquarium in a person's home twice a month.

What is the name of your business?

Fred's Aquarium Cleaners

What is the competitive advantage of your business?

The price for my service will be lower than my competitors' price.

| Name | Fred Marshall | Business | Fred's Aquarium Cleaners | Date | 1/4/00 |

Marketing

....

Type of business you are in (please circle)

Manufacturer	Wholesaler	Retailer	Service Retailer
Sells to	Sells to	Sells to	Sells to
↓	↓	↓	↓
Wholesaler	Retailer	Consumer	Consumer

Consumer Description

Describe your target consumer   a home aquarium owner who is too busy to care for it, or someone who would buy an aquarium if there were a service to care for it

Expected age of consumer   any age   Expected gender of consumer   M or F

What need or want will your product fulfill?   save time

Financial status of consumer   making enough money to afford an aquarium

Promotion/Advertising

How will you reach this consumer?   Flyers

What is the slogan for your business?   A clean fish is a happy fish.

Will you make sales calls?   ☑ Yes   ☐ No   When I start expanding to offices and restaurants.

Write a four-sentence sales presentation:

For only $30 a month my professional cleaning service will keep your fish healthy and happy and your aquarium sparkling. You won't have to buy or store cleaning supplies. My service saves you time and money. You can feel confident that the very latest techniques and supplies are being used to care for your fish.

Economics of One Unit:
Service Company

Fill this out if you have a service business.

Economics of One Unit

Note: A service unit is typically defined as one hour of service or one job.

Define your unit: ___One month of cleaning service for one aquarium.___

_____

_____

Selling price per unit $ _____30.00_____ **A**

Cost of services sold per unit

(Cost of services sold per unit must include both your labor and supplies.)

Labor

What value are you placing on your entrepreneurial time per hour?

$ _____6.00_____ **B**

How long does it take to perform your service (in hours)?

_____2 hours_____ **C**

Labor cost per unit = B × C $ _____12.00_____ **D**

Supplies

What is the supply cost per customer? $ _____5.00_____ **E**

Cost of services sold per unit = D + E $ _____17.00_____ **F**

Gross profit per unit = A − F $ _____13.00_____ **G**

Selling Price per Unit	−	**Cost of Services Sold per Unit**	=	**Gross Profit per Unit**
A	−	**F**	=	**G**

Market Research

....

Competition

Ask two people these questions about your business and write their answers in the space provided:

Do you like the name of my business?

#1 _Yes_

#2 _Yes_

What do you think of my logo?

#1 _like it_

#2 _a little confusing_

Where would you want to go to buy my product?

#1 _I like that you come to the home._

#2 _I wouldn't want a stranger in my home._

Do you think my product/service has value?

#1 _Yes_

#2 _Yes_

How much would you pay for my product?

#1 _$25 a month_

#2 _$35 a month_

How would you improve my business idea?

#1 _offer fish food, supplies_

#2 _service office, restaurant aquariums_

Who is my closest competitor(s)?

#1 _don't know any_

#2 _Manhattan Cleaning Services_

Do you think my product/service is better or worse than that offered by my competitor(s)?

#1 _don't know_

#2 _better, less expensive_

Why is your product/service going to beat the competition?

My service is cheaper and I will try to develop a good personal relationship with each

customer.

Below is a sample strategy for a business selling handmade jewelry. Can you add other locations or methods of selling?

MARKETING PLAN LOCATIONS (WHERE TO SELL)

S E L L I N G M E T H O D S	Door to Door	Flea Markets	School/ Church Functions	Street (Street Vendors)	Through Local Stores	Your Own Home	Internet Marketing	Other
Business Cards	no	no	yes	no	yes	no	no	no
Posters	no	no	yes	yes	yes	no	yes	no
Flyers	no	no	yes	yes	yes	yes	yes	no
Phone	no	no	no	yes	yes	yes	no	no
Sales Calls	no	no	no	yes	yes	yes	no	no
Brochure	no	no	yes	yes	yes	yes	yes	no
Mailings	no	no	no	yes	yes	yes	yes	no
Other	no	no	no	yes	yes	yes	yes	no

Legal Structure

Is your business a sole proprietorship, a partnership, a regular corporation, a subchapter S corporation, or a not-for-profit corporation?

sole proprietorship

Explain your decision:

I am the only employee and the owner.

How much will you be paying for legal fees?

Explain: _$33 to register as a sole proprietorship._

What permits and/or licenses will you need for your business?

I will need a sales tax identification number and a business certificate. I will look into any other permits.

What are the names, addresses, and phone numbers of the local official(s) in charge of the permits and licensing you need?

Name	Address	Phone
Business Permits Office	State Office Building, Albany, NY	800-342-3464
Tax Forms Office	State Office Building, Albany, NY	800-462-8100

Start-Up Costs   (These are the items you need to earn your first dollar of sales.)

....

What are your estimated start-up costs? Itemize:

Item	Where Will You Buy This?	Cost
Cleaning Equipment	Petland	$150
Medicine (Water Treatment)	Hertz	$ 61
Tools	Hunter Hardware	$ 25
Cart	Hunter Hardware	$ 42
Business cards	Kinko's	$ 20

Estimated Total Start-up Costs _____$298_____

List your sources of financing below. Indicate with a check mark whether each source is offering equity, debt, or a gift.

	Amount	Equity (Investment)	Debt (Loan)	Gift
Personal Savings:	$150	✓		
Relatives:	$100		✓	
Friends:	$48		✓	
Investors:				
Grant:				
Other:				
Total:	$298			

If you receive equity financing, what percentage of ownership will you give up? _20%_

If you receive debt financing, what is the maximum interest rate you will pay? _10%_

Operating Costs (Fixed & Variable)

Monthly Fixed Costs

Monthly Operating Costs include USAIIR: utilities, salaries, advertising, interest, insurance, and rent. In a small business, many operating costs are usually fixed, although a few may be variable, depending on your business.

Type of Fixed Costs	Monthly Fixed Cost
Advertising (Flyers and Posters)	$26
Monthly Fixed Costs	$26

Variable Costs

(Estimate those operating costs (USAIIR) that fluctuate with sales and cannot be directly assigned to a unit of sale. Example: utilities = 1% of sales.)

Type of Variable Costs	Estimated Variable Cost as a % of Sales
	$0
Estimated Variable Costs as a % of sales	_____ %

Remember . . . to get total monthly variable costs you must multiply variable cost as a percentage of sales by total monthly sales. Note: you may set variable costs equal to zero._

Monthly Budget: Projected Income Statement for a Service Company

	Jan	Feb	Mar	Apr	May	Jun	Jul	Aug	Sep	Oct	Nov	Dec	Total
Units Sold	2	4	6	8	8	16	18	20	8	8	8	6	112
Unit Selling Price	30	30	30	30	30	30	30	30	30	30	30	30	30
Total Sales	60	120	180	240	240	480	540	600	240	240	240	180	3,360
Cost of Services Sold per Unit	17	17	17	17	17	17	17	17	17	17	17	17	17
Total Cost of Services Sold	34	68	102	136	136	272	306	340	136	136	136	102	1,904
Gross Profit	26	52	78	104	104	208	234	260	104	104	104	78	1,456
Fixed Costs	26	26	26	26	26	26	26	26	26	26	26	26	312
Variable Costs	0	0	0	0	0	0	0	0	0	0	0	0	0
Total Operating Costs	26	26	26	26	26	26	26	26	26	26	26	26	312
Profit/(Loss) before Taxes	0	26	52	78	78	182	208	234	78	78	78	52	1,144

Less Taxes (25%, Estimated)   286

Net Profit   858

Total Sales = Units Sold × Unit Selling Price

Total Cost of Services Sold = Units Sold × Cost of Services Sold per Unit

Gross Profit = Total Sales − Total Cost of Services Sold

Variable Costs = Multiply Variable Costs as a % of Sales by Sales

Operating Costs = Fixed Costs + Variable Costs

Profit/(Loss) = Gross Profit − Operating Costs

Taxes = Profit × .25

Name _Fred Marshall_ **Business** _Fred's Aquarium Cleaners_ **Date** _1/4/00_

Budgeted Yearly Income Statement for a Service Business

Sales	Amount	
Units Sold	112	
Unit Selling Price	$30	
Total Sales	$3,360	Total Sales = Units Sold × Unit Selling Price

Costs	Amount	
Cost of Services Sold per Unit	$17	
Total Cost of Services Sold	$1,904	Total Cost of Goods or Services Sold = Units Sold × Cost of Goods or Services Sold per Unit
Gross Profit	$1,456	Gross Profit = Total Sales − Total Cost of Goods or Services Sold
Fixed Expenses	$312	
Variable Costs	0	Variable Costs = Variable Costs as a % of Sales × Sales
Operating Costs	$312	Operating Costs = Fixed Costs + Variable Costs

Profit	Amount	
Profit/(Loss) before Taxes	$1,144	Profit/(Loss) = Gross Profit − Operating Expenses
Less Taxes (25%, Estimated)	$286	Taxes = Profit × .25
Net Profit	$858	Net Profit = Profit − Taxes
Net Profit per Unit	$7.66	Net Profit per Unit = $\dfrac{\text{Net Profit}}{\text{Units Sold}}$

BUSINESS PLAN WORKBOOK

Your Business Idea

. . . .

Describe your business idea:

_____

_____

_____

_____

_____

_____

_____

_____

_____

_____

_____

What is the name of your business?

_____

_____

What is the competitive advantage of your business?

_____

_____

_____

_____

_____

_____

Marketing

· ·

Type of business you are in (please circle)

Manufacturer	Wholesaler	Retailer	Service Retailer
Sells to	Sells to	Sells to	Sells to
↓	↓	↓	↓
Wholesaler	Retailer	Consumer	Consumer

Consumer Description

Describe your target consumer _____

_____

_____

Expected age of consumer _____   Expected gender of consumer _____

What need or want will your product fulfill? _____

Financial status of consumer _____

Promotion/Advertising

How will you reach this consumer? _____

What is the slogan for your business? _____

Will you make sales calls? ☐ Yes ☐ No

Write a four-sentence sales presentation:

_____

_____

_____

_____

_____

Economics of One Unit:
Manufacturing Company

....

Fill this out if you have a manufacturing business.

Economics of One Unit

Define your unit: _____

_____

_____

Selling price per unit $_____ A

Cost of goods sold per unit

(Cost of producing one additional unit must include both your labor and supplies.)

Labor

What value are you placing on your
entrepreneurial time per hour? $_____ B

How long does it take to make your product
or perform your service (in hours)? $_____ C

Labor cost of goods sold per unit = B × C $_____ D

Raw materials

What is the raw material cost of goods sold
per unit? $_____ E

Cost of goods sold per unit = D + E $_____ F

Gross profit = A − F $_____ G

Selling Price	−	Cost of Goods Sold per Unit	=	Gross Profit per Unit
A	−	F	=	G

Economics of One Unit:
Wholesale Company

· ·

Fill this out if you have a wholesale business.

Economics of One Unit

Note: A wholesale unit is typically measured in dozens, because wholesale items are sold in bulk.

Define your unit: _____

_____

_____

_____

_____

_____

_____

_____

Selling price per unit $_____ A

(Price at which you plan to sell one unit.)

Cost of goods sold per unit $_____ B

(Cost to you of producing one unit.)

Gross profit per unit (A − B) $_____ C

(Gross profit of one unit.)

Selling Price per Unit	−	Cost of Goods Sold per Unit	=	Gross Profit per Unit
A	−	B	=	C

Economics of One Unit:
Retail Company

....

Fill this out if you have a retail business.

Economics of One Unit

Define your unit: _____

_____

_____

_____

_____

_____

_____

_____

_____

Selling price per unit $_____ **A**

(Price at which you plan to sell one unit.)

Cost of goods sold per unit $_____ **B**

(Cost to you of producing one unit.)

Gross profit per unit (A − B) $_____ **C**

(Gross profit of one unit.)

Selling Price per Unit	−	Cost of Goods Sold per Unit	=	Gross Profit per Unit
A	−	B	=	C

Economics of One Unit:
Service Company

....

Fill this out if you have a service business.

Economics of One Unit

Note: A service unit is typically defined as one hour of service or one job.

Define your unit: _____

_____

_____

Selling price per unit $_____ A

Cost of services sold per unit

(Cost of producing one additional unit must include both your labor and supplies.)

Labor

What value are you placing on your
entrepreneurial time per hour? $_____ B

How long does it take to perform your service
(in hours)? $_____ C

Labor cost per unit = B × C $_____ D

Supplies

What is the supply cost per customer? $_____ E

Cost of services sold per unit = D + E $_____ F

Gross profit per unit = A − F $_____ G

Selling Price per Unit	−	Cost of Services Sold per Unit	=	Gross Profit per Unit
A	−	F	=	G

Market Research

··

Competition

Ask two people these questions about your business and write their answers in the space provided:

Do you like the name of my business?

#1 _____

#2 _____

What do you think of my logo?

#1 _____

#2 _____

Where would you want to go to buy my product?

#1 _____

#2 _____

Do you think my product/service has value?

#1 _____

#2 _____

How much would you pay for my product?

#1 _____

#2 _____

How would you improve my business idea?

#1 _____

#2 _____

Who is my closest competitor(s)?

#1 _____

#2 _____

Do you think my product/service is better or worse than that offered by my competitor(s)?

#1 _____

#2 _____

Why is your product/service going to beat the competition?

_____

_____

_____

_____

_____

_____

Below is a sample strategy for a manufacturing, wholesale, retail, or service company. Can you add other locations or methods of selling?

MARKETING PLAN LOCATIONS (WHERE TO SELL)

S E L L I N G M E T H O D S	Door to Door	Flea Markets	School/ Church Functions	Street (Street Vendors)	Through Local Stores	Your Own Home	Internet Marketing	Other
Business Cards								
Posters								
Flyers								
Phone								
Sales Calls								
Brochure								
Mailings								
Web Sites								
Other								

Legal Structure

....

Is your business a sole proprietorship, a partnership, a regular corporation, a subchapter S corporation, or a not-for-profit corporation?

_____

_____

Explain your decision:

_____

_____

How much will you be paying for legal fees?

Explain: _____

_____

_____

What permits and/or licenses will you need for your business?

_____

_____

_____

_____

What are the names, addresses, and phone numbers of the local official(s) in charge of the permits and licensing you need?

Name	Address	Phone

Start-Up Costs (These are the items you need to earn your first dollar of sales.)

....

What are your estimated start-up costs? Itemize:

Item	Where Will You Buy This?	Cost
_____	_____	_____
_____	_____	_____
_____	_____	_____
_____	_____	_____
_____	_____	_____
_____	_____	_____

Estimated Total Start-up Costs _____

List your sources of financing below. Indicate with a check mark whether each source is offering equity, debt, or a gift.

	Amount	Equity (Investment)	Debt (Loan)	Gift
Personal Savings:				
Relatives:				
Friends:				
Investors:				
Grant:				
Other:				
Total:				

If you receive equity financing, what percentage of ownership will you give up? _____

If you receive debt financing, what is the maximum interest rate you will pay? _____

Operating Costs (Fixed & Variable)

. . . .

Monthly Fixed Costs

Monthly Operating Costs include USAIIR: utilities, salaries, advertising, interest, insurance, and rent. In a small business, many operating costs are usually fixed, although a few may be variable, depending on your business.

Type of Fixed Costs	Monthly Fixed Cost
_____	_____
_____	_____
_____	_____
_____	_____
Monthly Fixed Costs	_____

Variable Costs

(Estimate those operating costs (USAIIR) that fluctuate with sales and cannot be directly assigned to a unit of sale. Example: utilities = 1% of sales.)

Type of Variable Costs	Estimated Variable Cost as a % of Sales
_____	_____
_____	_____
_____	_____
_____	_____
Estimated Variable Costs as a % of sales	_____ %

Remember . . . to get total monthly variable costs you must multiply variable cost as a percentage of sales by total monthly sales. Note: you may set variable costs equal to zero.

Monthly Budget: Projected Income Statement for a Manufacturing, Wholesale, Retail, or Service Company

	Jan	Feb	Mar	Apr	May	Jun	Jul	Aug	Sep	Oct	Nov	Dec	Total
Units Sold													
Unit Selling Price													
Total Sales													
Cost of Goods or Services Sold per Unit													
Total Cost of Goods or Services Sold													
Gross Profit													
Fixed Costs													
Variable Costs													
Total Operating Costs													
Profit/(Loss) before Taxes													

Less Taxes (25%, Estimated) _____

Net Profit _____

Total Sales = Units Sold × Unit Selling Price

Total Cost of Goods or Services Sold = Units Sold × Cost of Goods or Services Sold per Unit

Gross Profit = Total Sales – Total Cost of Goods or Services Sold

Variable Costs = Multiply Variable Costs as a % of Sales by Sales

Operating Costs = Fixed Costs + Variable Costs

Profit/(Loss) = Gross Profit – Operating Costs

Taxes = Profit × .25

Budgeted Yearly Income Statement for a Manufacturing, Wholesale, Retail, or Service Business

Sales	Amount	
Units Sold		
Unit Selling Price		
Total Sales		Total Sales = Units Sold × Unit Selling Price

Costs	Amount	
Cost of Goods or Services Sold per Unit		
Total Cost of Goods or Services Sold		Total Cost of Goods or Services Sold = Units Sold × Cost of Goods or Services Sold per Unit
Gross Profit		Gross Profit = Total Sales − Total Cost of Goods or Services Sold
Fixed Expenses		
Variable Costs		Variable Costs = Variable Costs as a % of Sales × Sales
Operating Costs		Operating Costs = Fixed Costs + Variable Costs

Profit	Amount	
Profit/(Loss) before Taxes		Profit/(Loss) = Gross Profit − Operating Expenses
Less Taxes (25%, Estimated)		Taxes = Profit × .25
Net Profit		Net Profit = Profit − Taxes
Net Profit per Unit		Net Profit per Unit = $\dfrac{\text{Net Profit}}{\text{Units Sold}}$

EPILOGUE

I hope this book will help you to understand and apply the simple concepts of entrepreneurship to your life. It has been a great joy for me to teach entrepreneurship. I have watched my students succeed in business and develop mental strength and self-esteem.

I've always encouraged my students to memorize the poem "Invictus" by William Ernest Henley. It expresses, better than I ever could, my belief that knowing how to start and operate a small business will make you master of your own fate.

Invictus

Out of the night that covers me,
Black as the pit from pole to pole,
I thank whatever gods may be
For my unconquerable soul.

In the fell clutch of circumstance
I have not winced nor cried aloud:
Under the bludgeonings of chance
My head is bloody, but unbowed.

Beyond this place of wrath and tears
Looms but the Horror of the shade,
And yet the menace of the years
Finds and shall find me unafraid.

It matters not how strait the gate,
How charged with punishments the scroll,
I am the master of my fate:
I am the captain of my soul.

William Ernest Henley

GLOSSARY

asset any item of value owned by a business. Cash, inventory, furniture, and machinery are examples of assets.

audit a formal study of accounts conducted by the Internal Revenue Service to determine whether the taxpayer being investigated is paying appropriate taxes.

balance 1. the difference between the credit and the debit side of a ledger; also, the difference between the assets and liabilities sides of a financial statement. 2. to calculate such differences; to settle an account by paying debts; to keep books properly so credit and debit sides of an account equal each other.

bankrupt the condition of a business that is unable to pay its bills. A business declared legally bankrupt may have its property confiscated by the courts and divided up among its creditors.

board of advisers a group of people who agree to meet regularly to advise an entrepreneur about his or her business and to share contacts and make introductions that will help the business.

brand a name (sometimes along with a symbol or trademark) that distinguishes a business from its competition and makes it and its competitive advantage instantly recognizable to the consumer.

browser software used to "surf" or browse the Internet.

business the buying and selling of goods and services in order to make a profit.

capital money or property owned or used in business.

cash flow cash receipts less cash disbursements over a period of time. Cash flow is represented by the cash balance in an accounting journal or ledger.

cause-related marketing marketing that is tied to a social, political, or environmental cause that the entrepreneur wants to support.

checking account a bank account against which the account holder can write checks. Some banks pay interest on checking accounts that maintain a minimum balance.

compound interest the money an investor earns on interest that was earned by the investment in a previous period, enabling the investment to grow exponentially.

compromise a settlement in which each side has given in on some demands.

consumer a person or business that buys goods and services for its own needs, not for resale or for use in producing goods and services for resale.

copyright exclusive right to a literary, dramatic, musical, or artistic work or to the use of a commercial print or label, as granted by law.

corporation a legal "person" or "entity" that is composed of stockholders, is granted the right to buy, sell, and inherit possessions, and is legally liable for the entity's actions.

cost an expense; the amount of money, time, or energy spent on something.

cost of goods sold the cost of selling one additional unit.

credit in bookkeeping, a recording of income.

credit card an account that allows carrying a debt indefinitely, as long as interest is paid to the account holder.

creditor a person who extends credit or to whom money is owed.

customer service the maintenance and servicing of a product once it has been sold; the act of keeping customers happy and loyal to one's business.

database information (data), such as customer addresses, stored in a computer.

debit in bookkeeping, a recording of an expense.

debt an obligation or liability to pay back a loan.

debt ratio the ratio of debt to assets.

debt-to-equity ratio a financial ratio that expresses the financial strategy of a company by showing how much of the company is financed by debt and how much by equity.

deduction expenses incurred during the course of doing business. A business owner may subtract deductible amounts from income when figuring income tax due.

demand the desire for a commodity, together with the ability to pay for it; the amount consumers are ready and able to buy at all the prices in the market.

demographics population statistics.

diversification a method of decreasing risk by spreading an investor's money among many different investments.

Dow Jones Averages three averages of stock market prices that represent how well the stock market (and, therefore, the economy) is performing. The three averages comprise: (1) thirty industrial stocks, (2) twenty transportation stocks, (3) fifteen utility stocks.

electronic storefront   a Web site set up as a store where consumers can see and purchase merchandise.

e-mail   short for electronic mail, or messages sent between computers using the Internet.

employee   a person hired by a business to work for wages or salary.

encryption   code used to scramble information sent over the Internet.

endorsement   signature on the back of a check, rendering it payable.

entrepreneur   a person who organizes and manages a business, assuming the risk for the sake of the potential return.

equity   ownership in a company received in exchange for money invested in the company. In accounting, equity is equal to assets minus liabilities.

expense   cost of doing business.

file   when referring to taxes: to fulfill one's legal obligation by mailing a tax return, and any taxes due, to the Internal Revenue Service or a state or local tax authority.

finance   to raise money for a business.

fixed costs   business expenses that must be paid whether or not any sales are being generated; USAIIR: utilities, salaries, advertising, insurance, interest, and rent.

flame   an angry e-mail sent in response to "spam," which is unsolicited e-mail hawking a product or service.

foundation   an organization that manages money donated to it by philanthropists.

franchise   a business that markets a product or service developed by the franchisor, in the manner specified by the franchisor.

franchisee   owner of a franchise unit or units.

franchisor   person who develops a franchise or a company that sells franchises.

free enterprise system   economic system in which businesses are privately owned and operate relatively free of government interference.

goodwill   an intangible asset generated when a company does something positive that has value—goodwill can include the company's reputation, brand recognition, and relationships with community and customers.

gross   total or entire amount before deductions, as opposed to net.

gross profit   total sales revenue minus total cost of goods sold.

immigrant   a person who settles in a new country or region, having left his or her country or region of birth.

incentive   something that motivates a person to take action—to work, start a business, or study harder, for example.

income   money received from the sale of products or services, from a job or gift, or from a deferred payment fund such as a trust, annuity, or pension.

income statement   a financial statement that summarizes income and expense activity over a specified period and shows net profit or loss.

infringe   to violate a copyright, trademark, or patent.

insolvent   the condition of a business that is unable to pay its bills.

interest   payment for using someone else's money; payment you receive for lending someone your money.

interest rate   money paid for the use of money, expressed as a percentage per unit of time.

Internal Revenue Service   the federal government bureau in charge of taxation.

investment   something into which one puts money, time, or energy, in the hope of gaining profit or satisfaction, in spite of any risk involved.

investor   person who purchases securities or puts money into a business venture in hopes of earning a satisfactory return.

invoice   an itemized list of goods delivered or services rendered and the amount due; a bill.

keystone   to buy an item wholesale and sell it for twice the wholesale price; to double one's money.

leveraged   financed with debt, not equity.

liable   responsible for any lawsuits that arise from accidents, unpaid bills, faulty merchandise, or other business problems.

license   (1) authorization by law to do some specified thing; (2) to grant the right to use the licensor's name on a product or service.

licensee   person granted the right to use the licensor's name on a product or service sold by the licensee.

licensor   person who sells the right to use his or her name or company name to a licensee; unlike the franchisor, the licensor does not attempt to dictate exactly how the licensee does business.

liquidity   the ease with which an investment can be converted into cash.

management   the art of planning and organizing a business so it can meet its goals.

manufacturing   the activity of a business that makes or produces a tangible product.

market   a group of people interested in buying a product or service; any situation or designated location where trade occurs.

market clearing price   the price at which the amount of a product or service demanded equals the amount the supplier is willing to supply at that price; the price at which the supply and demand curves cross. Also called "equilibrium price."

mentor   a person who agrees to volunteer time and expertise, and to provide emotional support to help another person reach his or her goals.

middleman   descriptive often substituted for "wholesaler"; a trader who buys commodities from the producer or wholesaler and sells them to the retailer.

modem   device that connects a computer to a phone line and translates the digital information coming from the computer into a form that can be transmitted over the phone.

monopoly   a market with only one producer; the control of the pricing and distribution of a product or service in a given market as a result of lack of competition.

mutual fund   a company that collects money from investors and invests it for them; the goal of the investors is usually to achieve greater diversification than they could afford to achieve on their own.

negotiation   discussing or bargaining in an effort to reach agreement between parties with differing goals.

net   final result; in business, the profit or loss remaining after all costs have been subtracted.

networking   the act of exchanging valuable information and contacts with other businesspeople.

newsgroup   an on-line discussion group focused on a specific subject.

notary public   person authorized to witness and certify the signing of documents.

operating cost   each cost necessary to operate a business, not including cost of goods sold. Operating costs can almost always be divided into US-AIIR: utilities, salaries, advertising, insurance, interest, and rent. Operating costs are also called "overhead."

optimist   a person who consistently looks on the bright side of situations or outcomes.

overhead   the continuing fixed costs of running a business; the costs a business has to pay just to have a place from which to operate.

partnership   an association of two or more persons in a business enterprise.

patent   an exclusive right to produce, use, and sell an invention or process.

percentage   literally, "a given part of every hundred" or "out of one hundred"; a number expressed as part of a whole, with the whole represented as 100 percent.

perseverance   the ability to keep trying, even when that effort is difficult.

philanthropy   concern for human and other beings that is expressed by giving money to charities and foundations.

principal   the amount of a debt or loan before interest is added.

privatization   the transfer of ownership of a government-owned business to a private owner.

product   something that is made by nature, human industry, or art, and is sold on the market.

profit   the sum remaining after all costs are deducted from the income of a business.

profit and loss statement   an income statement, showing the gain and loss from business transactions and summarizing the net profit or loss.

profit per unit   the selling price minus the cost of goods sold of an item.

promissory note   a written promise to pay a certain sum of money on or before a specified date.

prototype   a model or pattern that serves as an example of how a product would look and operate if it were manufactured.

public domain   free of copyright or patent restrictions.

rate of return   the return on an investment, expressed as a percentage of the amount invested.

receipt   a written acknowledgment that goods or services have been received; includes the date and amount of purchase.

repeat business   revenue that is generated because a customer returns more than once to a business.

resource   something that can be used to make something else or to fill a need.

retail   (1) to buy from a wholesaler or manufacturer and sell directly to the consumer; (2) the goods sold to a consumer by a retailer.

return on investment   profit on an investment, expressed as a percentage of the investment.

revenue   money earned by a business from sales of products or services.

risk   the chance of loss.

royalty   a share of the proceeds of the sale of a product, paid to a person who owns a copyright; also refers to a fee paid to a franchisor or licensor.

sales tax   tax levied on items that are sold by businesses to consumers. States raise revenue through sales tax.

savings account   a bank account in which money is deposited and on which the bank pays interest to the depositor.

service   intangible work providing time, skills, or expertise in exchange for money.

share   a single unit of stock in a corporation.

shareware   free software available on the Internet; shareware is usually the test or "light" version of the software.

sole proprietorship   a business owned by one person. The owner receives all profits and is legally liable for all debts or lawsuits arising from the business.

startup costs   the expenses involved in getting a business started; also called the original investment.

statistics   facts collected and presented in a numerical fashion.

stock   an individual's share in the ownership of a corporation, based on how much he or she has invested in the corporation.

stock market   market where shares of stock are traded.

supply   the amount of a product or service made available by sellers.

tax   a percentage of a business's gross profit or of an individual's income, taken by the government to support public services.

tax evasion   deliberate avoidance of the obligation to pay taxes; may lead to penalties or even to jail.

tax-exempt   the condition of an entity that is allowed to produce income sheltered from taxation.

technology   new tools made possible by scientific breakthroughs.

test the market   to offer a product or service to a very limited, yet representative, segment of consumers in order to receive customer feedback and improve the product or service as necessary, before attempting to sell it in a larger market.

trademark   any word, name, symbol, or device used by a manufacturer or merchant to distinguish a product from a competitor's.

tradeoff   an exchange in which one benefit or advantage is given up in order to gain another.

variable cost   any cost that changes based on the volume of units sold; sometimes used instead of "cost of goods sold."

venture   a business enterprise in which there is a danger of loss as well as a chance for profit.

venture capital   funds invested in a potentially profitable business enterprise despite risk of loss.

venture capitalist   investor who provides venture capital for a business; typically expects a high rate of return and equity in exchange for the capital investment.

wholesaler   a business that purchases goods in bulk from the manufacturer and sells smaller quantities to retailers.

NOTES

Prologue

1 Interestingly, I had had a premonition of my future as a teacher in 1980 when I spent a day with the philosopher Ayn Rand, who had been a close friend of my grandfather, Lowell B. Mason. We debated for hours over my deep belief in God, and at one point she got a little frustrated with me and said: "Don't keep talking to me like you're teaching me." We became friends.

2 Special thanks to the New York Institute of Entrepreneurship for making this possible.

Chapter 1

1 *New Venture Creation: Entrepreneurship For the 21st Century* by Jeffry A. Timmons (Irwin, 1994).

Chapter 2

1 J. Gregory Dees, "The Meaning of 'Social Entrepreneurship,'"

2 The "Four Roots of Entrepreneurial Opportunity" are based on publications by the Council of Economic Education.

3 Thanks to Chris Meenan, NFTE Divisional Director of Pittsburgh, for developing this distinction between internal and external opportunities.

Chapter 3

1 Adapted from the *Master Curriculum Guide: Economics and Entrepreneurship,* edited by John Clow et al. (New York: Joint Council on Economic Education, 1991).

Chapter 4

1 The Jane Hirsh story came from *Enterprising Women: Lessons from 100 of the Greatest Entrepreneurs of Our Day* by A. David Silver (New York: American Management Association, 1994).

2 Adapted from the *Master Curriculum Guide: Economics and Entrepreneurship,* edited by John Clow et al. (New York: Joint Council on Economic Education, 1991).

3 The MCI story is told in *Entrepreneurial Megabucks: The 100 Greatest Entrepreneurs of the Last Twenty-Five Years* by A. David Silver (New York: John Wiley & Sons, Inc., 1985).

4 *Capitalism, Socialism and Democracy* by Joseph Schumpeter (New York: Harper & Row, 1942).

Chapter 5

1 From *Dave's Way* by David Thomas (New York: G.P. Putnam's Sons, 1991).

2 With thanks to Joseph Mancuso, founder of the Center for Entrepreneurial Management.

3 Adapted from The National Federation of Independent Business, *The Entrepreneurs Series,* 1983.

Chapter 6

1 Details of the Microsoft–IBM negotiations are taken from *Gates* by Stephen Manes and Paul Andrews (New York: Touchstone Press, 1994), and *Hard Drive: Bill Gates and the Making of the Microsoft Empire* by James Wallace and Jim Erickson (New York: HarperBusiness, 1993).

2 With thanks to Joseph Mancuso.

Chapter 8

1 The story of Jacoby & Meyers was drawn from *Enterprising Women: Lessons from 100 of the Greatest Entrepreneurs of Our Day* by A. David Silver (New York: American Management Association, 1994).

Chapter 9

1 For the Charles Schwab story, see *Entrepreneurial Megabucks: The 100 Greatest Entrepreneurs of the Last Twenty-Five Years* by A. David Silver (New York: John Wiley & Sons, Inc., 1985).

Chapter 10

1 With thanks to NFTE teacher Frank Kennedy.

2 Adapted from *The Wall Street Journal.*

Chapter 11

1 Adapted from materials prepared by *The Wall Street Journal* and Dow-Jones Co.

Chapter 12

1 Special thanks to Bart Breighner, president of Artistic Impressions, and to NFTE teacher Glenn Swanson for this acronym.

Chapter 13

1 From *Have You Got What It Takes?: How to Tell If You Should Start Your Own Business* by Joseph Mancuso (Englewood Cliffs, NJ: Prentice-Hall, 1982).

Chapter 16

1 Special thanks to Sylvia Stein, co-founder of Consumer Eyes, Inc., for ideas in this chapter.

Chapter 17

1 Special thanks to Liza Vertinsky of Hill & Barlow for reviewing this chapter.

Chapter 18

1 From an article by Rita Ciolli in *New York Newsday,* July 6, 1995.

Chapter 19

1 *Forbes* magazine, May 1989.

Chapter 20

1 The Sue Scott story is from *Enterprising Women: Lessons from 100 of the Greatest Entrepreneurs of Our Day* by David Silver (New York: American Management Association, 1994).

Chapter 21

1 See *How to Get a Business Loan Without Signing Your Life Away* by Joseph Mancuso (Englewood Cliffs: Prentice-Hall, 1990) for more helpful hints on how to develop a great relationship with a banker.

Chapter 24

1 Thanks to Katie Treveloni, NFTE director of curriculum marketing and on-line development, for this insight.

ABOUT THE
NATIONAL FOUNDATION
FOR TEACHING
ENTREPRENEURSHIP
(NFTE)

The National Foundation for Teaching Entrepreneurship, Inc. (NFTE) is a nonprofit organization founded in 1987. Its mission is to introduce young people—including at-risk youth, the physically challenged, and those in detention—to the world of business and entrepreneurship. In partnership with academic partners such as the University Community Outreach Program, Babson College, Columbia University, Stanford University, Georgetown, The Wharton School at the University of Pennsylvania, and corporate partners such as Koch Industries, Artistic Impressions, Princess House, and NFTE (pronounced "Nifty") presently conducts entrepreneurship programs in fourteen American cities. Through licensing agreements, NFTE is also developing entrepreneurship programs in other countries.

NFTE teaches young people, through hands-on experience, to start and operate their own small businesses. We believe that many young people have extraordinary potential for business success and possess many of the characteristics of successful entrepreneurs, such as mental toughness, the willingness to take risks, resiliency, and sales ability. We also believe that each young person has unique knowledge about his or her market that can be a competitive advantage. These beliefs have been proven correct many times over by the enthusiasm and success of NFTE's young entrepreneurs.

By teaching business through demystifying, hands-on experience, NFTE seeks to encourage the economic participation of young people in their local communities as well as in society at large. Through their entrepreneurial initiatives, they can begin to make changes in their lives and their neighborhoods.

NFTE's "product" is a business-literate young entrepreneur who has experienced buying and selling in the marketplace and keeping accurate financial records. The larger goal, however, is to help renew the spirit of enterprise in America's inner cities through cutting-edge youth training, teacher training, curriculum research and development, and public education forums.

NFTE PRODUCTS

As an educational nonprofit foundation, NFTE produces a variety of products for young entrepreneurs. All proceeds from the sale of the products described below go to support its programs.

The NFTE "Core" Curriculum: *How to Start and Operate a Small Business: A Guide for the Young Entrepreneur* by Steve Mariotti and Tony Towle. This three-module, fifty-chapter course in entrepreneurship for classroom use is the foundation of NFTE's programs. It provides a thorough guide to entrepreneurship complete with exercises and the NFTE business plan workbook, and is widely viewed as the standard in high school entrepreneurship education.

Entrepreneurs in Profile by Steve Mariotti and Jenny Rosenbaum is a collection of fascinating profiles of outstanding entrepreneurs from a wide variety of backgrounds. Included are current favorites among young people, such as Spike Lee, Russell Simmons, and Anita Roddick, as well as historically important entrepreneurs such as King C. Gillette and Henry Ford.

The NFTE BizBag™ is a great asset for any young entrepreneur. This attractive black canvas shoulder bag contains the NFTE "Core" Curriculum, *Entrepreneurs in Profile,* a calculator, memo pad, receipt book, watch, record-keeping book, and deluxe datebook.

NFTE PROGRAMS

NFTE runs entrepreneurship educational programs in partnership with schools and youth-service organizations. The programs range from weekly after-school seminars to intensive in-school classes and summer BizCamps™. We train teachers and youth-service workers in the NFTE curriculum and offer a wide variety of participation options, including organization and city-wide licenses. For more information on any of its products, or to inquire about making a tax-deductible contribution or bringing the NFTE to your community, please contact the national headquarters at:

The National Foundation for Teaching Entrepreneurship, Inc. (NFTE)
120 Wall Street, 29th Floor
New York, NY 10005
(212) 232-3333
Fax (212) 232-2244

ACKNOWLEDGMENTS

I would like to thank my writing partners, Tony Towle, who from NFTE's very beginning helped me organize my thoughts and experiences, and Debra DeSalvo, without whose gift for organization and rewriting, this book would never have been possible. I am also grateful to literary agent Jeff Herman, for introducing me to our editor at Random House, John Mahaney, and his assistants, Eleanor Wickland and Luke Mitchell, who have helped us take this book to another level. I would also like to acknowledge the large contribution by Pittsburgh Metro director Chris Meenan and former NFTE Northern California director Duane Moyer, who, along with former NFTE teachers Juan Casimiro and Kevin Wortham, provided invaluable field testing of NFTE's curriculum as it developed. Former NFTE divisional directors Cindy Kelley, Kevin Greaney, and Kari Davis have also had a profound impact on this book via their helpful suggestions and work in the field. So have current directors Ted Tyson, Del Daniels, Elsa Huaranca, Julie Silard Kantor, and Dorian Johnson.

In addition, I want to thank my brother, Jack, the best CPA I know, and my father, John, for financing much of NFTE's early work and for their continuing love and guidance. I'd also like to acknowledge my colleague on NFTE's Executive Committee, Mike Caslin, for bringing organization and discipline to the field of entrepreneurship education and for invaluable counsel in building our organization and helping me learn the finer points of vision and leadership. I also look forward to continuing to work with Maximo Blake, who is helping to fulfill NFTE's dream of building student business incubators. Thanks are due, also, to Alaire Mitchell for her educational expertise; to Peter Eisen for helping me get the accounting sections "right"; and to all the other teachers, students, experts, and friends who were kind enough to review this book and help me improve it.

I'd also like to thank Jenny Rosenbaum for helping me write many of the profiles of entrepreneurs that are included in this book (and are adapted from our book *Entrepreneurs in Profile*). Thanks, also, to

Howard Stevenson, Jeff Timmons, Steve Spinelli, and Bill Bygraves for their academic and business expertise; my first three students—Vincent Wilkins, Josephine Reneau, and Howard Stubbs; and Lisa Hoffstein, executive director of the University Community Outreach Program, who gave us our first contract and has been instrumental in NFTE's development. The efforts of Richard Fink of Koch Industries, Michie Slaughter of the Marion Kauffman Foundation, Verne Harnish of the Young Entrepreneur's Organization, Tom Hartocolis of Microsoft, and Jean Thorne, Mike Hennessy, and John Hughes of the Coleman Foundation, Inc. have also been crucial to NFTE's development. I also greatly appreciate the efforts of Jim Holden, Al Abney, Joe Dolan, Andrew Sherman, Bella Frankel, and Jack Stack from NFTE's national board, and the guidance provided by our national advisory board's executive committee: William Crerend, Ted Forstmann, Bernie Goldhirsh, Jack Kemp, Elizabeth Koch, Alan Patricof, Ray Chambers, and Jeff Raikes

I also want to thank visionary philanthropists including: Vicky and Max Kennedy, Diana Davis Spencer of the Shelby Collum Davis Foundation, The Scaife Family Foundation, The Heinz Endowments, James H. Herbert, Jr. and The First Republic Bancorp, the W. H. Donner Foundation, The W. K. Kellogg Foundation, The R. K. Mellon Foundation, The Clark Foundation, The New York Community Trust, The J. M. Kaplan Fund, Loida Nicholas Lewis of the Reiginald F. Lewis Foundation, the Argidius Foundation, and a number of anonymous donors.

Finally, I want to thank my mother, Nancy, a wonderful special-education teacher who taught me that one great teacher affects eternity; my friends and mentors, Ray Chambers and John Whitehead; Gloria Appel, for funding NFTE teacher training and being a good friend; Julian Robertson, Tref Wolcott, and John Griffin of the Tiger Foundation for funding NFTE's research project; and Clara Del Villar, Laurel Skurko, Bill Tkacs, Liza Vertinsky and Terry Mahoney of Hill and Barlow, Ken Dillard, Cynthia Miree, Peter Janssen, Elizabeth Wright, Andrea Bonfils Leavitt, Christine Chambers, Janet McKinstry Cort, Leslie Koch, Jane Walsh, Sue Dubester, Carol Tully, Kathleen Kirkwood, and Dilia Wood who provided so many insights into how to encourage children to become business-literate.

Steve Mariotti

INDEX